Canada-United States Relations

edited by
H. Edward English

Published for
the Academy of Political Science

The Praeger Special Studies program—utilizing the most modern and efficient book production techniques and a selective worldwide
distribution network—makes available to the
academic, government, and business communities significant, timely research in U.S. and
international economic, social, and political
development.

Canada-United States Relations

PRAEGER SPECIAL STUDIES IN INTERNATIONAL POLITICS AND GOVERNMENT

Praeger Publishers   New York   Washington   London

Library of Congress Cataloging in Publication Data

Main entry under title:

Canada-United States relations.
  (Praeger special studies in international politics and government)
  Includes index.
  1. United States—Relations (general) with
Canada—Addresses, essays, lectures. 2. Canada—
Relations (general) with the United States—Address-
es, essays, lectures. I. English, Harry Ed-
ward, 1924- II. Academy of Political Science,
New York.
E183.8.C2C38   301.29'73'071   75-38067
ISBN 0-275-23300-6

PRAEGER PUBLISHERS
111 Fourth Avenue, New York, N.Y. 10003, U.S.A.

Published in the United States of America in 1976
by Praeger Publishers, Inc.

© 1976 by the Academy of Political Science
Library of Congress Catalog Card Number: 75-38067
Printed in the United States of America

Material in this book previously appeared in the
Proceedings of the Academy of Political Science
Vol. 32, No. 2

Contents

Foreword   vii

Preface   ix

Contributors   xi

PERSPECTIVES ON THE CANADA-UNITED STATES
RELATIONSHIP

The American Perspective   1
     Willis C. Armstrong

The Canadian Perspective   14
     Peyton Lyon

CANADA'S DOMESTIC CONCERNS—NATIONAL
UNITY AND FOREIGN "CONTROL"

Quebec and the Bicultural Dimension   27
     Dale C. Thomson

Western Disenchantment and the Canadian Federation   40
     Walter D. Gainer

Constitutional Aspects of the Canadian Economy   53
     Eugene Forsey

The Response to Cultural Penetration   63
     Davidson Dunton

Foreign Investment in Primary Industries   75
     A.E. Safarian

Foreign Investment in Manufacturing   88
     H. Edward English

CANADA AND THE UNITED STATES IN AN INTERDEPENDENT WORLD

Deterrence, Détente, and Canada?   100
    Roger Frank Swanson

The Energy Challenge   113
    Philip H. Trezise

The Evolving Trading System   124
    Harald B. Malmgren

Conflict Over Industrial Incentive Policies   137
    Sperry Lea and John Volpe

Canada-United States Environmental Relations   149
    David LeMarquand and Anthony D. Scott

The Optimum Use of Canadian Resources   164
    Carl E. Beigie

Index   177

Foreword

In recent months a number of issues have arisen that place considerable strain on relations between Canada and the United States. Some Americans have been disturbed by actions of the Canadian federal and provincial governments in the pursuit of independent economic and cultural objectives. Canadians, on the other hand, have reason to be concerned about "foreign control." The purpose of this book is to define the issues that threaten the long-standing friendship between the two countries and to promote a better understanding of their mutual interests.

Most of the essays in this volume were discussed at a conference jointly sponsored by the Academy of Political Science and the Center of Canadian Studies, School of Advanced International Studies, The Johns Hopkins University, in Washington, D.C., on October 23 and 24, 1975. The conference was organized by H. Edward English, director of the Center of Canadian Studies. Chairmen for the various sessions included Bruce Rankin, Canadian consul general in New York City; Richard J. Schmeelk, cochairman, American-Canadian Committee; A. Randolph Gherson, minister counsellor, Canadian Embassy; and Robert H. Connery, president, the Academy of Political Science.

In the interest of promoting better understanding between the United States and its neighbor to the north, the Exxon Corporation and the International Nickel Company, as well as the Gulf Oil Foundation, the Texasgulf Corporation, the Bank of Montreal, and the Royal Bank of Canada provided financial support that made the project possible. The Academy is deeply grateful for their assistance.

The Academy serves as a forum for the dissemination of informed opinion on public questions, but it makes no recommendations on political issues. The views expressed in this volume do not necessarily reflect those of tthe Academy, the editor, or the institutions with which the authors are affiliated.

ROBERT H. CONNERY
President of the Academy

Preface

Although most Americans continue to think of Canadians as more or less distant cousins, there is an increased awareness, especially in the border states, that Canadians want to be independent and different from Americans. This awareness has been heightened by a number of issues that have emerged over the last two or three years. In mid-December 1975, on the eve of his departure for another post, the United States ambassador to Canada, William Porter, held an informal meeting with the press in Ottawa to put on the record his views on outstanding issues in Canadian-American relations. He is quoted as saying that Canadian nationalistic attitudes are causing alarm and suspicion, if not hostility, in some quarters in the United States and that the prime minister and president should get together before "the majority opinion developed in the U.S. that Canada was no longer a friendly ally, or even a friendly country that could be trusted."

Unfortunately, there was no text of his statement, and, as Prime Minister Trudeau pointed out, this made it difficult to react to the media reports. Since neither the State Department nor Mr. Porter sought to correct the reports on any substantive issue, however, one may conclude that the particular issues highlighted were those that the State Department wished to stress. They included six items identified in the *Washington Post* and other news reports:

1. Canada's decision to charge the United States the full world price for oil and gas and the gradual elimination of oil and gas exports to conserve what Canada claims are dwindling supplies.

2. Saskatchewan's plan to take effective control of the $1 billion potash industry by buying on the open market or nationalizing private mining companies, many of which are American-owned.

3. Legislation that could lead to shutting down Canadian editions of Time, Readers Digest, and several foreign medical publications by removing what is, in effect, honorary Canadian citizenship for tax purposes. The measure, aimed at strengthening the financial base of Canadian media, would deny Canadian advertisers the right to claim 100 per cent tax deductions for the cost of advertising in the American magazines or on border television stations.

4. The Canadian Radio and Television Commission's plan to have Canadian cable television operators block out commercials on signals from American stations.

5. A new agency that screens foreign investment to make sure it is of significant benefit to Canada.

6. Canada's efforts to broaden its foreign relations to become less economically and culturally dependent on the U.S.

All of these issues are discussed in this volume. For example, Philip Trezise reviews the issues related to the energy crisis. Carl Beigie and A.E. Safarian examine the natural resources development policies and foreign investment issues that underlie the questions about the control of basic industries and sharing of the revenues, such as the potash issue. Davidson Dunton deals with the media and related cultural distinctiveness questions. H. Edward English and Willis Armstrong discuss the Foreign Investment Review Agency and, like Malmgren, touch also on the efforts of the Canadian government to broaden its external relations with overseas countries.

The essays go beyond the Porter list to deal with other bilateral issues. LeMarquand and Scott discuss environmental relations along the border. Lea and Volpe examine the implications of national policies for regional development on the possible subsidization of trade in manufactures between Canada and the United States. Other essays (Thomson, Gainer, and Forsey) stress domestic issues relating to national unity that preoccupy many Canadian political leaders and result in some neglect of international affairs. Finally, some focus on multilateral issues, such as trade policy (Malmgren) and détente (Swanson) that often bring the North American countries to the same side of the bargaining table but may also result in divergences of viewpoint between them.

As Peyton Lyon indicates at the end of his essay, "Canadians . . . seem unlikely to initiate dramatic changes in the continental relationship. They will seek stronger ties with other countries and, if successful, should become more confident and less irritable in dealing with Americans. They will look critically at new proposals that appear integrative, and may take further steps to reduce the predominance of the American media. It is not inconceivable, however, that trends in the global environment will persuade the two nations to move closer together."

H. Edward English

Contributors

WILLIS C. ARMSTRONG, formerly minister at the United States embassy in Ottawa and former assistant secretary of state, is now adjunct professor of international economics at Georgetown University.

CARL E. BEIGIE is executive director of the C.D. Howe Research Institute in Montreal and the author of *The Canada-U.S. Automotive Agreement: An Evaluation.*

DAVIDSON DUNTON is director of the Institute of Canadian Studies at Carleton University, Ottawa, of which he was previously president; formerly he was chairman of the Canadian Broadcasting Corporation and cochairman of the Royal Commission on Bilingualism and Biculturalism.

H. EDWARD ENGLISH, formerly professor of economics at Carleton University, is director of the Center of Canadian Studies at the School of Advanced International Studies, The Johns Hopkins University; he is the coauthor of *Canada in a Wider Economic Community.*

EUGENE FORSEY, a political scientist and former research director of the Canadian Labour Congress, is a member of the Senate of Canada.

WALTER D. GAINER is professor of economics at the University of Alberta in Edmonton and the author of articles on Canadian public policy.

SPERRY LEA is an economist and director of research for the British North American Committee, National Planning Association, and the author of books and articles on Canada-United States economic relations.

DAVID LEMARQUAND is a research associate with the Westwater Research Centre at the University of British Columbia in Vancouver.

PEYTON LYON is professor of political science and international affairs at Carleton University in Ottawa and the author of *Canada-United States Free Trade and Canadian Independence.*

HARALD B. MALMGREN, formerly deputy special representative for trade negotiations in the Executive Office of the President, is a fellow at the Woodrow Wilson International Center for Scholars at the Smithsonian Institution and the author of *Trade for Development.*

A. E. SAFARIAN is professor of economics and dean of graduate studies at the University of Toronto; he is the author of *Foreign Ownership of Canadian Industry*.

ANTHONY D. SCOTT is professor of economics at the University of British Columbia and a former member of the Canadian section of the International Joint Commission, and the author of *Natural Resources: The Economics of Conservation*.

ROGER FRANK SWANSON is assistant professor of international relations at the Center of Canadian Studies at the School of Advanced International Studies, The Johns Hopkins University, and the author of *Canadian-American Summit Diplomacy, 1923-1973*.

DALE C. THOMSON is vice-principal of McGill University in Montreal and the author of *Louis St. Laurent* and other books on Quebec and Canada.

PHILIP H. TREZISE, formerly United States ambassador to the OECD, is senior fellow at the Brookings Institution and the author of *Atlantic Connection*.

JOHN VOLPE is director of research (Washington, D.C.) of the Canadian-American Committee of the National Planning Association.

The American Perspective

WILLIS C. ARMSTRONG

Canada is far from the minds of most Americans most of the time, and probably it is fair to say that most Americans have no perceptions of Canada at all. It is hard to say why this should be so, when the United States does more business with Canada than any other country, when the largest proportion of its foreign investment is in Canada, and when 20 million Canadians live within easy reach of the United States.

Consciousness of other countries begins in school. American children are exposed to teachings about Europe, Asia, and Latin America, and now there is an emphasis on Africa. Canada may be mentioned a few times in courses in the early history of the Republic—but only in passing, as the area where American efforts at liberation failed, for unexplained reasons. Perhaps in Louisiana there is reference to the Canadian origin of the early settlers. In New England and upstate New York and Michigan, there may be some attention to Canada in the curriculum. But it is fair to conclude that the average American's elementary and secondary education is bereft of any fundamental knowledge of Canada. Nor does one find much in college offerings. There are courses in the history of the British Empire and now and then a course or so on Canada, but they are not among the more popular offerings. Again there are exceptions in New England, upstate New York, Michigan, and elsewhere, and there are some who strive to introduce Canadian studies in American universities and colleges. Johns Hopkins University and the Donner Foundation deserve much credit for their efforts to keep a voice crying in the wilderness of ignorance that pervades all United States perceptions of Canada. One would hope more Americans would hear it.

So, by education, Americans are devoid of training on Canadian matters. Some areas of experience may be worth examining. Recreation comes first, because it is the primary reason for most American visits to Canada. Fishing, skiing, golf, summer cottage sojourns by the lake or sea or mountains, visits to Canadian national parks, boating visits on the Ontario and Quebec waterways, glimpses of the Gaspé—all these are cherished objects of many Americans who find the clean air and pleasant summer or winter weather refreshing. Some learn a little about Canada's history, if they visit Ottawa, Quebec, Kingston, Halifax, or Montreal. Some go for cultural reasons—the theaters at Stratford and Niagara, or the museums and busy life of Toronto. But basically, the word is recreation, and who wants to be serious about one's playground, if it satisfies the felt needs of the vacationist?

There are other forms of American experience with Canadians. The businessman who sells in Canada, the banker who deals in Canadian finance, the executive of a company with subsidiaries in Canada, the oil and gas or mining entrepreneur, the buyer of Canadian goods—all these have substantial experience with Canada and Canadians. They also learn a great deal about the Canadian government as its regulations and laws affect their business. When they encounter problems, as they often do, their curiosity may be aroused enough to compel them to seek a deeper understanding of Canadians so they can determine how to advance their business interests. Such curiosity also may lead them into concern with official United States government relations with the government of Canada—a rather arcane field dominated by specialists and mostly unknown to the average citizen.

A third type of American experience with Canadians is what might be called the comparative professional. Americans and Canadians are great joiners of organizations, and there is a tendency for there to be either one organization for both Canadians and Americans, or at least a friendly relationship between two national organizations with similar aims for their members and possessed of a common body of knowledge. Thus one sees historians, economists, political scientists, librarians, musicians, doctors, lawyers, scientists, university administrators, students, and all sorts of professional people, as well as what might be called local small-business men, engaged in conventions, meetings, and gatherings of varying degrees of utility, always including Canadians and now and then having a distinct Canadian component. The exchange of experience among counterparts is always useful and can be enjoyable, and Americans get to know Canadians in this way.

In the business field there are contacts through the two national Chambers of Commerce, within the framework of the International Chamber of Commerce, and in the work of the two Conference Boards. There are also comparable contacts between national associations in some business areas, and, of course, there is a significant element of Canadian labor which is linked with the AFL-CIO and the UAW, whose internal Canadian-American relations could well be the subject of a special study. The comparative professional experience blends at the edges into the business experience.

One interesting area of comparative professional experience is among politicians. Few issues in Canadian-American relations have attracted American legislators' interest in recent years, apart from the Columbia River Treaty and the agreement on the St. Lawrence Seaway. Thus there have been few American legislators with any interest in the actual issues or transactions between the two governments, handled almost exclusively by the executive branch. But the Congress authorized United States participation in a Canadian-U.S. Parliamentary Committee, following an initiative of Canadian legislators who wanted more involvement in Canadian-United States relations. These gatherings of Canadian and American legislators do discuss issues of political or economic importance between the two countries. A review of the record, however, might lead to the conclusion that more time had been spent comparing notes on the life of a North American politician than on the issues of the day. The institution of a joint parliamentary committee is of some utility in intergovernmental relations, but thus far it has not been a major element in the structure.

The Public View

The experience of the general public in the United States, apart from those who visit Canada, those who do business with Canada, and those who compare notes with their Canadian opposite numbers, is very limited indeed. There is probably an awareness of the Royal Canadian Mounted Police, the Arctic, the French segment of Canada, the price of oil, the dominance of Canada in hockey, the Rockies, the Seaway, the queen, and Mr. Trudeau and his social life. Beyond this there is not much more. The American public does not understand its own business world, let alone business with Canada. The public is conscious of the fact that there are intergovernmental relations, but sometimes wonders why there is an American Embassy in Ottawa, because it is not clear to them that Canada is a country, let alone a foreign country.

This impression of Canada, based on hearsay, television, snips of information about Canada from the media, some novels or short stories, and a general feeling that the "Canadians are like us"—and therefore good people—is one of ignorant friendliness and good will. To say this is not to imply a critical judgment. Perhaps ignorant good will is the most desirable attitude for a public regarding a neighboring country. It is certainly an improvement on comparable national public attitudes about neighbors in other parts of the world.

There is nothing seriously erroneous in the vague, well-intentioned set of perceptions of Canada shared by most Americans, including those who have recreational or comparative professional experience, but it is essentially incomplete in one major respect. It does not recognize the disparity in size between the two countries. Not many Americans realize that the United States has ten times the population of Canada and that such a disparity between neighboring countries cannot avoid creating an attitudinal difference between them. Ignorance of this basic fact, coupled with American unawareness of the striving of Canadian elites for some identifiable set of qualities to distinguish Canada from the United States, can lead to misunderstanding. Americans do not in general perceive Canada as very different in quality from the United States. Why should they? English-speaking Canadians and Americans share the same basic educational, legal, ethical, and material values, and the French Canadians differ primarily in language. Canadians live in large and pleasant cities close to the United States border, and everyone knows Canada has an enormous land area.

From the standpoint of the American public, there is probably no reason to be at all interested in official Canada-United States relations. But there is vital importance in the classic sense to the United States of its economic and political relations with Canada, for reasons too obvious to mention, and whether or not there is public awareness of them. There is great public awareness on the Canadian side, another element in the asymmetry that characterizes the relationship. On the United States side, there is a small group of people in the State Department and other departments, augmented by a few in congressional circles and by a few academics as well as persons in such bodies as the Council on Foreign Relations, who are deeply concerned with Canadian-American relations and who expend much effort on the subject, as a matter of either official responsibility or basic interest and awareness.

In addition, there is the business community in the United States whose relationship with the official community is rather inchoate, since business and government are seldom partners in the United States (or Canada either) in the sense they are in Europe and Japan. It is with these two elements in the United States and their perceptions that one must deal if one is to be realistic about perceptions that count. But, in so dealing, one must recognize that almost nobody except those business and government people who deal directly with these matters either knows or cares much about what is going on. Consequently, this limited group of business and government actors are compelled to deal with matters they think vital with almost no public understanding or appreciation at home, while they are the objects of intense interest from a wide public on the other side of the border.

Business Perceptions

What are the perceptions of business people regarding the relationship with Canada? The answer, of course, depends on what business one may be in. The banker surveys the well-organized Canadian banking system and perceives that he has little or no chance to enter it, because of restrictive legislation and the dominance of the big Canadian commercial banks. So he finds that business must normally be done with and through these banks. A large American bank, one may recall, made an effort at investment in Canada and found the experience painful; its conduct was not the most astute possible, and the event aroused a nationalist reaction that many Americans found unbelievable, primarily because of their own ignorance of the state of affairs in Canada.

Merchant bankers in the New York market, however, find Canadians welcome customers. Canada's industries, provinces, municipalities, and state-owned enterprises find the New York market indispensable, and float their issues there. New York is used to the pilgrimages of Canadian provincial ministers who come to urge investment in their provinces. New York financiers are assured that what Ottawa says about controlling foreign investment in Canada should not be taken too seriously, because "in the Province of Saskascotia, we have fine resources ready for exploitation, Americans are treated in a friendly fashion, and we have no problem with French Canadians." The Quebec people come also and say they welcome American capital as a hedge against domination by Toronto and Ottawa. In most cases, Canadian issues floated in the New York market get a good rating.

Between New York and the cities of Toronto and Montreal the flow of capital is easy, and in many respects one could say that a common market in money exists—in securities, loans, capital stock issues, and in commercial paper. There are some governmental formalities on both sides, but they are minimal, and presumably the advantage of the arrangement is mutually appreciated. Thus, the merchant banking fraternity should be pleased with its Canadian opportunities. So should security dealers and stockbrokers, although their range is restricted by nationalist regulations on both sides of the border. Such limitation, however, does not prevent a vigorous trade in securities with relatively little difficulty over nationality. The Securities and Exchange Commission has friendly working relationships with the securities commissions and regulatory authorities of the provinces.

Investors are of various kinds. The American portfolio investor who chooses to buy Canadian securities may find the experience somewhat more complicated than buying domestic American issues, but the differences are not serious, and there have been times when Canadian issues were extremely attractive. The direct investor is, of course, in a different situation, and his experience is a major element in the Canadian-American relationship.

Ever since Prime Minister Macdonald established his national policy over a hundred years ago, Canada has had a protected manufacturing industry. The market has been relatively small, and economies of scale have not been possible as they are in Britain and the United States. A high tariff, especially for goods of a class or kind not made in Canada, has encouraged the development of domestic industry, which could not easily survive in the rough waters of worldwide competition. Inducements to foreign capitalists to invest have been attractive and numerous. In fact, the Canadian government has had a service that watches the flow of imports and, as soon as a particular firm's shipments are large enough, suggests politely that the firm might well consider building a plant and manufacturing in Canada. These national inducements have been supplemented by a wide range of grants and bounties which may be obtained by investing in some of the more remote and less favorable areas, comparable to concessions available in the United Kingdom. American manufacturers have not been loath to take advantage of a prosperous, protected market, a friendly atmosphere offered by local, provincial, and federal authorities, and plants have sprouted all over Canada, bearing familiar American corporate names. Other foreign manufacturers have been there too, but the Americans are by far the dominant group. Despite what many say, this movement has not obliterated a vigorous indigenous industry that has developed satisfactorily without being linked to American counterparts.

Of course, the manufacturer who invests in Canada has problems. He has to deal with Canadian governmental regulations, but these are not much different from those he encounters at home. He has to pay taxes, pay attention to local community affairs, encourage hockey teams, subscribe to police benefits, and do all the other things one does in the United States. He also has to remember that Canadian businessmen are just as competent as Americans, and in due course he finds he has hardly any Americans left in his Canadian enterprise. He also has to realize that his employees are not Americans and expect to be so recognized. After a while, Canadians begin to appear in the home offices of American multinational corporations and in positions in European or Asian subsidiaries. This is the true world of the multinational enterprise in its more generally accepted form, and within it Canadian-American relations seem to work fairly well, when the attitude of the home company is enlightened and open. Of course, this whole process works the other way too. There are Canadian companies with subsidiaires in the United States.

Although there are low or zero tariffs on a number of items that cross the border, in only one industry have Canadian-American relations developed to the point where there is almost a North American common market. American automobile manufacturers dominated the Canadian market for years with branch plants, and this developed into an integrated industry because of the automobile pact, designed as a response to the aspirations of the Canadian government for more manufacturing in Canada. The result has certainly been more manufacturing in Canada and a larger market for the automobile companies in both countries. This situation seems a happy one for the manufacturers, although grumbling is now and then heard from both governments, preoccupied with the examination of statistics rather than the larger question of economic efficiency, whose aims seem well served by the transaction.

Generally, the American investor in a manufacturing plant in Canada has had a good experience, with stable conditions, a government whose regulations were no more difficult than those of his own, and with the usual problems of labor relations, community welfare, and responsiveness to local people experienced at home. Manufacturers have responded to the pressures of Canadianism in its various manifestations, and have rolled with the punches. They have also adjusted to French Canadianism, at once more obvious and less easy to handle. By and large they have coped, and they keep their complaints to themselves. The relations with Canadian-owned businesses are generally cooperative, within the Chamber of Commerce, the Canadian Manufacturers Association, and other bodies.

The American direct investor in Canadian natural resources has also had a generally satisfactory experience, although here one encounters the problems of federal-provincial relations more acutely, and here one realizes that many Canadians regard with more nationalist fervor the exploitation of what might be found underground than they do the manufacture of widgets for the Canadian market. Obviously, however, there has been an enormous flow of United States capital to Canada for resource exploitation, and the experience has been not unattractive to those who participated, including the various Canadian governments. In recent times there has been some change in mood, noticeable by American entrepreneurs, and the hand of government has become heavier on the producer of oil and gas, in particular, because of the political importance of energy and because governments want more of the profits. The resulting disincentive has been followed by a decline in oil and gas exploration in Canada, but the experience is not peculiar to American investors. The drilling rigs have been moving south, where in due course similar discouragement will doubtless occur, as a result of a high-minded Congress that seems to prefer scarce energy to successful corporate enterprise.

Recently the investing community has become aware of the new Foreign Investment Review Act, which has thus far considered take-overs only. No serious complaints have been heard from investors whose projects have been disapproved, and most people feel that the regime of Richard Murray, a broad-minded and perceptive businessman, has given the act enlightened administration, under the very different condition that the only standard is the vague formula "what is good for Canada." What happens next, now that his successor has said he intends to oper-ate in accordance with the so-called third option of Canadian foreign policy, is a matter of concern and serious conjecture, especially since the act will now bring within its purview all new investments in Canada.[1] In a world of capital shortage, capital disallowed in Canada can doubt-less find a profitable home in the United States or elsewhere, so to a large extent the rulings of a subjective administrator can well lead to economic activity in some other country.

The business community also contains people who buy from or sell to Canada both goods and services. Exporting to Canada is not difficult, al-though Canada Customs is rather rigid about some of its rules; in any event, it is probably easier than exporting to other countries, and a great amount of traffic occurs. Buying from Canada is also easy enough. Much of the import and export trade is through intracompany transactions, in raw materials, oil, forest products, and the like, and so one who has the mental picture of the small exporter or importer must recognize that this is not characteristic of Canadian-American trade, although a good deal of it does occur. U.S. Customs is at least as difficult as Canada Customs, and imports and exports are comparable in volume.

What of the future, in the view of the American businessman with large investments in Canada or with a great stake in Canadian trade, or both? So far he has not been badly served or badly treated. He is aware of Canadian economic and political nationalism, and of its vigorous growth in recent years. He can understand nationalism, but he finds it hard to understand Canadian actions that are manifestly—in his view—contrary to Canada's economic interests. He wonders where a trend in this direction may lead. He is aware of pressures for greater investment in Canada for what might be called the ends of Canadian industrial poli-cy, designed to increase economic activity of an industrial nature in Canada, and quite possibly to transfer manufacturing from the United States to Canada for the production of goods for the American market. The investor can presumably make money this way, but perhaps at the

---

[1] The "third option" refers to the choice among principles governing Canadian for-eign policy. The first two options are the status quo and closer economic integration with the United States. The third option implies less emphasis on Canada-United States interdependence.

expense of his manufacturing establishment in the United States and its market in Canada.

Nothing extraordinary has occurred as yet, but intentions in this direction are easy to read, and industry may look to government in the United States for support and help, so the issue can become one of intergovernmental relations. There have been some discussions of the matter between governments, but it is an amorphous type of thing about which Canadian officials do not appear very forthcoming.

Generally, American business with an eye on Canada probably feels that Canadian nationalism and the growth of statism will make life more difficult and expensive for Americans doing business with Canada or in Canada, although there will be many mitigating circumstances, because the American businessman hears not only the voice of the nationalist but also the reassuring tones of those who want him to invest in a given province, or who want his goods, or who want to sell goods to him. In fact, there are many voices in Canada, as there are in most countries, and it is hard to know which to heed. The businessman will be aware that the government of Canada is more distant from the United States government than it used to be, that neither government is very friendly to business, and that one must take one's chances when trying to make an honest dollar in between such forces. Businessmen will probably be particularly careful about the implications of internal problems in Canada and not be anxious to get caught between any Canadians in a domestic argument. In sum, the businessman will have to adjust to the political and administrative circumstances that prevail. These will be more difficult in the future, and he knows it. But this is also true at home.

American farmers are, in respect to many products, competitors of Canadian farmers. In grains the prospect for a seller's market remain good, thanks to the weather, the inefficiency of the USSR, and the growth rate of the world's population. Each country sells the other a good deal of produce, however, and every so often the respective agricultural authorities realize the interdependence and so remind their farmers who are clamoring for protection. Minor and short-lived crises over given products are normal, since each country has its own system of protecting producers, but they are not significant factors affecting long-term attitudes.

Government Perceptions

It is somewhat difficult to give an account of United States government perceptions of Canada if one is no longer in the government or engaged in handling relations with Canada. On the other hand, if one is so engaged, one is either reluctant to talk about the matter in full view of the people with whom one is dealing, or one is tempted to use the occasion to advance one's own cause. Retirement from the scene but maintenance of an active interest can give perspective, which is perhaps what is desired.

Official relations between the two governments, from the American viewpoint, refers to the work and attitudes of a handful of officials who are fully engaged, of a comparable handful who are now and then engaged because the Canadians discuss problems with them and of senior government officials whose duties make official contact with Canada obligatory. In this last category, one finds the president, the secretary of state, other cabinet officers, and the heads of regulatory and other agencies such as the Federal Energy Agency. The top and middle-level officials usually depend on briefing papers from the officials who are regularly engaged in Canadian matters, and their opinions and impressions are modified or strengthened by what they gain from direct contact. Some of them may even have had some impression of Canada through some other means—as tourists, fishermen, or golfers, or because they live in Michigan, Maine, or Minnesota. But essentially they depend on their officials.

Over time a modest but growing number of United States officials have been involved in Canadian affairs. Usually, at the beginning, they had a rather mild curiosity about Canada and progressed to an intense interest, because the consideration of Canada and its affairs can indeed be absorbing.

Perceptions of Canada watchers usually start with the internal situation in Canada. First and foremost, one is struck by the importance of the relationship or nonrelationship between French Canada and the other Canada. The problems and issues arising from the fundamental fact of two separate communities in the same country is sometimes almost overwhelming. The secular revolution in Quebec beginning in the 1950s and 1960s, the development of a separatist movement, the political struggles within the province and within the country, the efforts at bilingualism, the occasional outbursts of violence, and what seems to many as the widening gap between the French consciousness and the apparent unity of one Canada are profoundly important to Americans, who live next door. Although most government officials may not want to admit it, this is an area about which an American should not even have an opinion.

Nevertheless, one's opinions are solicited. French Canadians try to get Americans to agree with them. Anglo-Canadians seek support from Americans for their views. The views of each run across the spectrum from intelligent and friendly mutual appreciation to bigotry and ignorance. The subject is fascinating, though not well understood except historically by Americans, but it should be strictly off limits. All the Americans can do is watch and hope that everything comes out all right. If one says that a unified and united Canada is in the interest of the United States, one is accused of being unsympathetic to the wishes of a strong and assertive minority. If one expresses sympathy with the minority in its aspirations, one is accused of Machiavellian intentions designed to encourage subversion. American officials generally stay out of this discussion, and they should. So should all other Americans. How Canadians arrange things between different major groups in the population or areas of the country is strictly their business. But Canadians will understand if the informed watchers are now and then a bit nervous.

Canadian politics, including but apart from the Quebec matter, are colorful and fascinating to those Americans who understand them. The play of provincial forces, the variety of provincial opinion, the populist attitude of the prairies toward Toronto, the independent attitudes of British Columbia, the very different Newfoundland experience, and the solid comfort and economic success of Ontario all have to be a part of a knowledgeable official's understanding without which he is not fully capable of dealing with Canada officially. Of course, the reverse is also true in some measure of the United States with its many regions and variations, but the differences in attitudes and aspirations in Canada are far greater and more likely to come in conflict with one another, or so it seems to the American. Again, people everyhere seek to enlist the sympathetic support of the American, and again he must refrain. Canada has its own peculiar provincial-federal structure. Many times it has seemed on the verge of serious fissure, and many times the crack has been sealed. The qualitative difference between the Canadian political structure and that of the United States is indeed great, although both are federal states.

The major problem in official relations is determining the Canadian attitude toward the United States. The United States normally waits to see what Canada is going to do, decides whether the action or policy is likely to be injurious to some specific United States interest or policy, and acts accordingly. The reaction of the United States is seldom sharp, but if it is, there is usually a good reason. In rare instances there is a United States initiative on a bilateral matter or on some global issue. If the American public hears of problems in relations, which it sometimes does, it usually sides with the Canadian government against its own. In recent years this has changed somewhat, as Americans have become better informed and as Canadian action in the energy field has been generally perceived as injurious to the United States.

The fundamental determinant in United States perceptions of Canada at the official level is thus what Canada wants, or has decided, or has done. All actions are analyzed by knowledgeable officials, tea-leaves are read, oracles consulted, precedents hunted, and hypotheses developed. Questions are asked: Why? How much will it hurt us? What kind of public or local reaction can we expect? Should we do anything? If so, what? Would this produce a new and different problem? If we do not do anything, what will they think? Are we a paper tiger? What comes next? Is it part of some deep and complex plot? Does anybody here care?

Fundamentally, of course, the question is, What does Canada want, and where is it going? The evidence is mixed, as Americans hear it. Some Canadians continue to express the warmest possible sentiments of friendship. Some others propound what sound to Americans like unfriendly views. Some are socialists because Americans are capitalists; some are seriously socialist; some say they must buy the Yankees out; some say they want more capital. What Americans in the year 1975 see is a Canada that is unbelievably wealthy in resources, with a strong nationalist movement among a part of its elite and in parts of its government; a Canada that would like to be more independent of the United States but without making any economic sacrifice; a Canada that does not want the capital flow to stop but would like to have more say about what the capital does; a Canada that has strong views about the United States and its policies and wishes to express them, but without much interest in American views of Canada; a Canada that has serious internal political problems, that is sometimes torn between a serious effort to solve them and a tendency to blame the Americans; a Canada that is preoccupied with American attitudes, looking over its shoulder at the United States and hoping at one moment that it will not notice and the next hoping that it will; and above all, a Canada of great diversity, where all kinds of views are heard, and where the American's problem is to know what to take as valid signs of Canadian directions and intentions.

It takes a lot of patience for American officials to deal successfully and sympathetically with Canada. Canadian officials are tough, competent, well-organized, and briefed. Their seniors in the cabinet are usually vigorous in a negotiation, whereas their opposite numbers in the United States are often underbriefed on the specifics and frequently have not had time to read their briefing books. Moreover, the material is less than absorbing, since the stuff of Canadian-American official relations is often rather tiresome in its recital of facts about wood, water, rock, oil, gas, tariff, or subsidy. The United States suffers the disadvantage also of being ten times as big, and North America is always for the little guy. If the United States were to use its economic power to cow the Canadians, it would immediately suffer major psychological damage and not be able to carry through with its muscle. So American policy is normally reactive, nonaggressive, and patient. Sometimes there is a personality on the

United States side who strikes a spark over some issue, and then there is great excitement. Normally, the best American defense is to be slow, to yield but gradually if there is no perceptible damage, and to state its position firmly but quietly if there is. This is presumably a sort of elephantine behavior, to go back to Mr. Trudeau's figure of speech about sleeping with an elephant. But the aggressive and positive Canadian sleeping partner should also bear in mind that the elephant is reputed to have a good memory.

There is a special problem in Canadian relations with the United States. In bilateral relations one is arguing about specific problems and a difference in view is normal. In the dimension of views of the world from Ottawa and from Washington, however, which is an essential component of the relationship, Americans have from time to time detected a Canadian psychological compulsion to avoid the appearance of full agreement with the United States, on issues in the United Nations, in NATO, in any other multilateral fora, or in views on the situation in any given part of the world. Obviously, Americans are long past thinking that Canadians ought to agree with them because they are Canadians; they would, however, like the assurance of reciprocal treatment, to the effect that Canadians will examine issues honestly and if they agree with the United States will say so, both privately and publicly. Stating a different view is entirely Canada's prerogative. But it must be a view that is different for clear and persuasive reasons. If Canada takes an opposite view for the sake of being different, where will it be if it persuades the United States to change its mind?

Americans perceive Canada as moving away politically from the United States. They perceive Canada as wanting to move away economically but not knowing how, in a world that is increasingly interdependent. They perceive Canada as in the throes of a delayed nineteenth-century nationalism, which comes in two languages, sparked by the new generation and the new universities. They see Canada having a hard time reconciling its internally conflicting pressures. They will wait, and watch, and feel that it is necessary increasingly to treat Canada as a foreign country. This is counter to the trend of interdependence prevalent among developed countries, and counter to the normal instinct of Canadians and Americans in their social contact. It is the Canadians, however, who set the tone of the relationship. They can have almost any kind of relationship they want, from hostility to friendship. The Americans will not do anything except when assaulted or sworn at, and even then they will react slowly and with some bewilderment (unless they are still smarting from a previous episode that their elephant's memory brings to mind), because basically they have no hard feelings about Canada.

The Canadian Perspective

PEYTON LYON

From a Canadian perspective, it is less than self-evident why foreigners, especially Americans, should be encouraged to focus their attention on Canada-United States relations. The reason can scarcely be the differences in the characteristics of the two peoples. Important distinctions do exist, and foreigners cause offense by overlooking them. However, the distinctions are either obvious, such as the disparity in population, wealth, and military muscle, or less significant than those that differentiate most other pairs of countries. Similarly, while Canada is one of the most important of the secondary powers and a leading actor in such issue areas as trade, food production, and control of the ocean bed, the consequences of ignoring it would be less deleterious to the interests of the United States than those that would be caused by the neglect of a dozen other international actors or issues. Relatively speaking, from an American perspective, Canada can be taken for granted.

Nor is it necessarily in the Canadian interest that Americans should concentrate their attention on their northern neighbors. It is, of course, hard on the pride of Canadians, most of whom fancy themselves to have been born knowledgeable and wise about the United States, to discover that Americans know little about Canada. And there have been occasions when the "mouse" has suffered because the amiable "elephant," oblivious to the existence of its tiny bedmate, has rolled over, or merely twitched. On the other hand, it is not quite obvious that to know Canadians better is to love them more.

The benign ignorance about Canada that tends to prevail throughout the United States may, in fact, be one of Canada's most precious diplomatic assets. Close attention to the relations within this disparate dyad might raise doubts about which is the elephant and which the mouse.

Apart from more real estate and a richer per capita resource base, Canadians lay claim to a more invigorating climate, greater social stability, a sounder political system, and even, now that the CN tower is in place, the biggest erection. It may be argued, moreover, that these advantages are reflected in the historical record; many Canadians are wont to cite such facts as which nation led the other into two world wars, which invented NATO, which initiated détente, which rediscovered China, and which first floated its dollar. In a significant number of bilateral conflicts, such as those over Arctic waters, the Mercantile Bank, trade with Cuba, and the automobile pact, Canada's position has clearly prevailed. Even the substantial American lead in per capita income is being eroded.

That Canadians are born losers, a nation for which mere survival is a triumph, remains the theme of much of Canada's rather depressing literature, and the current vogue for the nationalistic novels of Richard Rohmer testifies to the persistence of an underdog mentality. A balanced assessment, however, suggests not only that Canada has fared remarkably well in its relations with the United States, but also that the disparity in crude power is offset in good part by the greater attention that Canadians can and do devote to the dyadic relationship. This is not to say that the quality of Canadian research on the United States is high—it is not—or that American scholars have ignored Canada; some of the most thorough and perceptive studies are from American pens. The fact remains, however, that the United States constitutes for Canadians the major part of their external environment, and its actions, or failure to act, can be of decisive importance. The reverse is rarely the case, even when it is noted that the United States's longest land frontier is the Canadian, and the largest portion of its trade is with Canada. Nothing could be more natural than the greater attention paid by Canadian than by American decision makers to the conduct of the continental relationship.

Gallup data suggest that Americans have a considerably higher regard for Canadians than for other foreigners, if indeed they perceive them as foreigners.[1] This condition is not immutable, however, as evidenced by the anti-Canadian sentiment in the areas threatened by cuts in the supply of Canadian oil and gas and by the irritation in Congress concerning the automobile pact. There are good grounds for the belief, moreover, that anti-Canadian feeling in the United States Treasury influenced the implementation of the emergency measures taken in August 1971. Since it is widely acknowledged in Canada that Washington's policies are vital to the well-being of the Canadian economy, the mystery is why Canadians appear so eager to risk augmenting such irritation by attracting American attention to their economic and other relations with Canada.

During long periods, the Canadian-American interaction has been quiet, and much of the credit has been attributed to the tradition of tackling transborder issues in a factual, problem-solving spirit, the approach

---

[1] John H. Sigler and Dennis Goresky, "Public Opinion on United States–Canadian Relations," *International Organization* 28 (Autumn 1974), 639-40.

exemplified by the International Joint Commission (IJC) established in 1909 to deal primarily with the complex net of boundary waters. This success has inspired some authorities, chiefly American, to urge that the characteristic handling of Canada-United States issues should be studied as a model for all nations. While not necessarily as impressed by the civilized quality of the relationship, other writers have also stressed its alleged uniqueness as the reason why it should be studied.

Joseph Nye came close to taking the opposite position in making what is perhaps the most persuasive case for wide interest in the Canada-United States dyad. "There are large areas of world politics," he reasons, ". . . in which economic objectives are more salient than military security objectives, force is not very useful in achieving positive objectives, and unified governments are not the only significant actors".[2] This development may well have gone furthest in North America. With increasing interaction between industrialized societies, coupled with strong determination to preserve national identity and autonomy, the Canada-United States dyad can best be seen not as an interesting oddity but rather as an example of a relationship that is likely to become increasingly common.

Students of international integration should also be interested in the Canada-United States case as one in which the normative assumptions underlying most of the literature must be reversed, at least from the perspective of one of the two actors. In most Canadian eyes, integration with the United States is an evil to be resisted, or at best to be tolerated with extreme care in those limited instances where the costs of refusal would clearly exceed the costs of further integration.

For three years the Canadian government's policy toward the United States has been encapsulated in the "third option".[3] This has been interpreted as a comprehensive attempt to reduce Canada's dependence on its superpower neighbor through intensified relations with third countries, the rejection of further measures that would facilitate economic integration with the United States, and increased state intervention in the form, for example, of regulations to control foreign investment. The third option seems to enjoy general support, but there is less consensus concerning the phenomenon that it is designed to control. About two-fifths of the Ottawa foreign policy decision making elite believe that the overall trend in continental interactions is disintegrative; nearly a third perceive continuing integration; almost as many estimate that a state of equilibrium has been attained.[4] Relatively few believe that the adoption

---

[2] Joseph S. Nye, "Transnational Relations and Interstate Conflicts: An Empirical Analysis," ibid., 961.

[3] Mitchell Sharp, "Canada-U.S. Relations: Options for the Future," *International Perspectives*, Special Issue, 28 (Autumn 1972).

[4] This and subsequent estimates of the current attitude of the Ottawa foreign policy-making elite are based on nearly two hundred interviews that the author con-

of the third option has resulted in significant change, except perhaps in elite attitudes.

Considering the importance attached to autonomy in official rhetoric, and in some governmental actions, it is remarkable how little serious study is being devoted to the phenomenon of continental integration by Canadian scholars and decision makers. Histories of the Canada-United States relationship abound, and a number of economists have dealt professionally with the trade and investment linkages. Political scientists, however, have as yet contributed little of a nonpolemical character.[5] Few researchers, in or out of the government service, are attempting to comprehend the relationship in its entirety, or to gauge the prevailing tendencies.

As a preliminary step, it would appear useful to disaggregate the concept of international integration in a manner that reflects Canadian concerns and to estimate the trend within each of the seven relevant dimensions. Although it is not the most significant, one might start with the formal legal framework governing the transborder exchange of goods and factors. This consists largely of the rules accepted under GATT by both countries, coupled with an approximation of free trade in automobiles, auto parts, farm machinery, and arms. About 70 percent of Canada-United States trade bears no tariff, but rates on processed goods are often substantial. The latest sectoral free trade arrangement, the automobile pact, was concluded in 1965.

Although it resulted in considerable rationalization, and a big increase in Canadian production, neither Washington nor Ottawa is disposed to initiate further sectoral deals. The United States Congress is on record as favoring the negotiation of a general free trade arrangement with Canada, and the Economic Council of Canada has commended serious consideration of this option.[6] Neither government appears disposed to take the initiative, however, at least until the outcome of the current GATT negotiation becomes clear. The last word on the subject from the Trudeau government was a firm rejection of continental free trade on the traditional but fallacious grounds that it must lead to political union.[7] Ottawa has tightened its control over the inflow of capital through es-

---

ducted during the summer of 1975, as part of a study of elite images directed by Roddick Byers, Thomas Hockin, David Leyton-Brown, and Peyton Lyon. The interviewing is not yet complete, and precise computation and analysis have not been undertaken.

[5] Exceptions include A. Axline et al., editors, *Continental Community?: Independence and Integration in North America* (Toronto: McClelland and Stewart, 1974); and the special issue of *International Organization*, "Canada and the United States: Transnational and Transgovernmental Relations" 28 (Autumn 1974).

[6] Economic Council of Canada, *Looking Outward: A New Trade Strategy for Canada* (Ottawa: Information Canada), 1975.

[7] Sharp, p. 15.

tablishing the Foreign Investment Review Agency (FIRA), and both governments have become more restrictive concerning the movement of labor.

Similarly, if one turns from the legal forms to the actual flows of goods, capital, people, and communications, the current trend can hardly be described as integrative. The inflow of United States capital, and the volume of trade in both directions, increased dramatically in the postwar decades. By the criterion of economic transactions, a substantial degree of integration has already been attained and is likely to persist. In absolute terms, moreover, American ownership of industrial assets in Canada and the flow of goods continue to increase. As a proportion of total assets or flows, however, a plateau appears to have been reached, and there is a net decline in the movement of labor.

Integration for some authorities is largely a matter of formal intergovernmental structures to achieve joint or harmonized policies. These have always been kept to a minimum in Canada-United States relations, and they did not increase significantly over the past decade. Less use, moreover, has been made of the long-established structures that continue in existence. The last meeting of the cabinet level committee on trade and economic affairs, for example, was in 1969; the equivalent committee on defense last met in 1964. The responsibilities of the IJC for the control of pollution in the Great Lakes have increased, and a useful new committee to publish agreed statistics on Canada-United States trade was set up in 1973. On balance, however, the formal institutionalization of the relationship has declined.

This could, of course, easily be deceptive. Given the ease of informal communication across the border and the profusion of transgovernmental and transnational actors, an increase in overall policy harmonization is conceivable in spite of the decrease in formal structures. Impressionistic evidence, however, suggests that this is not the case. A number of interpersonal links were severely strained during the Connally tenure in the United States Treasury, and not all are fully restored. United States officials have complained that middle level Canadian officials, notably in the Department of External Affairs, now seem to delight in being difficult. Another complaint is that Canadians at all levels are too wrapped up in their own concerns to be able to contribute, as so often in the past, ideas of general relevance.

While the bulk of the transgovernmental links may well be as easy and effective as ever, however, a quick survey of policy outputs suggests a diminished determination on both sides to arrive at common approaches. This is apparent in such internal matters as automobile pollution standards. It is even more obvious in external behavior. Canada's unilateral extension of jurisdiction over Arctic and coastal waters, for example, was strongly resented in Washington. So too was the halving of the Canadian military contingent stationed in Europe and Canada's decision to initiate diplomatic relations with Peking. It is a fallacy, of course, to assume that similar policies must be the product either of joint decision making or dictation. Different governments may well perceive their interests and the external situation in such a way that they arrive quite independently at similar policies. This is frequently the case when Canadians and Americans participate in multilateral economic negotiations. Similarly, governments may choose to understate in public declarations severe differences of opinion that are more effectively conveyed through diplomatic channels. In vital respects, Canadian and American assessments of cold war issues coincided, but, when they did differ, as on tactics during the Korean war, the Canadians often played down their reservations in public in order to maximize their capacity to moderate American behavior through quiet persuasion. Even when full allowance is made for such considerations, however, there appear to be adequate grounds for the conventional assessment that, from the perspective of policy outputs, Canada and the United States are less integrated today than they were a decade ago.

A similar trend appears to characterize transnational linkages. The relations within such entities as corporations, trade unions, and sports leagues are increasingly politicized, and the impact of Canadian public concern is to augment the differentiation between the Canadian and American subunits. Canadian affiliates of predominately American concerns have also been rendered more subservient to Canadian wishes as manifested in federal policies and, in some cases, those of the provinces. As with transactions, a remarkable degree of integration has been attained in the transnational dimension, but the current trend is most probably one of moderate disintegration.

As for the attitudinal dimension, the disposition of Canadians to identify with Americans, or to look to Washington for leadership, has clearly declined. They are much more inclined to think in "we-they" terms, and the rhetoric of partnership no longer strikes a responsive chord. Canadians are much quicker to perceive direct conflicts of interest, and the traditional problem-solving approach is frequently viewed with suspicion. The extent, indeed the novelty, of overinvolvement in Indochina and the Watergate scandals are fading into history, and concern is rising about global economic conditions. It may even be that the peak of the current wave of Canadian nationalism, too often difficult to distinguish from anti-Americanism, has passed. Compared to a decade ago, however, there can be little doubt that Canadians and Americans are less prone to regard themselves as one people.

The last of the relevant dimensions, cultural homogenization, is the most difficult to comprehend. In spite of the growing Canadian consciousness of being different and the steps being taken by Ottawa to protect the media and subsidize the arts, the objective differences between the two societies may in fact be diminishing. A substantial proportion of Canada's intellectual sustenance continues to come from the United States. What does it profit a nation, it may well be asked, if it preserves political sovereignty and a generous standard of living but permits its value system to be largely determined from without its borders?

The problem is not that the American media flooding into Canada or even the American teachers in Canadian universities are out to promote a love of all things American. The media can hardly be accused of presenting recent American performance in an excessively charitable light, while many of the American professors, considering themselves to be political refugees, have fanned the anti-Americanism latent in Canadian society. Moreover, the most ardent nationalists among Canadians are often the most absorbed in American affairs and the most likely to engage in the latest American fad, especially if it entails an apparent rejection of American values. With considerable justification, one observer has written of the "Americanization of Canadian anti-Americanism."

A more valid objection to the preponderence in Canada of the American media is that it diverts Canadians from the problems and opportunities peculiar to their own country, including activity involving peoples on other continents that is both distinctive and rewarding. The difficulty of preserving, or creating, a Canadian culture is no less acute for being part of a global development. The homogenization of values that is perceived and deplored is less a case of spreading Americanism than the values that seem to be inherent in industrialized societies.

"The fact is," Frank Underhill wrote in 1960, "that, if we produced Canadian movies for our own mass consumption, they would be as sentimental and vulgar and escapist as are the Hollywood variety. . . . It is mass-consumption . . . which produce[s] the undesirable aspects of 'mass-communications,' not some sinister influence in the United States."[8] Canada has made progress in the production of quality films, but the few that have succeeded at the box office and on Canadian television tend to confirm Underhill's pessimistic prognosis. Indeed, considering the popularity in Canada of American magazines, films, and television, it is remarkable that striking differences in beliefs and behavior still persist. Not all of these are attributable to the "French fact." The lower incidence of violence in Canada, for example, has probably increased in recent years the differences in the life-styles characteristic of urban communities on the two sides of the border.

In three of the seven dimensions that have been identified—transactions, transnational linkages, and cultural homogenization—a substantial degree of international integration has occurred. In three others—

---

[8] Frank Underhill, *In Search of Canadian Liberalism* (Toronto: Macmillan Co. of Canada, 1960), p. 212.

formal economic arrangements, policy harmonization, and attitudes—the level of integration is more modest. In one, formal intergovernmental structures, it is relatively trivial. Of more immediate concern, however, are the prevailing trends. In three of the dimensions—formal economic arrangements, transactions, and transnational linkages—a state close to equilibrium appears to exist. In three others—formal intergovernmental structures, policy harmonization, and attitudes—the trend is clearly disintegrative. The dimension of cultural homogenization, arguably the most basic as well as the most difficult to gauge or control, is the only one in which integration seems likely to be proceeding.

It may well be objected that these are guesses, but the objection simply underlines the complaint already registered about the absence of serious, comprehensive research to understand and measure a phenomenon that the government, with considerable support at least from elite groups, has identified as posing a threat to national survival and has undertaken to combat by decisive measures. Even a cursory examination of the available evidence, however, casts doubt on the nationalists' claim that Canada is experiencing galloping integration and must be approaching the threshold beyond which its total absorption into the Great Republic becomes inescapable. Similarly, although the data prove little about causal linkages, they do tend to disconfirm theories of economic determinism. Along with substantial economic integration, North America has witnessed a degree of political and attitudinal disintegration. The temptation will be resisted to advocate further measures of economic integration as means to stimulate Canadian self-awareness and political autonomy. Current trends in North America, however, as well as experience elsewhere, suggest that Canadians would be irrational to rule out further collaboration in economic matters on the sole ground that this would entail serious political risks. Proposals, such as those of the Economic Council of Canada for continental free trade, deserve to be assessed seriously, very largely on their economic merits.

As Canadians have become conscious of their relative strength in natural resources and the gap in per capita income between the two countries narrows, the fear of losing out in any negotiation with Washington may be diminishing. Confidence has also been strengthened by the evident failure of the United States Treasury to muster the coordinated action that might have forced significant economic concessions from Canada. Some well-placed officials in both capitals believe that Canada characteristically comes closer than the United States to achieving its objectives whenever the two governments engage in disputes; this belief has been supported by the recent research of Joseph Nye, who has studied all the Canada-United States conflicts known to have received presidential attention during the past half-century. He concludes that "outcomes were closer to the American government objectives in five-eighths of the prewar cases, and in nearly half the cases in the 1950s, but in only a quarter of the cases in the 1960s."[9]

Canada, of course, could be winning the battles and losing the war. The automobile pact, for example, considered at the time to be a triumph for Canadian diplomacy, now appears to many to have left Canada more firmly locked into the American embrace.[10] It almost certainly caused a further concentration in Detroit of the management and research functions. "We may win a lot of games," a Canadian official said recently, "but we are playing in the Americans' ball park, in accordance with their rules." Ottawa may seem to do well in terms of conflict outcomes, another has reasoned, but only because it exercises extreme caution in choosing the issues on which to take a stand. For these and other reasons, the high level conflicts surveyed by Nye may yield misleading conclusions concerning the bulk of Canadian-American transactions. The trend in outcomes at lower levels could be in the opposite direction, especially if one thinks of multinational enterprise as an element of American power.

Nye suggests that this is unlikely. In the cases he has examined, Canada was better able than the United States to make use of transnational entities to buttress its negotiating position. United States based oil companies, for example, assisted Ottawa in achieving increases in the United States quota on oil imports, back in the days when Canada wanted to sell more in the American market. Similarly, the American automobile manufacturers, worried about their stake in Canada, served as an effective Canadian lobby in Washington during the passage of the automobile pact. Canadian officials believe that they fare reasonably well in dealings with their American counterparts, and there may well be grounds for this belief. Certainly most observers of the IJC have concluded that its technique for depoliticising issues has served Canada well. The Progressive Conservative party, traditionally the most cool toward closer ties with the United States, is now advocating the extension of the IJC approach to cover economic relations between the two countries.

Nye's findings offer some encouragement to the substantial minority in the Ottawa foreign-policy elite who now challenge the efficacy of quiet diplomacy in dealings with the United States. By showing Canada to have fared better in the 1960s than in the 1950s, he suggests that as the cold war eased and Canada became more openly self-centered and assertive, it fared better in high-level conflict outcomes than when it had

---

[9] Nye, p. 980.

[10] This point is disputed by some Ottawa officials who contend that the Canadian automobile industry is now in a stronger position to go it alone than in 1964, and they have seriously considered the possibility that Ottawa would take the initiative in abrogating the automobile pact.

perceived itself, and had been perceived in Washington, as a more vital and cooperative ally. In the 1950s, however, Ottawa was far more conscious than it is now of the potential danger to Canada in misguided United States policies in matters of global security and more confident of the superiority of Canadian common sense.

In seeking to moderate the behavior of a powerful neighbor directed largely toward third countries, the argument for quiet diplomacy is obviously stronger than when strictly bilateral issues are on the table. "A strong case," John Holmes has written, "can be made that the United States was in fact defied more stubbornly by the St. Laurent-Pearson policies of the fifties" than by those of contemporary Ottawa. In 1975 there appears to be less need, as well as less opportunity, for a Canadian input in the making of United States global policies. With but few exceptions, Washington is now pursuing the sort of policies that Canada has advocated for many years. If, however, Henry Kissinger is the most Canadian secretary of state yet seen, it is not because he solicits Canadian views. Indeed, it took two years to persuade him to pay his first official visit to Ottawa.

Canadian self-interest dictates doing as little as possible to irritate decision makers in Washington. Hard-boiled Canadian nationalism, often assumed to coincide with anti-American postures, is in fact more likely to lead to policies that downgrade Canada's endeavors to influence American behavior toward third countries or international agencies. This has been the trend in Canadian diplomacy under Trudeau, but the rhetoric of Canadian diplomacy has changed more than the reality; in general, Trudeau is much more in the Pearson tradition than his early statements would suggest.

For several years, the leaders of both countries have been burying the notion of a special relationship. Secretary Kissinger went so far as to wonder if it had ever been more than a myth. For an oft-interred concept, however, the special relationship is remarkably reluctant to lie down. It is readily conceded on both sides that the relationship will remain very special in terms of extent, complexity, and intensity. Although Ottawa is seeking a better balance by increasing its relations with other countries, it evidences no intention to reduce interaction with the United States in absolute terms. Nor, it is stressed, is there any desire to reduce the warmth of the relationship. Canada has promised to improve the practice of consultation, which had become erratic, and seems to be keeping this pledge.

The only sense in which the special relationship has been clearly repudiated is the one that amounted to a claim by Canada for preferential treatment—preferential both in comparison with other countries and also compared to the treatment to be accorded the United States by Canada. Some senior Canadian officials deny that Ottawa ever engaged in this sort of special pleading, but Washington is not alone in feeling that the burden of the "special relationship" fell heavier on American shoulders. Many Canadians were pleased when President Nixon, speaking in Parliament, appeared to give Canada permission to be independent. In fact, what they were hearing was a second declaration of American independence.

Canada is one of the most fortunate nations on earth and among the dozen strongest. It should not need special consideration, and the relationship, whether or not one chooses to call it special, should be rooted in reciprocity. However, while about half the makers of Canada's external policies believe that the United States accords Canada less favorable treatment than it did in the past, two-thirds still consider that treatment to be better than that accorded other countries. A strong majority in both the elite and mass concur that "the United States is Canada's best friend."[11] Nearly half perceive no essential difference in the interests of the two countries in international affairs, and those that do frequently attribute the difference simply to the disparity in power and consequent global responsibilities. About a quarter believe the values of the two societies to be essentially the same. Approximately half perceive neither country as most often getting its way in Canada-United States relations; a majority of the other half see the United States as the most frequent winner, but often volunteer that the margin is far less than the discrepancy in crude power; the minority that holds that Canada does best includes a significant proportion of those who have had the most experience in the conduct of the relationship. Almost half the elite consider that Canada acts more independently in international affairs than most other countries, and they do not assess as serious the constraints on Canada's external activity arising out of economic interdependence with the United States. A high proportion give a positive rating to the overall impact of the United States on international affairs and would regret its decision to withdraw from most of its global involvement.

Along with this benign view of the United States, however, especially of its treatment of Canada, most of the Canadian decision makers articulate a firm resolve to strengthen Canada's autonomy *vis-à-vis* the United States. About three-fourths would give high priority to measures designed to increase Canada's control over its economy, even if this were to mean a reduction in living standards, and support further steps to limit the impact of the United States on Canadian cultural activity. The largest number, about one-third, consider that relations with the United States constitute Canada's most pressing external problem. The decision makers were asked to rank the six themes from *Foreign Policy for Ca-*

[11] The elite members who disagree generally object to the proposition that countries have "best friends"; only a small minority name another country, such as the United Kingdom.

nadians, the government's pretentious statement of national aims,[12] and the most popular first choice within the elite is "sovereignty and independence." The perceived threat to this value, needless to say, is not from the United Kingdom, the Soviet Union, or Iceland. Substantial majorities express opposition to further measures of North American relations characteristic of the decision-making elite and the stated support for policies to augment independence. In part it appears to be because a serious military threat to North America is no longer perceived; Canada, in consequence, can afford to give higher priority to relatively secondary concerns. In part it is because the policy makers, perhaps erroneously, believe that a more independent posture is what the masses want. A number of Mr. Trudeau's ministers, not including the prime minister himself, have become prominently identified with the nationalist cause, and many civil servants may deem it proper, or at least prudent, to get in step.

This is not to suggest that most of the decision-making elite see no danger to Canada emanating from the United States. They do perceive a threat, but it has more to do with the attractive features of American life than the negative. One is forced to the dull conclusion that much of Canada's official rhetoric is true. Its decision makers and its masses do like Americans and appreciate the United States as a good neighbor. Their apprehension was well articulated by the senior official who, having agreed that the United States was Canada's best friend, added "and the worst threat because it is so friendly." If Canadians possessed memories of brutal American treatment comparable to the Irish case against the English, they would be less insecure about their identity and independence.

A large majority of Canada's decision makers express agreement with the policy of strengthening ties with third countries, most notably the West Europeans and Japan, as a means to lessen Canada's vulnerability to changes in the United States. They are less certain, however, that the third option is likely to make much difference in the foreseeable future. Some openly question if a time of economic stress at home and abroad is appropriate for a campaign to increase national independence. Other countries, especially those that are forming the European Community, are not without sympathy for Canada's predicament but quickly become bored by its appeals for help. Most, in fact, would gladly exchange Canada's problems for theirs. To the extent that foreign countries are interested in Canada's economy, they tend to be more single-minded than the Americans in wishing to exchange processed goods for Canada's raw materials, and Canadians are weary, or so most of them say, of being "hewers of wood and drawers of water." The interest shown by France in Canada's uranium and by other countries in its nuclear technology, especially the CANDU, is disturbing to many Canadians who take pride in their country's advocacy of nonproliferation.

[12] *Foreign Policy for Canadians* (Ottawa: Information Canada, 1970.)

Some of the Canadian policy makers doubt that the masses would tolerate significant steps toward increased autonomy *vis-à-vis* the United States. Public opinion polls have indicated majority support for increased control over Canadian industry, even at the cost of a drop in living standards. On the other hand, the political parties, on the strength of private soundings, have steered clear of the issue in successive election campaigns. Although the Foreign Investment Review Agency has turned down relatively few takeovers by foreign firms, only nine respondents out of more than two thousand cited foreign investment as the issue most important to them in the 1974 general election; only two said it was an important reason for voting as they did.[13] Hostility to American investment is far stronger in Ontario than in other parts of Canada. In Quebec, indeed, there is considerable support for increased American investment as a means to reduce its economic subservience to Ontario, while in both the Maritimes and the western provinces measures to restrict foreign capital are perceived by many as devices to perpetuate the economic advantages of central Canada. It has frequently been argued that continental integration is a cause of disintegration within Canada; measures to counteract the phenomenon, however, are very likely to add to the tensions between the Canadian regions and groups.

Canadians appear to be fair weather nationalists; in a climate of economic uncertainty they are unlikely to insist on measures that would seriously disrupt relations with the United States. Donald Jamieson, Canada's new trade minister, evoked little protest when he called recently for an increase in trade with the United States, and the Economic Council's advocacy of continental free trade has met with surprising tolerance and even some sympathy. There are strong grounds for action to foster indigenous Canadian culture, but here, too, public support is doubtful; restrictions on the dissemination of American programs by cable television, for example, and the action to block the entry into Canada of the ill-fated World Football League were greeted with widespread resistance.

Canadians, therefore, seem unlikely to initiate dramatic changes in the continental relationship. They will seek stronger ties with other countries and, if successful, should become more confident and less irritable in dealing with Americans. They will look critically at new proposals that appear integrative and may take further steps to reduce the predominance of the American media. It is not inconceivable, however, that trends in the global environment will persuade the two nations to move closer together.

[13] The author is grateful to Professor Jane Jensen for this information. See also Sigler and Goresky, p. 652, for a discussion of the saliency of the foreign investment issue.

Quebec and the Bicultural Dimension

DALE C. THOMSON

Prime Minister Trudeau once remarked that the real importance of a minority group is not so much a function of its legal guarantees as its potential to disrupt the country in which it lives. On that basis, French Canada, with the political and administrative apparatus of the province of Quebec behind it, easily qualifies as important.

"Quebec" and "French Canada" are not synonymous terms. Almost 20 percent of the 5.5 million French Canadians live outside that province, and almost 20 percent of Quebec residents are not French Canadians; that is, their first language is not French. But the disruptive power Mr. Trudeau referred to is in the hands of those French Canadians within Quebec. So, for practical purposes, there is a high level of synonymy. And the bicultural dimension of Canada flows from the real power of French Canadians in the province of Quebec.

That is one way of looking at French Canadians—as a minority so troublesome that they might conceivably break up Canada. There are other ways: for instance, as one of the two "founding peoples," a concept utilized by the Royal Commission on Bilingualism and Biculturalism. That concept implies an equal partnership between the descendants of those hardy Frenchmen who first colonized New France and the British who conquered them in 1759. The other Canadians, notably the original settlers, the Indians and Eskimos, and the one-quarter of the Canadian population of origins other than English or French are attributed some lesser status. Those shortcomings acknowledged, the concept of two founding peoples does represent a sincere attempt to transcend psychological divisions that have existed in Canada for more than two centuries and that are still highly pertinent.

The view proffered here of French Canada is more positive than that of a great many, probably most, English Canadians. It challenges the con-

cept of nearly one-third of the total population as a minority to be tolerated only because of some legal guarantees or disruptive potential.
French Canada, it posits, is an integral and very important part of Canada,
a great asset to be preserved and developed.

The complexities and intricacies of such a pluralist society must be
acknowledged. No political leader would choose one if he did have a
choice. However, that is the heritage of history.

It is difficult for Americans to realize the full significance of the linguistic dualism of Canada. Many seem to consider it a historical vestige that
was illogical to perpetuate and that would disappear with time. There are
certainly Canadians who share this view, but it is unlikely to occur soon.
Indeed, both the Canadian and Quebec governments are taking steps to
see that the opposite occurs.

There is undoubtedly a price to be paid for maintaining biculturalism
in Canada, and statistics indicate that the highest price is being paid by
French Canadians. They are still the second-lowest income group, even in
the province of Quebec where they are a majority. Those who speak and
write English, particularly those who switch languages, generally do
better financially. And yet most French Canadians refer with sadness
and even pity to those who have abandoned the language of Molière for
that of Shakespeare, or the language of the vast majority of North
Americans.

The explanations of this attitude are too complex to deal with here, but
it is clear that the great majority of French Canadians feel the loss of
their language would be an unacceptable price to pay for the full benefits
of the American way of life. At the same time, they are attracted by
many of those benefits, both material and nonmaterial. The dilemma
facing French Canadians is how to find ways of enjoying the benefits of
life in North America while preserving their language.

Until the fairly recent past, material goals did not rank high for French
Canadians, or at least for their leaders. In fact, they preserved their language and customs by denying themselves the material benefits that
would come from greater integration with the rest of North America.
Even during the negotiations that led to the present federal system in
Canada, one of the primary goals of French Canadian leaders was to preserve and even strengthen their control over their own way of life. It is
too often forgotten, even by English Canadians, that Confederation, in
1867, not only laid the ground work for a country extending from sea to
sea but that it put an end to the previous regime, which placed both English and French Canadians under a single government and legislature.
This persistence and determination to survive unchanged led Arnold
Toynbee to remark that French Canadians would be one of the most durable peoples in human history.

Unfortunately for the French Canadians, the province of Quebec was not rich enough to support their rapidly growing population indefinitely on the basis of a primary economy. Faced in the nineteenth century with a situation described by historian Michel Brunet as "anemic survival," the excess population sought employment in the industrial towns of eastern Canada and New England, and became the urban proletariat working under English language bosses. Their lack of education, knowledge of the language of commerce and industry, and money severely restricted their upward mobility. Of course there was an affluent French Canadian elite, and the poverty level should not be exaggerated, but it cannot be denied that in cities like Montreal economic class and linguistic class cleavages were largely congruent.

Part of the pattern of conduct of French Canadians in Quebec today can be explained as a reaction against that situation. The dam holding this system in place broke as recently as 1959 with the death of Maurice Duplessis, the last provincial premier to stress the traditional nonmaterial values at the expense of economic growth. The arrival in power in Quebec City of the Lesage government in June 1960 marked the beginning of a new era of rapid modernization.

At the outset this "quiet revolution," as this modernization process was called, seemed designed primarily to enable Quebec to catch up to more developed parts of Canada, such as the province of Ontario. For this reason many English Canadians welcomed the change of government as likely to bring the objectives of Quebec closer to those of the other provinces and therefore to enhance national unity. However, it soon became evident that there were other ramifications to this process of modernization. It stirred new hope and pride in French-speaking Quebecois, and the Lesage government appealed to that sentiment to pursue its modernizing objectives. For instance, in 1962 it called an election to strengthen its position and campaigned in favor of nationalization of the electrical power companies in the province. Its slogan, which proved eminently successful, was *maîtres chez nous* or "masters in our own house." Lesage also carried on and intensified the struggle with Ottawa for a larger share of taxing powers and other financial resources. He surprised the rest of Canada even more, particularly since he was a former federal cabinet minister, by demanding increased legislative autonomy for Quebec as well. In 1964, Canadians witnessed a spectacle—certainly unanticipated by either man a few years earlier when they were members of the St. Laurent cabinet in Ottawa—of Prime Minister Pearson and Premier Lesage playing brinkmanship with Confederation in their dispute over control of social welfare legislation.

The quiet revolution of the 1960s in Quebec must be seen in the context of worldwide events and conditions. As British Prime Minister Harold Macmillan said at the time, "winds of change" were sweeping the continents. Its defenses already being eroded by industrialization, improved communications, and other factors, Quebec was no longer immune to these currents. For instance, news of national liberation movements in Asia and Africa struck a responsive chord among French Canadians and stimulated the centuries old dream of wiping out the British conquest. After years of acquiescence, separatist movements appeared once more, and public opinion polls in 1963 indicated that 13 percent of Quebecois openly favored independence. Acts of terrorism were committed by some extreme separatist groups that included at least one person who had had experience in Algeria and another in the Congo. The most infamous of these was the kidnapping in October 1970 of British diplomat James Cross and of Quebec Labour Minister Pierre Laporte. The latter was assassinated. It is significant as an indication of the state of public opinion in Quebec at the time that while many people thought the kidnapping of the British diplomat a good trick to play on *les Anglais*, the vast majority of French Canadians were horrified at the assassination of Laporte and approved the firm action of the Canadian and Quebec governments to restore order. Many expressed deep concern that foreigners, hearing perhaps of Quebec for the first time, would get a wrong impression of it.

Another facet of the quiet revolution was the renewal of links with France and the development of new links with other French-speaking peoples. French-speaking Quebecois have always had difficulty in accepting the Canadian government in Ottawa as "their" government, and that was probably a factor in the decision of the Quebec government to establish direct working relations with France rather than going through Ottawa. It must be pointed out that these relationships were restricted to fields of provincial jurisdiction, but at the same time they fell within the ambit of any reasonable definition of "foreign affairs" and consequently were of direct interest to the federal government. President de Gaulle, encouraged by a small group of politicians and officials in France, many of whom saw an analogy with contemporary events in French-speaking Africa, encouraged these direct contacts. By 1967, he had apparently become convinced that the independence of Quebec was inevitable, and he took the opportunity of his visit to Expo in Montreal in July of that year to *poser un geste* (make a gesture) in its favor. His adoption of the separatist cry, *Vive le Québec libre*, shouted from the balcony of the Montreal Hôtel de Ville, echoed around the world. He certainly did succeed in encouraging the separatists. On the other hand, he stirred the Canadian national sentiments of many millions of Canadians, both English- and French-speaking, and spurred the federal government to defend its prerogatives. Its first act was to declare his intervention in Canadian affairs "unacceptable" and force him to return to France the next day.

Since that time, thanks in part to changes in leadership in Paris, Ottawa, and Quebec City, a new *modus vivendi* has been reached, according to which Ottawa's overriding authority in international matters is recognized, but Quebec does have considerable interaction with other countries, including France, and the Quebec government has a special voice through participation in Canadian delegations when its interests are involved. The extent of Quebec's external relations astonishes some theorists of federalism, but they do reflect the ability of the Canadian federal system to adapt to political realities. To sum up on this point, it is fair to say that relations between France and Canada are once again normal, but the "normality" is rather different from the *status quo ante*. Each year thousands of Frenchmen and Quebecois cross the Atlantic under a variety of cooperative arrangements. Will these relations tend to weaken Quebec's ties with Canada and the rest of North America? There is a possibility, but there is also evidence that better knowledge of France and the French has led Quebecois to realize how very North American they are.

But the real measure of the quiet revolution and its long-range significance must be taken within Quebec and based on both material and nonmaterial changes. The Lesage government was defeated in 1966, but the Union Nationale party, which governed from 1966 to 1970, and the present Liberal administration under Robert Bourassa, a former lieutenant of Lesage, have carried the province forward along the same path. Quebec is now a highly industrialized province, with agriculture accounting for only 9 percent of production. A radically new system of education has been established, replacing the former highly elitist, churchsponsored one, which had been designed essentially to train priests and members of the liberal professions. Quebec now has a comprehensive system of social welfare, including Medicare. Regional economic development programs have greatly increased revenues in the poorer outlying regions, and the public service has grown rapidly.

More difficult to evaluate are the present norms, values, and attitudes of Quebecois. What, for instance, is their attitude toward the long-standing preoccupation with their survival as a group? Has this sentiment diminished? The evidence is contradictory. On one hand, qualified young Quebecois are not hesitant about demanding their place in the sun. They display a confidence that certainly seems new. On the other hand, there is no doubt that their society is more vulnerable to outside influences than ever before.

Politicians apparently still feel that the sentiment of insecurity is a factor to be reckoned with and do not hesitate to prey on it. René Lévesque, the leader of the separatist party, the Parti Québécois, declares at regular intervals that if independence is not achieved within ten years, no one will have the right to speak French in Quebec. And even Premier Bourassa evokes it in support of his policies to strengthen the position of

French by government action. Some might see in the growing popularity of the separatist movement an indication of continuing insecurity. Others interpret that phenomenon as a growth of self-confidence, a feeling that French Canadians in Quebec have reached a level of development where they can take charge completely of their own affairs and run their own country. The issue of separatism today no longer seems as emotional and as abstract as a decade ago, when it was often characterized by an outpouring of frustration and nourished by privation and inequality. Today, the possibility of separation is just another, though very serious, option in Quebec.

A related question is whether, having achieved a fair degree of modernization and competence, with greater opportunities for careers within the province of Quebec, French Canadians' attitudes toward Ottawa have changed. It is fortunate from the point of view of those who believe in a single Canada that throughout most of the period since 1960 its government has been in the hands of people able to understand this process of modernization and willing to support it. If the situation that pertained there in the 1950s still existed, when the working language of the federal public service was almost exclusively English and French was not allowed on public signs in the city of Ottawa, there is little doubt that modern day young French Canadians would be inclined to turn their backs on it.

Fortunately, the Pearson government and its successor, the Trudeau government, have taken significant initiatives, one of the first of which was the creation of the Royal Commission on Bilingualism and Biculturalism, set up in 1963, with Dr. Davidson Dunton as one of the two co-chairmen. That massive investigation resulted, among other things, in both English and French being made official languages within the areas of jurisdiction of the federal government. Associated steps, such as enabling citizens to be served by the federal public service in either language and enabling young French-speaking Canadians to be on a comparable footing when starting their careers in Ottawa, have had a salutary effect. In the Department of External Affairs, for example, a high level of bilingualism has been achieved, that is, officials are bilingual and may work in either language. In the circumstances and since much of the work that the federal government offers is more challenging than that in Quebec, some of the resistance to making a career in Ottawa has been overcome. The increasing self-confidence of young French Canadians has also had the effect of making them more inclined to accept the challenge of the federal public service.

Other types of measures must also be borne in mind, such as the regional economic development program, through which vast sums of money were poured into rural areas of Quebec. Another example is the system of equalization payments, through which taxes raised by the federal government are redistributed to the provinces in such a way that they can all provide a similar level of provincial services. Quebec is a very important beneficiary of this system. Generally speaking, the policy of the federal government has been to induce Quebecois to identify more with the rest of Canada, particularly with the national capital, and to perceive the advantages of remaining a part of Canada.

These policies have been pursued in the face of a substantial backlash, particularly in the western provinces, against the more visible French presence in Ottawa, the demands of Quebec, and the cost of programs such as bilingualization and federal payments that end up in Quebec. It is not easy to weigh the threat to Canada from Quebec separatism against the hostility of some other parts of Canada to measures designed to meet that threat. And in periods of economic austerity, the federal government's position is more difficult still.

A sobering thought for the federal government in determining its policies to meet the problem of Quebec and biculturalism is that there is no complete solution. Most of Canada will remain essentially "English" and, at best, Ottawa will be only half-French. By and large, French Canadians will continue to feel more at home in Quebec than elsewhere in Canada. Hence their first loyalty will be to Quebec, in contrast to residents of the other provinces, whose first loyalty is quite clearly to Canada as a whole. Other, more international, forces will also contribute to the outcome, such as future economic conditions, the future course of nationalism, regional regroupings, and world peace in general.

When the Liberal government of Robert Bourassa was elected in Quebec in 1970 on an unabashedly profederal ticket, there was widespread hope that he and Pierre Trudeau would work closely together to keep Quebec happy within Confederation. However, in many instances, the two governments have appeared to be at odds, even in their language policies. Bourassa first won election on the slogan of "profitable federalism," a somewhat cynical claim that he and his party could extract more money from Ottawa than anyone else. He was appealing to a majority sentiment in Quebec, carefully ascertained in advance by polls, that the primary concerns of the voters were material in nature and that these could best be solved within Confederation. In this vein, he promised to create 100,000 additional jobs in a short period. Because he was elected with such a clear commitment to federalism, many Canadians expected him to cooperate fully in the process of constitutional review then under way but long delayed because of Quebec's particular demands. However, when the crunch came following the constitutional conference in Victoria, British Columbia, in 1971, he found a pretext at the last moment to avoid placing the constitutional revisions before the Quebec legislature, and so the efforts of several years came to naught. He gained some political credit within Quebec for "standing up" to Ottawa. Whether or not he did Canada a great disservice in the long run will be determined by history.

As they prepared for new elections in 1973, Bourassa and his colleagues decided to add another dimension to their program and adopted the further slogan, "cultural sovereignty." It was clearly designed to undercut the Parti Québécois, the separatist party, and clearly the principal threat to the Liberals. Through this tandem of "profitable federalism" and "cultural sovereignty," Bourassa was borrowing at least the words of the first program devised by separatist leader René Lévesque, "sovereignty-association," or sovereignty of Quebec in association, presumably economic and financial, with the rest of Canada. Looked at another way, Bourassa was telling the Quebec electorate it could have the material advantages of Confederation and yet remain French. The appeal was not unlike that made by George-Etienne Cartier in selling Confederation to Quebecois in 1867. The strategy worked: the Liberals were returned with a fantastic majority of 102 out of 110 seats. However, the Parti Québécois, the separatist party, increased its popular vote to between 32 and 33 percent, but because of the single constituency system won only six seats.

The 1973 elections marked the clear polarization of the Quebec electorate, with separatism as the clear alternative to Bourassa-type federalism. This is a rather unsettling situation, for it appears to imply that keeping Quebec within Confederation requires keeping Bourassa in power. In other words, there appears to be no profederal alternative to the Bourassa government at the present time.

Bourassa's first major step in implementing his policy of cultural sovereignty was to rush through the legislature in the summer of 1974 a bill making French the official language of Quebec. The expression "priority language" would be more appropriate, since English still retains an important but reduced role. But for a man with Bourassa's keen political instincts, the word "official," even if less accurate, had greater value. In brief, the Official Language Act, or Bill 22, as it is commonly called, aims to make it possible for Quebecois to use French in their province, while respecting the rights of the English-language population to their educational system. The "English" may also use English in many other instances, but overall the official language is French. In the field of business, firms must undertake "francization" programs and open up as many jobs as possible to French-speaking persons. Provision is made for all French-speaking children to learn English as a second language, and vice versa; but it will be many years before the school system is able to carry out the terms of that provision.

Thus, while Ottawa has been moving to promote bilingualism, the Quebec government has moved toward greater unilingualism. Is this a case of the two governments working at cross-purposes? Perhaps to some degree. On the other hand, it can well be argued that the future of bilingualism in Canada depends on the viability of French in Quebec. If it is not made "secure" there, and here again is the historic French Canadian preoccupation with security, attempts to promote it elsewhere in Canada will be of no avail. One can also argue that if Quebec separates, then attempts to encourage bilingualism in the rest of Canada will certainly be futile. And one must recognize clearly that the language law is designed to reduce the appeal of separatism. From those points of view, then, the provincial and federal language acts are complementary and mutually supporting.

At the time it was passed, the Official Language Act raised a storm of protests, particularly from what Bourassa called both English and French extremists, that is, those who felt it repressed the English and those who felt it did not do so enough. Many in between were also unhappy about aspects of this legislation, either on the grounds of principle, common sense, or practicality. However, they had to recognize that Premier Bourassa had again pulled a political trump card out of his sleeve. Polls taken a few months after the law was passed indicated that he had succeeded in defusing the language issue among young French Canadians. By coincidence or not, the percentage of separatists among junior college students fell from about 80 to about 50 percent. The Parti Québécois continues to attack the legislation as mere "tokenism," but it is the English language population that has protested the most as it has been applied. And of course that helps to vindicate the government's position in the eyes of French Canadians.

At the beginning of the 1975-76 school year, a furor was caused in the Montreal area when children were obliged for the first time, in accordance with the new law, to take a language test to enter an English-language school. Some Italian immigrant children passed the tests but were not enrolled because the law also sets a quota for every school district, based on past enrollments. An English-language Montreal radio station seized on the issue and campaigned to have the law repealed. Bourassa met the enraged citizens in a public confrontation, stood firm—thereby improving his image among the French-speaking citizenry—and then set to work quietly to find a practical way of allowing the some 200 children who had been excluded by the quota system to attend an English language school. The premier's performance was not quite perfect: his minister of education, who had been growing increasingly unhappy with his place in the cabinet, resigned on the grounds that no such concession should be made and that the possibility of attending an English-language school should be restricted to children of proven English homes. Bourassa had no difficulty in finding another minister of education.

What are the likely long-term consequences of this language law? If Premier Bourassa and his colleagues had their choice, they would apply it gradually over a long period of time and moderate its provisions with large doses of common sense and realism. Because their aim was to remove the language issue from political debates, or at least to formulate the debate in terms favorable to them, they are anxious to have as few eruptions as possible in its application. Certainly they do not wish to amend the law before the next elections, two or three years away. However, their actions in this regard are being scrutinized by the Parti Québécois and other nationalist elements in Quebec, and it must always be remembered that the political threat to Bourassa comes from that direction. It is hoped that a majority of Quebecois, both English- and French-speaking, will recognize that the legislation is about as good as can be devised at the moment and will put it to the test of practice. A great deal of flexibility and discretion is provided for, and one can be confident that the government will use them to reconcile divergent interests and views. If a more nationalist Quebec government succeeds the present one, however, it might use that flexibility and discretion to "squeeze the English" without having to amend the law. Bourassa himself, if faced with a severe threat from the nationalist side, might not recoil before such tactics.

Thus a new pattern of bilingualism appears to be emerging in Canada, one that can be called *quid pro quo* bilingualism: as many rights for the English in Quebec as are accorded to the French in the other provinces and as much linguistic equality as possible in the national capital. Undoubtedly it will be difficult for the federal government to go further, or to encourage the other provinces to go further, in extending bilingualism throughout the other nine provinces. The backlash was strong before the Quebec law was passed; it has grown stronger since. However, there is real hope that progress can be made in improving the bilingual character of the national capital.

This trend suggests that Canada is moving away from the concept once advanced of integral bilingualism throughout the federation, with everyone having some knowledge of both languages. It will probably not even be possible to attain that goal within the federal public service, particularly outside of Ottawa. It is not a comparison that is appealing, but perhaps Canada is getting nearer to the Belgian model with two unilingual areas and a bilingual capital. Of course, come what may, whether they separate, partially separate, or whatever, French-speaking Quebecois will have a greater need to know English than the majority of English-speaking Canadians in other provinces will have to learn French.

One of the likely consequences of this linguistic legislation, combined with new arrangements between Quebec and Ottawa to discourage immigration to Quebec of persons who are not prepared to make French their principal language, is that Quebec will fall behind other parts of Canada in population and economic growth. By 1985, Quebec will be short of manpower, and neither immigration nor natural population increase seem likely to fill the gap. (One aspect of Quebec's modernization is that its birthrate has fallen to the lowest in Canada). There is a good chance that capital will not be as easily attracted to Quebec as to other parts of Canada, and this will increase the disparity in economic importance between Quebec and, say, Ontario. It is fairly safe to forecast that by the year 2000 Ontario will be at least twice as large as Quebec in terms of population and that Toronto rather than Montreal will be the financial capital of Canada. Quebec will constitute only about 20 percent of the population of Canada, and its representation in the Canadian Parliament will have to be adjusted accordingly. This last factor will again stimulate Quebecois' feeling of insecurity within Canada and may fuel separatism.

But those are rather long-term predictions. The question is whether the two sets of language legislation, Quebec and federal, and other actions will get Canada through another generation. Perhaps it would not be too optimistic to say they will. Much is made of the radical changes in Quebec since 1960, and particularly in the attitudes of French Canadians. Graphic illustrations are put forward of the decline in respect for authority, both of the church and of the state. Attention is drawn to the marked decrease in church attendance, the widespread use of the birth control pill, the frequency of abortions, the rising crime rate, and the numerous illegal strikes.

It is quite true that there has been a radical departure from past social patterns. And yet it can be argued that the new patterns only appear radical in today's world in comparison with the former traditional Quebec society. Compared to those of the youth of many other parts of the world, including English Canada and the United States, the attitudes and conduct of young French Canadians are relatively moderate. It must be remembered that the youth of today in Quebec are still the first generation to be "liberated" from the old constraints and are perhaps pursuing the enjoyment of that new liberty rather far, but that is a situation that will certainly correct itself with time.

For instance, there is concern with the low birthrate in Quebec, yet polls indicate that a high value is still placed on the family and on children. Almost certainly the birthrate will rise again, but childbearing will occur a few years later in a woman's life. In other words, the trend is not against the family unit and childbearing but in favor of a more relaxed, voluntaristic type of marital relationship and family planning, such as has become widespread in other parts of North America in the recent past. Similarly, with regard to public authority, or law and order, reference has already been made to the strong public reaction against the terrorist excesses in 1970. The same attitude was quite evident in the fall of 1975 in the case of strikes in the public service, including the post office and urban transport systems. In earlier days, resisting public authority was a way of thumbing one's nose at *les Anglais*; today, it represents a conflict between French Canadians.

Since World War II, it has been learned time and again that change breeds stress, and that progress is only accomplished at the price of some measure of conflict. Quebec is still engaged in a sweeping process of change and progress. It is far from having run its course. On balance, the results so far have been positive. Hence there is reason to be optimistic about the future. Fate has not been kind to French Canadians, making them a small linguistic minority on this continent; they merit understanding and even support in their legitimate goals, which are not essentially different from those of any other people.

Finally, in view of the title of this book, it must be asked what the state of Quebec and of the bicultural dimension of Canada means in terms of Canada-United States relations. Assuming first that Quebec will not separate from the rest of Canada, there are no major implications. The increased French Canadian input into Canadian decision making is scarcely likely to strengthen anti-American trends. Because they have the protective barrier of a different language, French Canadians feel less threatened by American influences and in a better position to take or leave what the United States has to offer. In other words, anti-American sentiment is much stronger in Toronto than it is in Quebec City. Ottawa's Foreign Investment Review Act resulted from pressures in English Canada and has not been received with enthusiasm by the government of Quebec, which is still trying to attract capital from south of the border for development projects.

American firms operating in Quebec will, of course, be expected to obey the Official Language Act, which means essentially opening up positions to French Canadians and giving them the opportunity to work in French. The day is gone when the American head of a big firm could say, as happened as recently as 1972, that as long as he was president no French would be used in the Montreal headquarters. Incidentally, he is no longer head of that firm. On the other hand, one cannot imagine the government of Quebec applying so much pressure on an American firm to "francisize" its operations that it will withdraw from the province. Persuasion, not coercion, is the order of the day. Generally speaking, American firms will be expected to see that their interests lie in adhering to the objectives of the Official Language Act. Past experience in other countries suggests that they will do so. Quebec officials are likely to continue to be happy to deal with Amerians in English, whether in Quebec or across the border. It is the English Canadians whom they want to force to use French!

Nor is the bilingualization of the federal public service likely to make much difference in the field of Canada-United States relations. In recent years, a French Canadian served as ambassador to Washington. He was able by his presence to draw attention to the fact that part of the population of Canada is French-speaking. He was also inclined to stand somewhat more on protocol than his immediate predecessor, and his *cuisine* was true *cordon bleu*! But it is doubtful that Americans he dealt with noticed many more significant differences. Certainly his concept of Canada was all-Canadian. Other French Canadians in the Canadian public service could not be expected to act differently.

Should the population of Quebec elect a government committed to separation from the rest of Canada, the position of the United States government might be delicate for a while. Some separatists argue that a Parti Québécois government would immediately move to establish close relations with the United States and that such a move would be welcomed in Washington. It is probable that the United States government would prefer to continue to deal with a single country on its northern border, since it is nearly always uneasy about political instability. Fears have been expressed, in view of some of the radical pronouncements in Quebec, of a Castro-type regime emerging in an independent Quebec. That seems unlikely. One can fear just as much a Batista-type regime, with the symbols but little of the true texture of independence.

But such comments verge on idle speculation. It would be better to conclude by saying that the recent evolution of Quebec and the growing bicultural dimension of Canada have had positive effects on Canada-United States relations. The modernization of Quebec has improved its capacity to contribute to the well-being of the whole continent. The assertion of the "French fact" in Canada has increased awareness of the distinctiveness of Canada from the United States, and a greater realization of this distinctiveness by American negotiators could make relations easier. Canadian negotiators have long complained that their American counterparts were not sensitive to such domestic factors. Finally, the total effect has been to strengthen Canada as a nation and as a partner of the United States on this continent.

Western Disenchantment and the Canadian Federation

WALTER D. GAINER

Much has already been written and said over the years concerning regional differences of outlook in Canada and the underlying influences conditioning the evolution of such differences. Richard Simeon, in more recent times, has summarized this thinking as follows: "The most salient characteristic of Canadian society is its regional diversity—geographic, economic, cultural, and historical. . . . These differences have led to great variations in outlook . . . and remain a prime source of conflict. . . . As a result, it appears reasonable to conceive of Canada as a collection of regional cultures rather than one 'national' culture."[1] Other authors have gone on to examine particular manifestations of these regional differences as evidenced in such things as electoral behavior, political party structures, attitudes toward language rights and provincial autonomy, stance on specific economic issues of concern to particular regions of the country at one time or another, and so on.[2]

Such an approach may carry a certain danger of concentrating too much on an analysis of particular regional symptoms and manifestations

---

[1] Richard Simeon, *Federal-Provincial Diplomacy: The Making of Recent Policy in Canada* (Toronto: University of Toronto Press, 1972), pp. 20-21.

[2] See, e.g., Mason Wade, ed., *Regionalism in the Canadian Community, 1867-1967* (Toronto: University of Toronto Press, 1969); Robert Alford, *Party and Society* (Chicago: Rand McNally, 1963); C. Brough Macpherson, *Democracy in Alberta: Social Credit and the Party System*, 2d ed. (Toronto: University of Toronto Press, 1962); Edward M. Corbett, *Quebec Confronts Canada* (Baltimore: Johns Hopkins University Press, 1967); H. A. and W. T. Easterbrook, "Fundamental and Historical Elements," in *The Canadian Economy: Selected Readings*, ed. John Deutsch, Burton Keirstead, Kari Levitt, and Robert Will, rev. ed. (Toronto: The Macmillan Company of Canada Limited, 1965), pp. 440-48; John Porter, *The Vertical Mosaic: An Analysis of Social Class and Power in Canada* (Toronto: University of Toronto Press, 1965).

of tension, rather than on an identification of the nature and regional distribution of the underlying sources of tension. Such underlying causes may possess a common denominator that does not demonstrate the same pattern of regional concentration suggested by symptoms alone, and these causes may give rise to different symptoms in different circumstances.

In any case, there is something about the above conclusion that would seem vastly to overdraw the extent of regional differences in economic, social, ethnic, and other circumstances and consequently of clearly distinctive regional cultures within Canada. With the one exception of the Quebecois section of the French-Canadian community, the substantial ethnocultural diversities to be found throughout the rest of Canada are rather well distributed throughout all parts of the federation. Only in Quebec are the dominant patterns sufficiently different and sufficiently concentrated geographically to qualify as a distinct regional culture—and then only with respect to the noneconomic aspects of the subculture. With respect to regional differences in fundamental economic attitudes, in contrast to economic conditions, it would seem more realistic to suggest that the dominant underlying determinant of Canadian regionalism is a common dissatisfaction on the part of all peripheral regions with the concentration of commercial influence, and all that goes with it, in central Canada—especially between Detroit and Montreal.

Such a bipolarization of attitudes in each region is of course reinforced by the particular circumstances of geography. Thus the real and psychic costs imposed by great distances from the center have been seared into the consciousness of individuals and organized groups in every peripheral region of the country. In the inbound and outbound movement of product and raw materials, the concern takes the form of dissatisfactions over the costs of transportation borne by peripheral residents. More important are the deep-seated attitudes engendered in all peripheral regions by feelings of psychic remoteness from the central establishments and "old-boy" networks of central Canada—the central administrative network of the federal government, the industrial and financial establishment of central Canada, the academic and government research establishment, and that of the arts and communication media. These are the personnel networks concentrated and activated at the center, and only randomly and sporadically accessible to the periphery—given the difficulties of building and maintaining casual human contact over great distances and through several layers of a national establishment of any kind. With respect to economic and geographic underpinnings of this kind, then, the conditioned outlook and attitudes of mainland Quebec, for instance, are little different from those characterizing other peripheral regions of the country. On these counts, only the populous nerve center of central Canada stands isolated from other regions.

It is therefore suggested that this ongoing tendency to economic bipolarization in regional attitudes, which can be characterized in terms of the periphery versus the center, has been an important underlying source of observed differences in the behavior of some regional institutions and spokesmen. Thus regional political party structures, electoral behavior, public pronouncements, and posturing on particular issues can easily take on seemingly incongruous patterns. But such anomalies can often be explained by the need to project the appearance at least of independence, whereas the basic values, mores, and attitudes in the peripheral society may differ but slightly from those in the dominant region.

It is perhaps more useful, then, to view certain characteristic regional poses or attitudes on particular issues as symptoms of a certain frustration over failure to win at a game in which there can be only one winner. Thus one can visualize a number of regional communities, each possessing essentially the same economic values and goals, but where each region is striving to improve its economic position *relative* to the others. The problem is that this must necessarily be a zero-sum game so long as it is relative positions that are at stake. Hence regional frustrations will show up as incipient attitudes of discontent voiced as open rationalizations concerning the reasons for regional disadvantage in the periphery. In short, there is no way that such underlying frustrations leading to periodic conflict can be eliminated so long as every hound is willing to chase the same rabbit, or so long as the lead hounds cannot be persuaded to hang back somewhat in favor of those in behind.

Thus, it is argued here that the underlying basis of regional frictions within the Canadian federation stems more from the pursuit of common economic growth and development goals by each section of the country than it does from any great regional differences in dominant values, attitudes, and behavior patterns. At the same time, within this general framework, it is also the case that history and geography have combined differently in the development experience of the various regions, often in a way that has led to a predominance of certain economic group interests identified with a particular industry or occupation. As a result, when various spokesmen for the region voice positions on a variety of policy issues, they frequently project a certain stereotype of regional outlook that is closely identified with the dominant economic interest groupings of the region. But again, such stereotyped regional positions on particular issues are often tangential to the main sources of complaint and a mere reflection of deeper-seated attitudes of regional paranoia over the seemingly intractable centralization of control of the economic and associated power centers of the country.

Moreover, every peripheral region of the country is acutely conscious of its relative position within the national economic hierarchy. Each tends to rationalize its own position of disadvantage and its aspirations for change within this hierarchy in terms of the familiar themes of history and geography that appear to have the most to do with shaping the regional destiny. But regardless of static or changing positions within the hierarchy, every region is nevertheless shooting for the same prizes —relative improvement in per capita incomes, more industrial job opportunities for a dwindling or growing local population, more industrial development to diversify and stabilize the regional income base, greater local participation and ownership in the regional industrial base, and so on.

The traditional conflict areas between western Canada and Ottawa are over policy issues such as protective tariffs, banking and finance, transportation, agricultural stabilization, and more recently returns from natural resources and regional economic expansion policies. Much of this conflict finds its common roots in a certain resentment over the lack of spontaneous spread of secondary industry and therefore of induced support for population and commercial activity and of political and economic influence in the peripheral regions. Such feelings are no different, and probably no more strongly held, in the western provinces of Canada than in the Atlantic provinces, or in the northern territories, or in mainland Quebec. Nor do they differ in kind from the sometimes bitter attitudes expressed by spokesmen for the Third World with respect to the continuing static or widening economic gaps between the less and more developed countries.

It is easy and perhaps natural for the lagging countries, and for slow-growth regions within a country, to imagine and possibly even to see at times some sinister hand of human conspiracy working behind the free play of market forces—especially when the impact of such market forces seems not to be resulting in a desired decentralization of developmental gains. Even where the sinister hand of the established power centers is not held to be the villain of the piece, there remains the easy tendency to reject the impersonal workings of competitive market forces as inadequate for local growth and diversification. Hence there is a tendency to press for a withdrawal from such forces in particular markets or sectors. However, sometimes it may suit the regional interests to decry any interference with the free play of competitive markets where these are working to the development advantage of the region.

Articulated attitudes in western Canada have displayed all of these seemingly inconsistent tendencies at one time or another on recurring issues of importance to the western provinces. Virtually all such divisive issues with the federal government have arisen over matters of economic rather than social concern, many of them of an economic developmental kind. This is perhaps not surprising in the light of the foregoing discussion. In any event, using the above discussion as a general framework, the remainder of this essay is an attempt to distinguish real from superficial aspects of a number of issues that may be said to constitute the present basis of western Canadian disenchantment with Ottawa and the center.

Most such issues over the years have revolved around questions of tariffs, freight rates, commercial bank activities and central bank monetary policy, the concentration of manufacturing activity in central Canada, and the taxation and exploitation of provincially administered nattural resources. With respect to several of these issues, a stereotype of the traditional, widely held western Canadian attitude is well expressed once again in a recent joint submission by the premiers of the four western provinces to the federal-provincial Western Economic Opportunities Conference held in 1973: "the pattern of settlement and development has been influenced by economic, financial and tax policies of the federal government, which early assisted the concentration of the nation's business and industrial activity in central Canada. These policies which have led to this concentration of financial and industrial resources and population have worked against the allocation of financial and production resources to bring balance to the economies of all regions of Canada."[3]

The argument goes on to recognize that the commercial branch banking system will ordinarily seek out those lending opportunities that show promise of the highest net return; that these are likely to be concentrated with the long-established, larger, and lower-risk enterprises located in the major commercial centers; and that the great bulk of such centers is to be found in central Canada. It is argued further that the result has been a continuous drain of savings and bank deposit funds from the peripheral regions as bank credit subsequently made available in support of commercial and industrial expansion mainly at the center; and that this has reduced the development potential of western Canada, for instance.

Similarly, the generally dominant position of the West on Canadian tariff protection has been primarily beneficial to new and established industry in central Canada and not likely to nurture new industry in other regions of the country in the absence of political separation and a separate tariff. In fact, the implicit assumptions of a recent study commissioned by the Independent Alberta Association have projected an independent Alberta economy whose structure would be much more heavily weighted toward industrial activity than any model projected for Alberta within Confederation.[4] Thus such beliefs are still current and have always been grounded in something broader than mere political posturing.

[3] "Capital Financing and Regional Financial Institutions," Joint Submission of the Western Premiers to the Western Economic Opportunities Conference, Calgary, July 24-26, 1973, p. 3.

[4] Warren Blackman, "The Cost of Confederation: Part I," a private study commissioned and circulated by the Independent Alberta Association, Calgary, December 1974. See also the comment in response to the above study by Kenneth Norrie, "The Real Costs of Confederation," Edmonton Journal, January 4, 1975.

On another occasion, a spokesman for the premier of Alberta was recently quoted as saying that his government had no intention of "sending jobs East through the pipe," when commenting on the province's attempts to encourage the first stages of a petrochemical processing base within the province.[5] The reference was to the province's unwillingness to permit ethane stripped from natural gas to be pipelined east—at least not until processing facilities for the manufacture of ethylene and polyvinylchloride in Alberta were first ensured as the foundation for a petrochemical complex.

Only months earlier, Alberta and Ottawa were also in open conflict over plans of a federally backed crown corporation to construct large new oil refining facilities in Ontario. Plans called for using a small fraction of the usual refined product mix as feedstock to a new ethylene and derivative production facility to be constructed and to market the remaining conventional refined products in the usual way. The operation sought some assurances from the Alberta government of a long-term oil supply before proceeding. Such unequivocable assurances were not forthcoming from the province that was incensed over the choice both of location and of an oil-based rather than natural gas-based technology at a time when the life-index reserves for oil were even tighter than for natural gas.

These particular occasions are but recent examples of the issues that continue to illustrate the underlying nature of the basic economic attitudes of the peripheral region and the type of rationale underlying those attitudes. The economic purist, using the efficiency criteria spelled out by the neoclassical competitive model, finds little difficulty in calling into question the "rationality" of any such parochial attitudes or normative policy objectives that would violate the maximized efficiency criteria of fully competitive interregional and international market structures. Thus it can be argued that savings generated in any part of the country, including the hinterland, will quite naturally seek investment opportunities in those industries and regions where, all things considered, potential return and growth prospects appear the most buoyant, and that indeed it is the function of commercial banks and other financial institutions to smooth and encourage this process in the interests of savers and investors everywhere. It could also be argued parenthetically that to do so would not involve the management of such institutions in a conspiracy against savers or potential borrowers in any particular geographic region.

In the case of the tariff, the argument would point out that, whatever the degree of protection afforded to Canadian industry, such protection should be just as inviting to industrial growth in western Canada, for instance, as in central Canada, and that if new industry growth in the hin-

[5] Ibid., September 25, 1975.

terland regions has not responded sufficiently in these protected circumstances, then there are sound reasons why industrial management has chosen not to so expand but has preferred instead those locations where industry and population are already concentrated.

In short, the cost advantages provided to new secondary industry growth by already established commercial and market agglomerations are likely to be substantial. Of course, every new location decision will in turn induce further growth in population and in the commercial service sector. Thus, for the great bulk of footloose and market-oriented enterprises, the process of commercial and market agglomeration, once begun, tends to feed on itself. Late starters on the periphery will find it difficult to blossom in the presence of such a strong field of attraction to the center.

Thus it can be argued that the rudimentary industrial structure of interior western Canada is simply a reflection of the "natural" competitive economic disadvantages imposed by reason of geographic isolation from (earlier) established population and commercial centers, and by reason of a relatively small and scattered population base responding largely to the pattern of primary resource location. Therefore, to act in defiance of the relative cost patterns evolving out of the chronology of history and the facts of geography is, in this model, irrational in the sense that some loss of global efficiency in the use of given resources will be invoked.

Now this is difficult medicine, both for those older communities or regions whose aspirations may seem to have been by-passed by random events of history and by the more recently settled regions in which aspirations may seem to be largely preordained by the same train of historical events. This is the real basis of much of the frustration and discontent underlying attitudes and positions expressed by wide sections of the community in the peripheral regions. Such groups see their development aspirations permanently constrained not so much by the original circumstances and events leading to concentration at the center, as by the self-reinforcing advantages of even further agglomeration at the center, carried by "natural" economic forces working through private capital allocation in unfettered markets.

Given such a prognosis for hinterland regional development, it is perhaps not surprising to hear periodic voices out of the West and elsewhere alleging a conspiratorial breakdown in competitive interregional market forces, or at other times arguing for outright rejection of the full forces of competition as a regulator of industrial growth and location.

In the case of the transportation and freight-rate issue, western Canadian concerns have always centered on railway operations, and much of the conflict with federal agencies has arisen over rate-making principles and practices. Complaints have been registered over the years concerning widespread inconsistencies in rail rates on long-haul and short-haul traffic in the same commodities, on different commodity classes of freight moving over the same distances, and on carload rates applicable to small and large shippers where the latter may negotiate special "agreed charges" on a high and specified percentage of all traffic generated by the shipper and dedicated to the particular carrier.

All such complaints are objections to various types of price discrimination practiced by the railways within the fairly broad limits (100 percent to 250 percent of the variable cost of moving the traffic) set forth in the Railway Act. The specific character of these practices is legitimized by the Canadian Transport Commission's acceptance of the "value-of-service" principle (essentially whatever the traffic will bear) as an appropriate basis for regulating monopolistic rate-making. Individual rates are therefore only loosely supervised by the commission.

Rate discrimination involves charging some shippers, and therefore some ultimate consumers, higher rates than others. If the carrier can identify traffic where final demand for the commodity is insensitive to higher freight charges from traffic where the demand is very sensitive, then the carrier can increase revenues by picking up volume via lower charges on rate-sensitive traffic while raising charges on the near-constant volume of rate-insensitive traffic. For instance, the rail carrier might choose to charge higher rates on the same type of traffic when destined to intermediate points not subject to independent competition from ocean or inland water or highway carriers and lower through-rates to destinations subject to such competition. Or if the carrier should wish to offer a particular service at a loss so as to hold the traffic, or if it is in a position to make profits in the long run by sustaining a loss in the short run, it may subsidize the losing traffic with profits drawn from higher charges on rate-insensitive traffic. It can also mean that the carrier is able to move a commodity that would not otherwise move if full recovery of overhead costs were required on every type of traffic. The latter can be an important consideration to hinterland developments, and one that the western provinces of Canada appear to be overlooking in their recent call for a complete abandonment of the value-of-service principle in rate determination.

In any event, the prairie provinces of western Canada have always been highly sensitive to rate discrimination for any reasons by the rail carriers. Being sparsely populated and without inland water or ocean shipping alternatives, the West is much more dependent on the railways for longer haul traffic than are some other parts of Canada where intermodal competition is more evident. It is also heavily dependent on inbound shipments of finished and semifinished capital and consumer durable items, the great bulk of which must move in by rail as relatively high-rated traffic.

For all of these reasons, then, the interior sections of western Canada have always felt vulnerable to what can easily appear as arbitrary pricing by the railway companies in efforts to take full advantage of the near-captive position of western consumers and consignees. These long-standing hardened attitudes have again come to focus on the value-of-service principle as the center piece, and the prairie provinces have recently taken the official position of urging a wholesale switch to "cost-of-service" rate-making principles.[6] In general, under this proposal, rates would be established on all traffic solely on the basis of full unit costs (overhead and variable) of moving the traffic, depending only on distance and weight (or perhaps density) of the cargo moved.

Once again, it is not at all clear that the full implications of such an omnibus proposal to the prairie economy have been fully traced out. For one thing, the systemwide effects of the proposal are bound to lead to considerable rate-leveling or averaging as compared to the present spectrum of variation between high- and low-rated freight classifications. Any such general convergence of rates could lead to distressing effects on present large outbound movements of cereal grains, chilled and frozen meat products, coal, potash, sulphur, lumber, fertilizer, and the like, while removing some of the natural protection afforded to potential local industry via present higher rates on inbound manufactured items.

Space does not permit a fuller analysis, but it is evident on a number of economic grounds that the prairie position may well be overdrawn, based as it is on an incomplete analysis of total effects. In fact, it is more in the nature of a cumulative reaction to the inadequacy of current regulatory practices and to a basic suspicion and distrust of rate differentials of any kind. The position fails to recognize that rate discrimination may arise out of a variety of circumstances, some of which provide sounder grounds than others for regional complaint. But again, with only limited access to the information and manner in which particular rates are struck by the carriers, it is little wonder that such suspicions find fertile emotional ground in which to spread.

Whatever the future may hold, then, it seems clear that the National Transportation Act of 1967 has done virtually nothing to meet these kinds of long-standing suspicions and objections. The mandate that Parliament gave to the Canadian Transport Commission placing reliance on the general forces of competition to limit abuses to users makes little sense in a national railway industry characterized by duopoly—and a duopoly that now includes extensive subsidiary operations in "competing" modes of transportation. What is needed is more positive regulatory direction and carrier disclosure with respect to rate-making practices, rather than the present regulatory watchdog approach to monitoring complaints over particular rates after the act.

[6] "The Equitable Pricing Proposal," Submission on Transportation of the Province of Alberta to the Western Economic Opportunities Conference, Calgary, July 24-26, 1973.

Thus many of the long-standing complaints of the western provinces about freight rates have persisted because of the difficulty of evaluating the incidence of an enormously complex rate structure on different classes of users in different parts of the country. Why this is so is not difficult to understand when one considers the latitude available for rate differentials under the value-of-service principle pushed to the limit as a rationale for rate-making. In these circumstances, it is all the easier for parochial interests to cite the transportation issue as an example of national policy that is biased against the industrialization aspirations of the prairie region.

Finally, the provinces of western Canada have come into conflict with Ottawa more recently over certain aspects of national energy policy. Not all of these various facets can be explored here, but undoubtedly the most acrimonious exchanges have taken place as a result of the introduction in late 1973 of a federal export tax on crude oil, coupled somewhat later with a domestic price ceiling on oil at the wellhead. Later, this policy was further coupled to federal measures that would use revenues generated via the export tax to subsidize consignments of higher-priced imported crude to the Atlantic provinces and Quebec down to the designated price-ceiling for Canadian crude.

Given the domestic price-ceiling, export-tax, subsidy combination, the nature and distribution of effects can be summarized in the following manner. There are two direct benefits to Canadians. First, Canadian users of domestic oil receive the product at something less than world prices landed in Montreal and at something substantially less than the even higher opportunity prices available to Canadian producers in the United States midcontinent market (east- or gulf-coast prices plus transport in); and, second, the federal government acquires tax revenues for subsidy transfer to Canadian users of offshore oil.

The cost of the price package is reflected, in the first instance, in a reduction in wellhead prices to Canadian producers by the amount of the tax on all sales. This assumes that the export tax is shifted backwards fully (i.e., that refiners in the competitive United States markets will not pay more for Canadian crude after tax than for alternative supplies). It also assumes that the wellhead price must be the same to all buyers and that Canadian producers remain interested in selling to any part of the United States market that currently absorbs just over one-half of total Canadian production. (This interest conceivably could have been wiped out by the imposition of an export tax alone in the absence of an imposed price ceiling in Canada).

Given a reduction in Canadian wellhead prices by the amount of the export tax and if provincial royalties in the producing provinces can be figured at an average of 22 percent of the wellhead price (as in Alberta until 1974), then the provincial treasuries in these provinces (but mainly Alberta and Saskatchewan) stood to sacrifice 22 cents on every barrel of production for every dollar of oil export tax levied, i.e., $1 of export tax levy will reduce the wellhead price by $1 on both domestic and export sales. Federal and provincial governments as a whole stood to lose roughly another 12 cents of the remaining 78 cents as reduced income tax collections resulting from the dollar of export tax levied (using an estimated 15 percent rate based on effective average rates of corporate income tax on book profits from crude oil production activities varying from 9-13 percent over the three years 1969-71).[7] Of the remaining 66 cents of reduced revenue per barrel because of the export tax, foreign shareholders would sacrifice about 53 cents (80 percent of equity) in retained or distributed profits, and Canadian shareholders some 13 cents (20 percent of equity) in profits due to the $1 reduction in wellhead price.

As far as the federal appropriation of potential provincial royalties is concerned, it has already been indicated that this will approximate the provincial royalty rate on every dollar of Canadian oil produced and sold —not just that sold into export and taxed. Thus, with over one-half of the production moving into export, if an average royalty rate were to be, say, 50 percent, the loss in revenue to a producing province would equal the whole of the federal export tax revenues gathered. For comparison, the new (1974) Alberta royalty rates on "old" oil now run from 22 percent on the first $3.80 of price, plus 65 percent on domestic price in excess of this figure. Royalty rates on production from "new" reserves are roughly comparable at the same price, and the revised Saskatchewan rates are somewhat higher at the margin.

Thus the impact of the export tax package on the opportunity revenues otherwise available to the treasuries of the western oil-producing provinces was immediate and great. Nor were the blows sustained to the financial plexus eased much by the unilateral manner in which they were first administered by Ottawa. In addition, quite clearly the revenue losses sustained by the producer provincial governments on export sales represent a transfer from the provincial to the federal treasury and on to consumers outside these provinces, and the losses sustained on domestic sales represent a transfer from the same provincial treasuries to domestic user groups located largely, but not entirely, outside the producing provinces.

In the light of these circumstances, the producing provinces remain highly incensed over the introduction of a new federal tax and pricing policy. Since nearly 85 percent of oil production is generated on provincially held lands or mineral leases (in contrast to freehold) in the case of Alberta, for instance, that province has taken the position that it

---

[7] For more detailed calculations, see Walter D. Gainer and Thomas L. Powrie, "Public Revenue from Canadian Crude Petroleum Production," *Canadian Public Policy* 1 (Winter 1975), pp. 1-12.

should be entitled to a priority claim on whatever level of windfall gains or rents as may seem reasonable to appropriate on a depletable natural resource owned or administered by the province.

In any event, at the time the export tax was first imposed, the producing provinces were clearly caught with their royalties down. As a reaction to the federal measures, the provinces were quick to hoist their royalties up to the waist, which in industry parlance would mean up to the armpits. As a counterreaction, the federal government then moved to disallow corporate payments of provincial oil royalties as income tax deductible. Alberta has subsequently made several adjustments, including introduction of a program of special drilling tax incentives. As of the fall of 1975, that is where matters stood.

Space limitations preclude a full discussion of the several federal-provincial issues underlying this kind of conflict. Some are of the more usual public policy management kind, and here the producing provinces have questioned the wisdom of the federal tax and price-ceiling measures with respect to both domestic consumer demand and future development capabilities of the Canadian petroleum industry under the new conditions of world marketing. Some of the issues have to do with the financial obligations imposed on the federal government automatically under the current Federal-Provincial Tax Equalization Grant arrangements in cases where a public revenue source in any one or several of the provinces is allowed to skyrocket. Finally, and most important for the future, some of the issues may require a constitutional determination of the extent to which various kinds of levies imposed or revenues derived from the sale, lease, or direct exploitation of provincially held public lands or mineral rights constitute a form of taxation at all as distinct from ordinary commercial payments to a resource owner; and if so, whether a direct or indirect form of taxation.

The producing provinces have argued that the receipt of such revenues does not constitute taxation, but rather the price exacted by a public landlord for rights transferred to a private agent to use or extract and sell a natural asset. But even if this position were to be accepted, it might still be argued that the province as a public landlord should be subject to the usual joint federal-provincial levies of direct taxation on any such income, rent, profits, or capital gain derived from leasing or selling the natural asset as would be applicable to a private or freehold landlord engaged in similar transactions. But the possibility of this kind of intergovernmental taxation of each other's revenues appears already .to be prohibited explicitly under section 125 of the British North America Act.

Thus considerable scope for clarification and subsequent negotiation still remains, but it is urgent that the future position of all provinces be clarified with respect to these same general issues which are bound to recur. In the meantime, the western provinces of Canada remain unhappy about the imposition of ad hoc solutions of convenience applicable to provincial oil and gas resources alone. There is no doubt that these provinces would be willing to subscribe, as they have in the past, to any general scheme working in the direction of provincial revenue equalization. But any such arrangement would have to apply generally to like revenues from like sources and would have to recognize the special and ephemeral nature of a depletable resource base—especially in the case of provinces that do not have a broader and more permanent industrial-commercial base.

Constitutional Aspects of the Canadian Economy

EUGENE FORSEY

If the intentions of the Canadian Fathers of Confederation had been fulfilled, this essay would have been almost as short as the famous chapter on the snakes in Ireland. For the Fathers thought they had placed all the great levers for controlling the economy in the hands of the central government and Parliament. Section 91 of the British North America Act, Canada's written Constitution, explicitly gives the Dominion Parliament exclusive jurisdiction over "the regulation of trade and commerce," "the raising of money by any mode or system of taxation," "currency and coinage," "banking, incorporation of banks, and the issue of paper money," "savings banks," "bills of exchange and promissory notes," "interest," "legal tender," "bankruptcy and insolvency," "lines of steam or other ships, railways, canals, telegraphs, and other works and undertakings connecting [a] province with any other or others of the provinces, or extending beyond the limits of a province," "lines of steam ships between [a] province and any British or foreign country," and "such works as, although wholly situate within [a] province, are before or after their execution declared by the Parliament of Canada to be for the general advantage of Canada or for the advantage of two or more of the provinces."

Section 132 gave "the Parliament and Government of Canada ... all powers necessary or proper for performing the obligations of Canada or of any province thereof, as part of the British Empire, towards foreign countries arising under treaties between the Empire and such foreign countries." Section 95 gave Parliament and the provincial legislatures concurrent jurisdiction over "agriculture and immigration," with the Dominion law prevailing in case of conflict.

Nor was this by any means all. The British North America Act was based on the Quebec Resolutions. The Fathers drew up those resolutions while the American Civil War was raging. The result was a conscious revulsion from American experience. What was threatening to destroy

American federalism? "States' rights." The American Founding Fathers had given the Congress only a short list of specific powers; everything else was "reserved to the states and to the people." The verdict of Sir John A. Macdonald on this was unequivocal: the Americans had "commenced at the wrong end." "Here," he went on, "we have adopted a different system. . . . We have provided that everything not distinctly and exclusively conferred upon the local governments and legislatures, shall be conferred upon the General Government and Legislature. . . . This is precisely the provision which is wanting in the Constitution of the United States. . . . We thereby strengthen the Central Parliament and make the Confederation one people and one government, instead of five peoples and five governments, . . . one united province, with the local governments and legislatures subordinate to the General Government and Legislature." The provinces were given a short list of specific powers; everything else was reserved to the Dominion.

This principle was embodied in the act by giving the Parliament of Canada power "to make laws for the peace, order and good government of Canada in relation to all matters not coming within the classes of subjects by this act assigned exclusively to the legislatures of the provinces." The section then went on to list, "for greater certainty, but not so as to restrict the generality of the foregoing terms of this section," twenty-nine enumerated "heads" which were "declared" to be within "the exclusive legislative authority" of the Parliament of Canada. These "heads" included all the fields mentioned above.

Plainly, the twenty-nine "heads" were meant to be merely examples of the general "peace, order and good government" power, inserted so that wayfaring judges, though fools, might not err therein. Plainly also, if a new, unforeseen matter arose, the test for jurisdiction would be perfectly simple and clear: "If it's not explicitly assigned to the provinces, it's Dominion." "We have thus," said Macdonald, with incredible optimism, "avoided all conflict of jurisdiction and authority."

Furthermore, the act provided that the formal chief executive of each province, the lieutenant-governor, was to be appointed, instructed, and dismissible by the Dominion government; and he was to have the power not only to veto a provincial bill outright but also to "reserve" it "for the significance of the Governor-General's pleasure" (that is, send it to the Dominion government in a state of suspended animation). Unless the "reserved" bill received the assent of the governor-general-in-council (the Dominion government) within one year of its receipt at Ottawa, it would die. Moreover, every bill assented to by the lieutenant-governor was to be promptly sent to Ottawa, and at any time within a year of its receipt the Dominion government could "disallow" the act (that is, wipe it off the provincial statute books); and if the province repassed it, it could be disallowed again, as often as the Dominion government saw fit.

Both reservation of provincial bills and disallowance of provincial acts could be, and often were, used to prevent provinces from frustrating Dominion economic policies (for example, the twenty year monopoly of the Canadian Pacific Railway and Dominion immigration policies) by valid provincial legislation.

All these powers still remain in the written Constitution, and an amendment of 1940 added to the twenty-nine heads of exclusive Dominion jurisdiction, "unemployment insurance."

In the first seventeen years of the new Dominion's history the central government and Parliament exercised their powers, or what they believed to be their powers, vigorously. Parliament passed a Trade Unions Act (1872), with scarcely a question as to its constitutional validity. It passed a national Local Option Act, which was upheld by the highest court, the Judicial Committee of the British Privy Council. Sir John A. Macdonald's second government introduced into Parliament four factory bills (1881, 1882, 1883, and 1884) and argued strongly that they were within Dominion jurisdiction. Parliament passed a national Liquor Licence Act; but the Judicial Committee ruled it *ultra vires*, though without giving reasons. One lieutenant-governor was dismissed (1879); forty provincial bills were reserved, with only thirteen receiving the governor-general's assent; forty-one provincial acts were disallowed. The power to declare local works to be for the general advantage of Canada was used ninety times.

Macdonald thought he had given Canada "a powerful Central Legislature, and a decentralized system of minor legislatures for local purposes." Till 1892, the courts, on the whole, so interpreted the Constitution. But in 1872, Macdonald's political archenemy, Oliver Mowat, became premier of Ontario and began his long campaign to expand the powers of the provinces. In this he was joined, after 1886, by the French-Canadian "nationalist" premier of Quebec, Honoré Mercier. Their efforts to get provincializing amendments to the British North America Act failed. But the Judicial Committee of the British Privy Council (till 1949, Canada's final court of appeal) was soon to do their work for them.

Its decision in the case of *Liquidators of the Maritime Bank of Canada* v. *Receiver General of New Brunswick*, 1892, was a landmark. It did not touch the division of legislative power. But it did give the provinces a status that Macdonald had certainly never intended them to have. It declared that the province of New Brunswick was not a simple creditor of the defunct bank but a privileged creditor, because the lieutenant-governor was not a mere Dominion officer, as Macdonald had always insisted, but the representative of the Crown, enjoying, for provincial purposes, all the rights and prerogatives of the Crown. The British North America Act had not "reduce[d] the provinces to the rank of independent municipal institutions. . . . The object of the Act was neither to weld the provinces into one, nor to subordinate provincial governments to a central authority." Lord Watson, who delivered the judgment, could hardly have contradicted Macdonald more flatly; and, "in a series of masterly judgments" (to quote Lord Haldane's obituary of him) "he expounded and established the real Constitution of Canada." In effect, Watson was saying that the Canadian Fathers of Confederation who drafted the British North America Act, and the Canadian judges who had been interpreting it, had not understood the nature of federalism. What had been hidden from them had been revealed to the Judicial Committee (which was unhampered by any experience either of federalism or of Canada); and by this light it had found the act and the Canadian judgments sadly wanting. Watson, and still more Haldane, who took up the work after Watson's death in 1898, undertook to set matters right.

The material lay ready at hand. The Dominion had indeed been given jurisdiction over the "peace, order and good government of Canada." But each province had been given exclusive jurisdiction over "property and civil rights in the province" (section 92, head 13). As the Judicial Committee itself had said in 1882, in its decision on the Dominion's Canada Temperance Act (local option), "Few, if any, laws could be passed by Parliament for the peace, order and good government of Canada which did not in some incidental way affect property and civil rights." Similarly, the Dominion had been given exclusive jurisdiction over "the regulation of trade and commerce"; but (though the Judicial Committee did not say so) few, if any, laws could be passed by Parliament for the regulation of trade and commerce that would not affect property and civil rights.

There is good ground for believing that the Fathers had intended "property and civil rights in the province" to cover only such matters as wills and mortgages. Watson and Haldane, however, proceeded to work out a theory that reduced the Dominion's "peace, order and good government" jurisdiction to not much more than an emergency power, capable of exercise only in times of "war, famine or pestilence" on a nationwide scale; and the power over "regulation of trade and commerce" to little more than a prop that could be used to strengthen a Dominion claim to jurisdiction already shown to be valid on other grounds. "Property and civil rights in the province" became, in normal times, for most practical purposes, the real residuary clause of the Canadian Constitution. The enumerated heads of section 91, intended simply as examples of the "peace, order and good government" power, became the primary, almost the sole, source of Dominion jurisdiction; the examples swallowed almost the whole of the thing they were supposed to be examples of.

This brief and somewhat impressionistic summary of a long development covers the period from 1896 to 1949. It should be added that, in 1931, the Judicial Committee repudiated the "prop" interpretation of "regulation of trade and commerce." It is possible to produce a scholarly, not to say scholastic, defense of the Judicial Committee's reasoning, and distinguished minds have done so. But whatever the intellectual merits of the committee's performance, of its results there can be no doubt.

Some of these are both conspicuous and of great contemporary importance. First, labor relations. Parliament had passed a Trade Unions Act in 1872. In 1907 it passed an Industrial Disputes Investigation Act, providing for compulsory conciliation in public utilities and mines. In 1925, the Judicial Committee, in *Toronto Electric Commissioners* v. *Snider*, held it *ultra vires*. The act was *prima facie* a matter of property and civil rights. It was not withdrawn from that category by any enumerated "head" of section 91. The general "peace, order and good government" power could, indeed, operate to "interfere" with exclusive provincial powers, but only "in cases arising out of some extraordinary peril to the national life of Canada, as a whole, such as cases arising out of a war. . . . But instances of this . . . are highly exceptional." The committee was unable to find any proof of "an emergency putting the national life of Canada in unanticipated peril." It also explicitly rejected the argument that the legislation could be supported as "regulation of trade and commerce."

This judgment put the whole of labor relations and labor legislation generally under provincial control, except in industries that fell within one of the enumerated heads of section 91 (for example, banks and interprovincial and international railways and telegraph lines), which employ only about 10 percent of the nation's workers.

Second, social security. "Property and civil rights," plus another enumerated provincial power, over "hospitals, other than marine hospitals," put this also within the exclusive jurisdiction of the provinces. A constitutional amendment in 1940 took unemployment insurance away from them and gave it exclusively to the Dominion. A second amendment, in 1951, gave the Dominion concurrent power to legislate on old age pensions, and a third, in 1964, broadened this to include "supplementary benefits, including survivors and disability benefits"; but both of these latter amendments left the provincial power to legislate intact and provided that in case of conflict, the provincial law would prevail. (This is why there are two contributory pension plans in Canada: "Canada," applying to the nine provinces that have chosen not to legislate on the subjects, and "Quebec," applying to the tenth, which has legislated. Fortunately the two are so similar that there is complete portability across the nation, but the Dominion had to trim its plan to accord with the Quebec legislation to achieve this result.)

There is an exclusively Dominion "Old Age Security Act." But it is noncontributory, merely providing for payments from the Dominion treasury to people who have reached the age of sixty-five and meet certain other conditions. It is based not only on the 1952 constitutional amendment but also on the Dominion's "spending power." This latter derives from Parliament's authority to raise money "by any mode or system of taxation" and its exclusive authority over "the public debt and property." Since Parliament can raise money in any way it pleases and spend it in any way it pleases, there is nothing to prevent its paying out money to anyone it pleases: old people (Old Age Security), children (or their parents: Family Allowances), or the provinces.

This last is important, for it is the constitutional basis not only of a system of unconditional massive "equalization grants" to the poorer provinces (to enable them to bring their services up to an average national standard with no more than the average level of taxation) but also of a whole series of conditional grants to the provinces in such spheres of provincial jurisdiction as hospitals, medical care, and post-secondary education. It is thanks to the "spending power" that Canada now has nationwide public hospital insurance and nationwide public medical care and that in the universities something like the same standards now prevail all across the country. The provincial jurisdiction remains intact; nothing can happen unless the province passes the necessary legislation; but the Dominion has a powerful weapon to induce the provinces to adopt the kind of social legislation it approves: unless a provincial act meets certain conditions, no Dominion money is forthcoming. (The general principle is not materially affected by the fact that, for Quebec, the "shared cost," conditional grant programs are handled by the Dominion vacating a certain part of the income tax field and letting the province occupy it.)

In 1935, there was a brief Dominion attempt to legislate in the fields of minimum wages, hours of work, and social insurance by invoking section 132 of the British North America Act (the treaty-implementing power). It got short shrift from the Judicial Committee. In the *Weekly Rest, Minimum Wages and Hours of Labour Acts* case, and the *Employment and Social Insurance Act* case, both in 1937, the committee held that section 132 applied only to "Empire" treaties (treaties between the "Empire and . . . foreign countries"); that the ILO Conventions were not Empire treaties; that the legislation fell within "property and civil rights"; and that there was no national emergency taking it out of that category. As Empire treaties are now an extinct species, this means that, while the *government* of Canada may negotiate, sign, and ratify any treaties it sees fit, the *Parliament* of Canada may pass implementing legislation only where the subject matter falls within the enumerated heads of section 91 plus whatever further jurisdiction it may exercise under "peace, order and good government" (whose limitation to little more than an emergency power is not quite so certain now as it was at Lord Haldane's death).

This brings one to a third, highly contemporary matter: price and wage control. Parliament legislated in 1919 two price control measures: the Combines and Fair Prices Act and the Board of Commerce Act. The Judicial Committee, in 1922, in the *Board of Commerce Act* case, held both *ultra vires*. They "interfered" with "property and civil rights"; there was no national emergency, no "highly exceptional circumstances," no "altogether exceptional situation," "such as those of war or famine," which would bring them under "peace, order and good government." The subsequent judgment in the *Fort Frances Pulp and Power Company* case (1923) made it plain that "emergency" legislation must be purely temporary to be *intra vires*: "The continued exercise of an exceptional interference . . . becomes *ultra vires* when it is no longer called for." This was reaffirmed in the *Employment and Social Insurance* case, in which the committee noted that the impugned legislation was "an Act whose operation is intended to be permanent."

On October 16, 1975, the government of Canada introduced into Parliament a bill imposing controls on prices and wages. Its operation is limited to three years, though it may be continued for a further period or periods by parliamentary resolution. It unquestionably interferes with "property and civil rights." But it is also unquestionable temporary legislation, and it purports to deal with a national emergency, inflation. This would seem to free it from the Judicial Committee's restrictions in the *Board of Commerce* case, unless it can be shown that the present degree of inflation in Canada does not amount to a national emergency. But even Haldane, in the *Fort Frances* case, in which the Dominion was continuing, after hostilities had ended, certain wartime controls, said that the committee "would require very clear evidence that the crisis had wholly passed away . . . to justify the judiciary . . . in overruling the decision of the Government that exceptional measures were still requisite. . . . The problem . . . is essentially one of statesmanship . . . which no authority other than a central Government is in a position to deal with." In the *Japanese Canadians* case, 1947, Lord Wright, speaking for the committee, made the same point even more explicitly: "Very clear evidence that an emergency has not arisen or that the emergency no longer exists is required to justify the judiciary even though the question is one of *ultra vires*, in overruling the decision of the Parliament of the Dominion that exceptional measures were required or were still required."

It is, therefore, highly probable that the courts would uphold the validity of the current price and wage control legislation even on the Haldane criteria. But they might do so on broader grounds. The "emergency" doctrine of the scope of "peace, order and good government" no longer stands judicially unchallenged. Even Lord Watson, in the *Local Prohibition* case of 1896, had said: "Their Lordships do not doubt that some matters, in their origin local and provincial, might attain such dimensions as to affect the body politic of the Dominion and to justify the Canadian Parliament in passing laws for their regulation or abolition. . . . [But] the exercise of power by the Parliament of Canada in regard to all matters not enumerated in section 91 ought to be strictly confined to such matters as are of unqestionably Canadian interest and importance." This doctrine has never been repudiated, either by the Judicial Committee or the Supreme Court of Canada, and counsel for the Dominion might certainly argue that inflation has attained such dimensions as to affect the body politic of the Dominion and is a matter of unquestionably Canadian interest and importance.

Moreover, the Judicial Committee itself, in 1946, repudaited the "emergency" doctrine. The liquor interests were making a fresh attempt to overthrow the Canada Temperance Act. They failed, and in the judgment in the *Canada Temperance Federation* case, Lord Simon said that "the true test" of the validity of any legislation "must be found in the real subject matter: . . . if it is such that it goes beyond local or provincial concern or interest and must from its inherent nature be the concern of the Dominion as a whole . . . then it will fall within the competence of the Dominion Parliament as a matter affecting the peace, order and good government of Canada, though it may in another aspect touch upon matters specially reserved to the Provincial Legislatures. War and pestilence, no doubt, are instances; so too may be the drink or drug traffic, or the carrying of arms . . . or . . . the sale or exposure of cattle having a contagious disease. . . . An emergency may be the occasion which calls for the legislation, but it is the nature of the legislation itself, and not the existence of emergency, that must determine whether it is valid or not." He noted that the Canada Temperance Act, whose validity had been upheld in 1882 and was again being upheld "was a permanent, not a temporary, Act, and no objection to it was raised on that account" in 1882.

The Judicial Committee, in 1947, returned to the "emergency" doctrine. But the Supreme Court of Canda, since it became the final court of appeal in 1949, has shown a disposition to rely on this judgment, notably in the cases of *Johannesson* v. *West St. Paul*, 1952, and *Munro* v. *the National Capital Commission*, 1966.

One other highly contemporary matter remains to be dealt with: jurisdiction over minerals, notably oil and gas. The British North America Act vests the ownership of natural resources (section 109) and exclusive legislative jurisdiction over them (section 92, head 5) in the provinces. But, except perhaps for Newfoundland, this does not include offshore minerals. The Supreme Court of Canada in the *Offshore Minerals Reference* case, in 1968, ruled that British Columbia (and by inference the other provinces) did not own these minerals. The provincial legisla-ture may "mark the earth with ruin—its control / Stops with the shore": the offshore minerals belong to the Dominion.

Newfoundland may be a special case. The Statute of Westminster, 1931, listed it among the "Dominions." It was, therefore, a sovereign state. On February 16, 1934, it lost responsible government and was placed under a commission appointed by the government of the United Kingdom. But this was only a "suspension" of its Constitution, requested by the Legis-lature of Newfoundland and enacted in strict accordance with section 4 of the Statute of Westminster. Moreover, throughout the period of commis-sion government, Newfoundland remained under the Dominions Office, not the Colonial Office (though it was not represented at the 1937 Imper-ial Conference). Further, by Term 7 of the Terms of Union embodied in the British North America Act, 1949, No. 1, which brought the island into Confederation, "The Constitution of Newfoundland as it existed immediately prior to the sixteenth day of February 1934, is revived at the date of the Union." Therefore, runs the argument, even if Newfound-land had lost its Dominion status, its sovereignty on February 16, 1934 (which the Government of Newfoundland does not admit), it regained it for a split second just before it became a Canadian province. Therefore, it carried with it into Confederation the ownership of offshore miner-als which it had enjoyed as a sovereign state.

This argument, if valid, would certainly give Newfoundland owner-ship of offshore minerals to the edge of the three-mile limit. Whether such ownership would extend beyond that depends on whether, in 1949, international law had already recognized that offshore mineral rights beyond the three-mile limit belonged to the maritime state. There is au-thority for saying that it had; there is perhaps more for saying that it had not, that the present doctrine on the subject is a post-1949 development.

Beyond question, the provinces have complete power to legislate in respect to the oil and gas in the ground, the royalties, the rigs, installa-tions, refineries, storage tanks, pipelines, and so forth, within the prov-ince, subject, of course, to reservation and disallowance. They may even confiscate private property. Within the limits of subject and area prescribed by the British North America Act, said the Judicial Com-mittee in *Hodge* v. *the Queen*, 1883, the provincial legislatures enjoy "authority as plenary and as ample as the Imperial Parliament in the plenitude of its power possessed and could bestow." As Riddell, J. said in the *Florence Mining Company* case, 1908: "The probition 'Thou shalt not steal' has no legal force upon the sovereign body. And there would be no necessity for compensation to be given." (The Ontario courts had award-ed ownership of a certain mining property to one company; the legisla-ture passed an act awarding it to another, and the courts upheld the act. The same sort of thing happened later in Nova Scotia. The Supreme

Court of Canada decided that the property of a deceased Mr. MacNeil belonged to his creditors; the legislature passed an act giving the property to his sister. The creditors secured satisfaction only by successfully invoking the Dominion's power to disallow the provincial act, in 1923.)

But the Parliament of Canada may, by virtue of its power to declare any local "work" to be "for the general advantage of Canada," take exclusive jurisdiction over the rigs, installations, and so forth, in the province (though not, of course, over the oil or gas in the ground) by declaring any or all of them to be "works for the general advantage of Canada." No judicial decision has limited this power in any way, and it has been used 470 times, notably in the Canada Grain Act, 1925, which brought the grain trade under the exclusive jurisdiction of the Dominion by declaring every grain elevator in Canada, past, present, or future, to be a "work for the general advantage of Canada."

Parliament's jurisdiction over "the regulation of trade and commerce" certainly extends to all interprovincial and international trade. It has also exclusive jurisdiction over "works and undertakings connecting [a] province with any other or others of the provinces, or extending beyond the limits of a province." It can, therefore, undoubtedly regulate interprovincial and international pipelines and the price of oil or gas entering into interprovincial and international trade. By virtue of its "emergency power," it can certainly pass temporary legislation allocating energy supplies of any kind.

The province can not only charge such royalties as it sees fit, but also levy on the oil and gas industries (and of course any others) such "direct taxation within the province in order to the raising of a revenue for provincial purposes" as it sees fit (though probably subject to the limitation about to be noted). The Dominion can levy such taxes as it sees fit and can, by its "spending power," grant such subsidies as it sees fit (subject, again, to the limitation about to be noted).

The limitation is that the province could not charge royalties so high that they would leave little or nothing for the Dominion to tax; and, by the same token, the Dominion could not levy taxes so high as to leave the province little or nothing to charge royalties on. Any such action by either authority would perhaps be invalid, as being not "in pith and substance" (the Canadian courts' acid test) legislation "in relation to" royalties or taxes but a colorable attempt to prevent the other authority from exercising its valid authority. At what point the royalties or taxes would become colorable, and therefore invalid, the courts would have to decide.

The Response to Cultural Penetration

DAVIDSON DUNTON

A combination of conditions has drawn American culture into English-speaking Canada. The relatively small population north of the border speaks the same language as the much larger mass to the south. It has many of the same interests and habits of mind. Although political traditions are very different, to a large extent the two societies share a common cultural inheritance, and both have developed under North American conditions.

The majority of the Canadian population lives in widely separated regions along a narrow band crossing the continent just above the United States border. Each region has readier natural access to a neighboring part of the United States than it has to another Canadian region, and the resulting north-south intercourse across different sectors of the border is heavy.

There is an inherent pressure making for a cultural flow from a large society to a smaller, contiguous one; the pressure is especially strong when the larger is wealthy, vigorous, and powerful. It is not strange that some 16 million English-speaking Canadians absorb much from 220 million Americans with whom they are such close continental neighbors.

The pressure of cultural penetration from the United States is of course not as strong on French-speaking Canadians, especially those living in Quebec. Because 75 percent of Quebecois do not consider themselves bilingual, the spoken and written American word has much less appeal to them than to their English-speaking compatriots. French-Canadians are very North American in respect to their physical tastes and habits. But the language difference insulates them considerably from the penetration of American culture and supports creativity within their own society.

The penetrating powers of United States culture are strongly reinforced by the economics of mass communication. Costs for the initial production of most kinds of popular cultural material are high, while the cost per consumer of distributing the original is relatively low. In the United States, high expenditures for original creation and production can be recovered in a very large market and the material can be profitably distributed in Canada at a fraction of the original cost. In a great many cases the material attracts the English-speaking Canadian public because of similarities in taste. To be competitive, Canadian-produced material must have somewhat comparable strength of appeal. Because basic production costs are similar in the two countries, finding the money to develop something of equal appeal for a much smaller Canadian market is extremely difficult.

Thus Canadian cultural production has to struggle for the attention of Canadians against American competition with an economic base more than fourteen times as large. In international trade of physical goods, differentials in production costs of a few percentage points for each unit may have a large influence on flow. In popular cultural material, the financial advantage of importation from the United States is not in small percentages but in large multipliers. A Canadian organization can seldom obtain financial backing and the production techniques with the corresponding spreading of costs necessary for success in the American as well as the Canadian market. Without any question of cultural imperialism, commercial arithmetic favors the importation of American cultural fare into English-speaking Canada and works against Canadian production.

Canada, like the United States, has a long tradition of openness to imported cultural products. But concern has risen from time to time as it became apparent that nonintervention could lead to overwhelming American domination of some fields. The feeling has developed that if Canada is to exist as a truly independent country, in the long run, it must produce at least a reasonable measure of the food for its people's minds; Canadians must be able to communicate with one another, at least to some extent, through their media; and Canadian creativity must have a fair chance. Consequently, there have been some decisions designed to counteract partially underlying pressures by providing economic and financial conditions that would make possible a degree of activity in Canada. The field of broadcasting, first radio and then television, is an outstanding example.

Broadcasting

In the 1920s, radio broadcasting developed in Canada on much the same basis as in the United States. Privately owned commercial stations were licensed to use certain frequencies in given areas and were free to carry on their activities with few restrictions. They grew rapidly in number and output. A federal royal commission, under the chairmanship of Sir John Aird, examined the development of Canadian radio at the end of the decade and found that broadcasting was tending to become a mere extension of the American system. A very high proportion of the program material on Canadian transmitters was being brought across the border by recording or line connection. Some Canadian stations in major centers had become affiliates of American networks. There seemed little hope, therefore, for the development of Canadian programming or for east-west network connections that would link the regions of the country.

The Aird commission thought the only solution in the national interest was a publicly owned broadcasting system supported by funds coming directly from the public. The essence of its findings became the basis for Canadian broadcasting policy. Although the original Aird proposals have been greatly modified, their principles still hold to a considerable extent. The commission recommended that the national agency become the only broadcasting organization in the country and that private stations be eliminated. In fact, however, private stations were allowed to continue and grow in number, under the general regulatory supervision of the Canadian Broadcasting Corporation (CBC), the national agency. Many of these stations became network outlets in their areas for the CBC, which also built owned-and-operated stations in certain areas. The Aird commission also recommended that the national organization accept only a limited amount of "indirect" advertising. The CBC found, however, that the exigencies of economics and broadcasting in North America impelled it to go into commercial activities quite heavily, with direct advertising related to both Canadian and imported programs.

Television developed on essentially the same pattern as radio. The CBC established its own stations in some areas, obtained network coverage in others through private affiliates, and later other private stations and private networks were licensed. Because all television costs are much higher, pressures for importation of programs have been even stronger than in the case of radio. Even the CBC, with its substantial support from public funds, has had to take more American programming than it wished in order to survive and keep a defensible share of the potential audience. Private stations, without the benefit of public subsidy, have been even more prone to using imported material, and many tended to carry little else, apart from some network programming, local news, and a few other local productions.

Geography, as well as economics, reinforces the penetrating power of American television since a number of populated areas in Canada are within direct range of American stations. Thus, many Canadians are exposed daily to a full, rich diet of expensive fare from Hollywood and New York, powerful competition for Canadian programming. This direct form of penetration has recently been strengthened by the growth of cable television systems. Most of these, in addition to carrying the broadcasting of nearby Canadian stations, also relay from receiving stations near the border the programming of several American stations, including main American network services. In the last few years, Canada has become a leading country in coverage by cable television systems, largely because many Canadians want to have available to them full American as well as Canadian television services.

As television has grown in Canada, the viewing of American programs has tended to mount, both in absolute terms and in relation to viewing of Canadian programs. The latest pressure is coming through the cable systems that are bringing full American services to more and more areas. The growing fragmentation of the audience has caused much worry by Canadian network and stations operators and by those concerned about preserving a core of English-Canadian programming. American material tends to dominate the Canadian television screen despite the CBC and its support of over $250 million a year by taxpayers. Its response, possible with the funds provided to it, has not been a sufficient counterbalance in the eyes of many Canadians.

The Canadian Radio and Television Commission (CRTC), the regulatory body for both the CBC and private stations in recent years, has found it necessary to take additional measures to give Canadian programming better chances. It has adopted rules for minimum percentages of Canadian content on the CBC, on private stations, and on private television networks. It has also instituted provisions for minimum proportions of Canadian music, with a resulting upsurge in the production of popular recordings. In the licensing and relicensing of stations it is endeavoring to ensure minimal amounts of program origination. It is also encouraging cable systems to develop community programming.

For some time, Canadian commercial broadcasting interests have been concerned about advertising carried on some United States stations near the border and directed at viewers in Canada. Most of these advertisers are Canadian companies. It has been argued that this practice drains Canadian advertising dollars to the American stations and away from Canadian stations which need the revenue, partly to help them meet the Canadian programming requirements of the CRTC. In this case the Canadian government intervened, and placed before Parliament a bill that would forbid companies from claiming as expenses for income tax purposes the costs of any advertising placed on non-Canadian stations and directed at Canadian audiences. The proposed penalty is designed to be heavy enough effectively to end such advertising. The bill has drawn protests from American broadcasters and opposition from some Canadian advertisers who claim that in some of the areas in question there is practically no good time available on Canadian stations and they need the option of having their messages carried on transmitters across the border. American broadcasters strongly oppose another move by the CRTC permitting Canadian cable systems to delete commercials from United States broadcast services and to insert messages of their own. This would presumably give cable companies some opportunity to improve their financial position and to support community programming. The deletion provision is being tested before the Canadian courts.

The situation in radio and television has never been as serious in French-speaking Canada, because of the language difference. The 6 million French-speaking Canadians enjoy programming that is much more home-produced than that for the English-speaking majority. A certain amount of American television material is available in dubbed form, and some comes ready for transmission from France, but French-language operations have had to rely heavily on production in Quebec. This has been true both of the CBC—Radio Canada in its French form—and of private operators. Most French-Canadians are within range of plentiful American programming, but with the majority of Quebecois speaking only French, the competition is not great.

Therefore, French-language television has developed in Canada with a high degree of creativity and a strong appeal to the audience it serves. It is patently more effective than English-language television in drawing out the talents of and providing a means of communication among the members of its society.

Films and Magazines

From the advent of motion pictures the penetrating power of American films has been great around the world and nowhere stronger than in English-speaking Canada. During the period 1920-40, Hollywood provided a large part of its popular cultural fare. Since 1950 the relative importance of motion pictures has declined, and more films from Britain and Europe have been shown, but American films are still enormously predominant in English-Canadian theaters.

In this field also the Canadian government found it had to take some initiative, and just before World War II it established the National Film Board (NFB) as a producing agency. The NFB has since built up a worldwide reputation as a producer of documentary films, and in recent years it has been instrumental in the making of some good feature films, especially in French. In 1967 the government also established the Film Development Corporation to provide financing for the private production of feature films; a certain number of productions have resulted, both in English and French-speaking Canada. But it is still estimated that less than 2 percent of the films shown on theater screens in Canada are of Canadian origin. Recently there was an announcement of generous tax concessions for investors who put money into the production of films in Canada. But Canadian film producers and others interested in Canadian cultural development do not believe that such measures are nearly enough. They point out that the great majority of theaters in Canada are owned by interests controlled from the United States. They claim that these interests are heavily biased toward American films and that, consequently, Canadian productions have little chance of exhibition. The only hope, the Canadians claim, lies in the imposition of a quota system establishing a minimum showing of Canadian films in Canadian theaters. This system, however, would require provincial action, and some provinces seem unenthusiastic about it. In the summer of 1975 it was announced that two major theater chains had agreed to run four weeks of Canadian films a year. But more will probably be heard on this subject in the future.

In the field of periodical publications, penetration has also been extensive, although not as overwhelming as with motion pictures. English-speaking Canadians have long been avid readers of American magazines whose editorial content is so highly expensive in Canadian terms. It was estimated that in 1959 three of every four magazines read by Canadians were American or American controlled; by 1969 the proportion had risen to four out of five.

Life has always been hard for Canadian magazines that had to face heavy competition for circulation from the attractive publications across the border. In an attempt at rectification a Conservative government in the 1930s imposed an import tax on periodicals, but this tax did not last long because a penalty on the importation of cultural material is repugnant to many Canadians.

A new element was introduced in the 1940s when *Reader's Digest* and then *Time* established Canadian editions and began seeking Canadian advertising for them. Later, other American publishers established similar special editions or split their printing runs so that a part aimed at Canadian readers would carry Canadian advertising.

This development brought growing opposition from some Canadian publishers who claimed that the special editions constituted unfair competition for limited advertising dollars available in the country. They argued that most of the editorial content was "dumped," that it was expensive material produced for the American market and was available to the Canadian editions at little or no cost.

The Royal Commission on Publications (the O'Leary commission), appointed by the Diefenbaker government, examined the problem and in 1961 recommended disallowance for income tax purposes of expenditures for advertising directed at the Canadian market in any foreign-controlled periodical, wherever printed. This disallowance was aimed at diverting a large part of the domestic advertising revenues of the Canadian editions and split-runs to Canadian publications.

The Diefenbaker government did not act on the O'Leary proposal, but the Pearson government did later. In 1965, Parliament passed an act defining Canadian publications, including newspapers, as those at least 75 percent controlled by Canadians and not licensed by nor substantially the same as foreign publications. The act, however, contained a clause exempting the Canadian editions of *Time* and *Reader's Digest*.

The exemption of the two long-established Canadian editions caused considerable controversy at the time and more in the following years. There were allegations of heavy pressure from the U.S. State Department and suggestions that the move had been made to save the automobile pact between the two countries. One of the recommendations of a Select Committee of the Senate on Mass Media (the Davey committee) in 1970 was that the exemption be removed in the interests of the Canadian magazine industry. Some Canadian publishing interests and other groups also continued to agitate for removal.

In September 1974, Hugh Faulkner, secretary of state (the head of a department in Canada that deals with many cultural matters), announced that the *Time-Reader's Digest* exemption was to be lifted, and a bill to this effect was introduced into the House of Commons in January 1975. By early fall 1975 the bill had not been passed, but the controversy had been sharp for a year since the minister's announcement.

Proponents of the bill have argued that the Canadian editions of *Time* and *Reader's Digest* enfeeble domestic publications by taking a high proportion of total advertising money going to magazines in the country, that they are unfair competition because so much of their editorial content is expensive material imported at very low cost, and that it is unjustifiable to give two foreign publishers an opportunity closed to others.

The two organizations in question have countered in somewhat different ways. The Reader's Digest Association (Canada) Ltd. has emphasized that in recent years it has become a public company with over 30 percent of its shares open to Canadians, that a majority of its directors and all its management are Canadian, that it has a large Canadian staff and has all its production activities carried out in the country, that it has been increasing the Canadian content in both its English and French editions so that it will soon average 30 percent, and that through the world operations of its parent company articles about Canada are carried to many other countries. The *Time* arguments appear to have been more general, but it has said, unlike *Reader's Digest*, that if the bill is passed it will arrange to meet the provision for 75 percent Canadian ownership and will endeavor to comply with any Canadian content rules. If the bill is passed in its present form, the effect on content will depend on the interpretation of "not substantially the same as." There has been a suggestion that a construction of the phrase by the Department of National Revenue would mean that 60 to 80 percent of the editorial material in a magazine would have to be domestic or different from that in any foreign magazine for it to be counted as a Canadian publication. *Reader's Digest* has said that for its type of operation no more than 30 percent would be reasonable.

The progress of the bill to remove the *Time-Reader's Digest* exemption has been slow, and its fate remains uncertain, although Mr. Faulkner has reiterated that the government is committed to it. Some Liberal as well as Conservative members of the House of Commons have expressed vigorous opposition, and some members of the cabinet are said to be less than enthusiastic. In the fall of 1975 the bill will presumably be studied by a House committee where the discussion will undoubtedly be lively.

Canadian concerns and disagreements about magazine editions are probably not understood easily by many in the United States. To many Americans, brought up in the tradition of the First Amendment, any attempt to tamper in any way with activities of any periodical is abhorrent; to them, any press activities should be untouchable. Most Canadians adhere in general to the same principle, but many also want a reasonable chance for a Canadian periodical press to exist. There is wide agreement in the country on the need for general restrictions on Canadian editions of outside periodicals because of the drain they make on potential advertising support for Canadian publications. It is important to recognize that in Canada no voice is calling for restrictions or penalties on American publications entering Canada, since they are printed at home. If Mr. Faulkner's bill is passed and the *Time* and *Reader's Digest* head offices decide not to meet the provisions, the American editions of both will still be freely admissible to Canada and will undoubtedly be bought by large numbers of Canadians. The current issue is really the down-to-earth one of whether tough and perhaps unacceptable conditions should now be imposed on operations which have for years been carried on in good faith under Canadian law and which, in the case of *Reader's Digest*, have undergone a considerable measure of Canadianization.

Professors and Books

Another controversial form of penetration has been the appointment of large numbers of American professors in Canadian universities. In the latter part of the nineteenth and the early part of this century, British academics played a considerable part in the development of higher education. By the 1950s there were a number of very respectable universities in the country, but student enrollment was proportionately a good deal lower than in the United States and graduate work relatively much less developed. There was some good research and graduate teaching in a few centers, particularly in the sciences, but few opportunities for good advanced study in the humanities and the social sciences, especially the latter. A high proportion of the rather small number of young people who wished to work on the doctoral level went to other countries, chiefly the United States, to pursue their studies.

Around 1960, government authorities rather suddenly agreed with university leaders that there would have to be a swift and broad expansion of higher education. But who would staff the new or rapidly expanding institutions? There were not nearly enough Canadians available or in sight within the academic stream, studying either in Canada or outside. The answer was that large numbers of academics would have to be attracted from other countries.

That is just what happened. During the 1960s, universities expanded enormously, and to fill their fast-growing faculty needs appointed many non-Canadian professors. Immigration authorities readily admitted the newcomers to the country. Appointees seemed to be attracted by the rising salaries, good working conditions, and congenial academic atmospheres; many were excellent scholars, including a few of high distinction, and some were mediocre, as can be expected under conditions of very high demand. Statistics Canada has estimated that in 1973–74 66 percent of all professors in the universities were Canadian; 15 percent citizens of the United States; and 19 percent citizens of other countries.

Agitation about the foreign academics was begun in the late 1960s by James Steele and Robin Mathews, professors at Carleton University, Ottawa, who rapidly gained the ears of a substantial number of people across the country, inside and outside universities. The two professors and others who joined in the cause protested that the proportion of faculty members from outside was too great and should be reduced, with a corresponding increase in the proportion of Canadians. They concentrated most of their attention on the contingent from the United States, arguing that American faculty members could not have a basic understanding of Canadian society and traditions and would tend to bring their own values with them to be communicated to Canadian students. The situation was most serious, it was said, in the social sciences in which there had been especially large numbers of American appointments. In response to counter-arguments that an American element of 15 percent in total countrywide faculty strength was not frighteningly high, the protesters pointed to particular concentrations in certain departments of some universities. They claimed that in some of these cases "old-boy" networks were at work so that any new appointments tended also to be made from the United States, leaving little chance for qualified Canadians.

The question of American professors drew a considerable amount of public attention over several years and brought sharp dissension within a number of universities. Academic opponents of the crusade, including many Canadians, argued that faculty appointments should be made solely on merit, without consideration of citizenship. They also held that Americans who had accepted appointments in good faith when they were badly needed in Canada should not be subject to any discrimination. On the whole this view has prevailed, and there has not been evidence of American professors with continuing or tenured appointments being dropped. In the tight financial position of universities in the 1970s, with much less faculty hiring, there have continued to be appointments of some non-Canadians, including Americans. Some of these have brought protests. A certain number of those appointed from outside several years ago have decided to remain permanently in Canada and have taken out citizenship.

Public discussion of the issue has lessened recently, but there is still an undercurrent of concern. In contrast to the heavy deficit position of the early 1960s, there is now a surplus of Canadians with a Ph.D. degree in most fields, and many of these highly trained young people are unable to find academic or other posts suitable to their background. Some Canadians feel strongly about many of the positions held by non-Canadians. The Canadian Association of University Teachers, after wrestling with the question for several years, finally, in 1975, adopted guidelines providing that any new appointment should be offered to the best qualified Canadian who meets the stated requirements unless a universitywide review committee or the senior academic body is persuaded that the appointment of a non-Canadian is justified.

Canadian universities are all under heavy financial pressure, but all receive broad governmental support, and reduction in faculties have so far been less than in the United States. Because of the present academic employment situation south of the border, few of the American professors are leaving their Canadian posts to return home. If the financial squeeze worsens in Canada and establishing of substantial faculty "redundancies" becomes necessary, there will inevitably be proposals that the first to go should be non-Canadians. In the meantime, for the comparatively small number of places that do become open, appointment committees and administrators are probably taking more care than before to look for well-qualified Canadians, although some Americans and others are still being hired. The purist tradition of looking for the best person, regardless of citizenship, is still strong. At the present time, because of university appointment practices and immigration procedures, it is probably harder for a suitable Canadian scholar to be appointed to an American university than for the reverse to occur. After the great developments in higher education that have occured since 1960, a much higher proportion of new appointments than previously may be expected to go to thoroughly qualified Canadians.

Book publishing labors under the same basic difficult conditions as other cultural activities: two publics, one speaking English and the other French, in a country with a comparatively small population and great distances that result in high costs of distribution. Traditionally many publishing houses in Canada have done a large part of their business as agents for British, American, or French publishers. Large British and American concerns have also long had subsidiaries in Canada, and in recent years an increasing number of Canadian houses have been bought by large American companies. Books by Canadian authors have been published for generations, and in recent years the number has been growing healthily. Public interest has been growing in both English- and French-speaking Canada for Canadian writing, which at the same time has been developing markedly in quality and scope. Both independent publishers and foreign-controlled houses have participated in the production of Canadian books.

There is practically no opposition in Canada to the principle of allowing a free flow of imported books; nor to the publication of Canadian editions of works from other countries. Publishers of Canadian books have rather concentrated on the inherent problems facing their business and have asked for governmental assistance to offset some of their difficulties.

This assistance has been provided to some extent by the governments of Ontario and Quebec and by federal agencies. More may be forthcoming. One reiterated demand of Canadian publishers is for the prescription of more Canadian textbooks in schools to replace more of the many American series still in use.

A particular source of irritation lies in the field of paperback books, which are sold in many places other than bookstores. A number of the agencies handling distribution in this area have come under the control of large American organizations, and Canadian publishers claim that their products get little display on the racks among the host of titles from the United States. As in some other sectors, the strongest thrust of penetration seems to be at the lower cultural levels, and more will undoubtedly be heard about the paperback situation.

Conclusion

Much has been written about the "new nationalism" that has developed in English-speaking Canada since the mid-1960s. But important measures to offset cultural penetration were taken well before that. As has been pointed out, the establishment of a national broadcasting system was in large part such a response. In 1951 the Royal Commission on the Arts, Letters and Sciences, under the chairmanship of Vincent Massey, found that Canada was far too dependent on the United States in cultural matters. It confirmed that television should have a public national system structure and recommended the establishment of a federal body to support developments in the arts as well as scholarly work in the humanities and social sciences. As a result, the Canada Council was established in 1957, and it has been of major help in the healthy growth in recent years of theater, serious music, ballet, the plastic arts, and creative writing. In Quebec there has been a particularly vigorous development in the arts and creative writing during the 1960s and 1970s.

In English-speaking Canada the nationalist movement, particularly as embodied by the Committee for an Independent Canada, has concentrated much of its propaganda on the high degree of American control of corporations in Canada. It has paid rather less attention to general questions of cultural penetration and Canadian activities in these fields, except in the *Time-Reader's Digest* affair and the question of American professors. At the same time, many Canadians not members of nationalist organizations have become increasingly conscious of the immense cultural pressures from the United States and the need for measures to assure opportunities for Canadian creative abilities, for effective communication among Canadians, and so for the evolution of a culturally richer national society. As a result the federal and provincial governments have taken or contemplated various measures.

It must be said that there is plenty of ambivalence among Canadians in these matters, and there are no signs indicating that Canada will move to become anything resembling a closed society. Many people want the whole range of American television available to them by cable and still expect Canadian artists and Canadian interests to be well represented on the air. Strong nationalists still read the spreads of American comic strips and columnists in their local, Canadian-owned newspapers. Some members of the Committee for an Independent Canada are keen followers of the Canadian Football League, in which the great majority of the star players and coaches are American. Others read *Time* regularly but say they will be still happier to do so when they can get the original instead of a Canadian edition. Some purists get excited at a suggestion that public servants might officially drop the *u* when writing "labour" and "colour"— although their newspapers have been doing so for years.

Cultural penetration, particularly at more popular levels, does pose major questions for Canada, especially English-speaking Canada. The flood of material arriving by a multitude of channels tends to stifle Canadian forms of expression and consequently inhibits the growth of self-understanding and self-awareness. Surveys have shown that Canadian school children know more about American political figures than Canadian ones, know the names of few Canadian writers, are fascinated by early western life south of the border but ignorant of the story of their own West, and so on. Probably no country in the world draws so much of its daily mental fare from another.

In such a situation it seems justifiable, indeed necessary, for a state to take some action in the interest of self-preservation and rounded national development. While it is hard to imagine the United States in a similar position, one can well speculate that if it ever had been, Americans would have acted vigorously. In Canada, it is important to note that the measures taken have not been aimed at excluding the products of an external culture. There are no indications of a trend to cultural isolation or to any blockage of the free flow of ideas. Rather the aim of various moves has been to create economic and financial conditions under which there can be a reasonable amount of Canadian production and to provide some counterbalance to the enormous economic advantages of cultural material from the United States. More such steps may be taken in the future, but Americans can still be confident that their culture will still have an immense part in Canadian life.

Foreign Investment in Primary Industries

A.E. SAFARIAN

Six objectives of Canadian foreign policy—economic growth (and efficiency), independence, equitable income distribution, environment, peace and security, and social justice—were outlined in *Foreign Policy for Canadians*, prepared by the Canadian Department of External Affairs. This essay is concerned particularly with the first three of these objectives as they affect foreign investment in the primary resource sector and the relevant policy responses.

Economic growth reflects not simply increases in the agents of production and in technological change, but an efficient allocation of resources. "Efficient" means not only an industrial mix and technology that is as productive as possible in supplying the material needs of Canadians, but also one that is responsive to their other private and public demands, such as the demand for environmental control. In a federal state the resulting distribution of income must be regarded not only from the viewpoint of individuals or groups, but regionally as well. In a highly decentralized federal state the objective of increased regional equalization necessarily ranks high, especially in some of the recent discussions on the issues to be noted here.

Independence is the capability to implement policies considered to be in the national interest. Much can be written on this theme, but four points might be made for present purposes. First, independence is not an absolute in the sense that one can eliminate all external elements that may constrain policy making, without regard to the effects on the objectives of policy. Some issues, nevertheless, may rank higher on the independence scale than others. Second, it should not be assumed that a lessening in relations with other countries increases the degree of independence; it may in some cases, but in others it may have the reverse effect on both independence and other objectives. Third, the effects of foreign ownership with regard to independence can be made specific by analyzing the extent to which, given any policy, the implementation and persuasion costs are higher (or lower) in the case of foreign-owned companies. This approach has been developed by M. D. Steuer and his associates in their study, *The Impact of Foreign Direct Investment on the United Kingdom.* If a country is attempting to rationalize an industry so that it is competitive by world standards, for example, does the existence of a high degree of foreign ownership make it harder (or easier) to achieve the objective with any particular set of policies, or by reducing (or increasing) the available sets of policies? Finally, Albert Breton has emphasized in his studies that policies ostensibly designed to increase independence may be purely protectionist in their economic consequences—increasing the real incomes of some at the expense of others, often perversely in the sense of redistributing from low- to high-income groups. Both groups may gain "psychic" income, i.e., a greater sense of independence, but some also gain real income at the expense of others. He has also mentioned that governments not only serve the national interest in some Benthamite sense, but more directly, may also serve bureaucratic objectives, special interests, and the patronage-political system. Governments must ultimately speak for the people by way of public policy, but whether these policies serve the national interest and what that means in a particular case is a matter for conjecture.

It is well known that there is an unusually high degree of foreign ownership in Canada compared to other high-income countries. At the end of 1974, United States and other foreign interests had voting control of 58 percent and 17 percent respectively of the capital employed in Canadian petroleum and natural gas industries, 43 percent and 12 percent in other mining and smelting, and 44 percent and 14 percent in manufacturing. In the largest sector of manufacturing, the pulp and paper industries, United States and other foreign interests had voting control of 36 percent and 17 percent of the capital in 1972.

To what extent do these high degrees of foreign control of industry account for the problems of Canadian industry or impede the realization of policy objectives of Canadian governments? The questions are broad and complex ones that admit of no unqualified answers. It is particularly difficult to disentangle, in any given situation, those consequences due to the existence of large corporations involved in foreign trade and investments from those due to the economic characteristics of the industry and those due to domestic and foreign government policies. It is important from a policy viewpoint, nevertheless, to specify which of these three is mainly responsible for a given problem. In Canada today it has become all too easy for some segments of public opinion to blame the large foreign presence for what may be the result of one or more of the other factors. In the current wave of Canadian nationalism, that approach is likely to guarantee a good press but bad policy.

Issues in the Primary Resource Sector

A number of direct and indirect gains in national income and in tax revenue can accrue to a country from access to foreign investment in the development of natural resources, provided these gains are not fully offset by subsidies. The gains result partly from access to capital. Even when local markets eventually supply much of the debt capital, firms with long planning horizons have played an important role in exploration and development because of a high degree of risk and a long period of gestation until the product is available. The gains result also from a wide range of technical and managerial skills concentrated in international firms, skills that often cannot be secured at the time by other means, or perhaps only at much larger costs. Often there are important marketing skills arising from vertically integrated operations on a multinational basis. The regional development effects are particularly important in a federal state, notably for provinces and regions that may have few other development options in any given period.

It is important to add that not all of these benefits accrue equally in every sector of activity. Put differently, a state that seeks to secure these benefits from sources other than multinationals (such as domestic firms, joint ventures, and licensing) may find any given *net* benefit more easily realizable in some sectors than in others. In the growth of the Canadian petroleum industry, for example, there were quite different degrees of risk, transfer of skills from abroad, and gestation periods in exploration, development, production, transportation, refining, and marketing.

Against the gains, there are growing questions in Canada, as elsewhere, regarding the social costs involved in natural resource development with multinational firms, and there is a search for alternative approaches by way of greater regulation of such firms, the development of private or public domestic firms, and by other means. All of this is against a background of a set of concerns which are sometimes exaggerated. They carry enough persuasion to cause governments to intervene heavily in the natural resource industries, frequently treating them as a special case for purposes of both domestic and foreign-control legislation.

Raymond F. Mikesell and his colleagues, in their major study, *Foreign Investment in the Petroleum and Mineral Industries*, developed four reasons for conflict between foreign investors and the governments of host countries. While their case studies related to countries which are less-developed economically than Canada, a similar set of questions has been raised in Canada. These relate to: the division of net revenues between firms and governments, notably the attempt in Canada to secure the full economic rent by increased taxes and reduced subsidies; the control of prices and production over short and long periods, particularly in an attempt to regulate the rate of extraction of nonrenewable resources and to increase the degree of processing, all subject to environmental and regional concerns; the domestic economic impact of the firms' operations, that is, national income and employment effects; and the legal and other forms of public control of the firm, including securing adequate information for regulatory purposes.

These issues have greatly affected Canada-United States relations, not surprisingly in view of the high degree of United States ownership of the capital in Canadian resource industries and the still high volume of unprocessed raw materials in Canada's exports. Each reflects not only questions about foreign ownership, but also a much more general set of concerns regarding the impact in the natural resource sector of large privately owned firms, wherever owned.

Before considering these four concerns, it is important to note that the Canadian Constitution places the proprietary rights in publicly owned natural resources in the provinces, except for the Yukon and Northwest Territories. The provinces, as a consequence, play an important developmental role with regard to such resources. The federal government controls interprovincial and international trade, and it can levy both direct and indirect taxes, while the provinces are restricted to the former.

Division of Net Revenues

In the case of natural resources, conflict over the division of net revenues is inevitable over time. In Raymond Vernon's terminology, a contract between a foreign investor in raw materials and a host country is an "obsolescing bargain," since the terms to which a government agrees at the start of an uncertain venture when it may have few other options are not likely to be the same as those it would consider acceptable when and if the venture proves successful. The few other options noted here should be thought of in two senses: other development projects for a region and other sources of the necessary inputs of knowledge and capital.

In Canada, a long period of substantial tax and other subsidies for mining and petroleum industries, partly for purposes of regional development, began to be reversed as a result of the recommendations of the federal Royal Commission on Taxation. More particularly, the recent rapid increase in the price of petroleum has led the province of Alberta in particular to attempt to extract higher royalties, while several provinces increased royalties in the mining industries. This has led them into a confrontation with the federal government, which moved quickly to prevent the erosion of its corporate income tax base from such royalty increases, since these could be charged against income for tax purposes.

The entire situation is further complicated by the decision of the federal government to limit the impact of higher imported petroleum prices on the domestic price. The lower domestic price is maintained by a variable subsidy on petroleum imports into eastern Canada, a subsidy financed by a variable federal tax on such exports to the United States. This led to difficulties in some quarters in the United States, although one is hard put to understand why a policy aimed at maintaining a domestic price below the world level should be extended by Canadian-financed subsidies to United States consumers. More dramatically, it has led to a fierce battle within Canada, as Alberta in particular has attempted to raise both prices and its taxes while the major user, Ontario, has strongly resisted this. Meanwhile, the federal government, having rejected the price provided by the international petroleum market, has perforce had the awkward job of finding the right political and economic price.

What has this to do with the foreign ownership of Canadian industry? A few years ago one could argue that the effective tax rate was so low that price increases would benefit particularly the foreign shareholder by way of dividends or through increased asset values. One would have more difficulty in making that case since the recent increases in taxes of various kinds. Indeed, the argument put forward by the petroleum and mining industries is that the tax share has become so high that the investments necessary to assure future supplies are in jeopardy and that a number of firms may be forced to invest abroad as a consequence. The issue is the classical one of both measuring and taxing the economic rent on natural resources, that is, the surplus over the expenditures necessary to secure the output of natural resources. That simplified statement conceals a host of complex issues in taxation, including the problem of securing economic rent while also maintaining the desired rate of investment in new capacity and the desired stock, and also the problem of determining an optimal pattern of use for a depletable resource over time.

The ability of governments to extract economic rent from private developers of natural resources depends not only on accurate measurement and taxation, but also on a host of issues related to their relative bargaining strength. There may be few potential bidders for any specific resource rights in the exploration stage, if the technical skills are not yet widely known; a varying number of competitive alternatives elsewhere; more or less cooperation between resource owners, that is, the provincial or national governments; and more or less difficulty in securing market access. Given a range of uncertainty in determining economic rent, such bargaining issues become significant.

An important question here will be the prices that related firms charge one another for goods and services. To the extent that multinational firms can minimize their global taxes by pricing practices that place profits in lower tax jurisdictions, some governments lose tax revenues. Thus a firm might underprice its exports to a related firm abroad, or pay more for management services provided by the latter (in each case in relation to an arms-length price) in order to put more profits into a foreign country with a lower tax rate. The issue of transfer pricing inevitably comes to the fore as governments seek to tax economic rent more fully, and it is also relevant in manufacturing industries. One major difficulty is that the Canadian government has apparently done little systematic work on the magnitude and other aspects of the transfer-pricing problem, despite repeated recommendations from various government-sponsored studies that it do so.

Control of Industry Production and Investment

A second set of issues, partly related to the first, arises from increasing attempts by governments to control prices, output, marketing, and investment policies. There is a great deal of scope for state-corporation interaction and disagreement on the maximization of returns over time in the petroleum and mineral industries where large firms dominate, markets are often controlled privately or through agencies such as OPEC, conservation is an issue, investments are heavily subsidized by the government, and such investments have long gestation periods. Where multinational firms are involved, largely foreign-owned as in petroleum or both foreign-owned and Canadian-owned, as in mining, there is scope for further disagreement over transfer pricing, over comparative production rates from domestic and foreign sources, over investments at home and abroad, and so on. To put it bluntly, governments do not trust markets and large firms to make such decisions, either because the price system is not regarded as an efficient allocator of investment and production over long periods, or because of monopoly elements, or because governments prefer other outcomes such as more processing than the firm might provide, or because such intervention serves bureaucratic or partisan objectives.

These issues have become acute in Canada and elsewhere with the rapid increase in petroleum prices and the concern about supplies. They have also become major problems in Canada-United States relations. The attempt to maintain a Canadian price below the world price, involving a subsidy on imports of petroleum and a tax on exports, has led to serious misunderstandings with United States consumers. The Canadian government's concern with reserves and future supplies has led it to reduce exports of petroleum and to announce recently that both domestic and export supplies of natural gas, much of which is sold under contract to United States customers, will be reduced. The question of how to handle these cutbacks is clearly a sensitive one, with the United States government and purchasers insisting the cutbacks must be shared between Canadian and foreign purchasers, the federal government appearing to agree in principle, but at least one province appearing to take the view that the United States should bear the burden of any cutback in natural gas.

Differences of view on the appropriate long-term rate of development seem to be somewhat more muted in that both governments and firms are concerned about the need for increases in supply from Canadian sources. At the same time, some basic questions have been raised about the timing of major northern pipelines and the impact on the economy, on the environment, and on the rights of native peoples; about the appropriate price and subsidy arrangements for recovery of oil from tar sands; and about the appropriate degree of public participation via joint public-private ventures or government corporations. Underlying all of this is a basic question about how fast and in what ways the domestic prices should be allowed to rise in order to encourage the development of future supplies.

In all of this, large corporations in petroleum and mining, particularly multinational firms, find themselves in an unenviable position. It is not simply that there is more public scrutiny and regulation of their activities in order to realize a variety of public objectives; there is no lack of regulatory agencies, both federal and provincial, in the area of energy in particular. The difficulty lies partly in quite different pressures from producing and consuming provinces, between federal and provincial governments, and between Ottawa and Washington, as well as from a variety of private entities. The difficulty also lies in different expectations of appropriate energy policy and a different evaluation of the role of the multinational as a consequence.

Not long ago, it was the conventional wisdom in Canada that the multinationals were not lifting *enough* of the relatively high-cost Canadian supplies, preferring to use their lower-cost foreign supplies; that it was in Canada's interest to be given preferred access to the United States market for petroleum, at a time when quotas limited imports to the United States from other countries; and that the multinational firm in primary resources contributed to a higher rate of growth because of its easier access to capital, marketing, and technology, and its long planning horizon. Preferences have changed, and the desire for conservation, for more processing of raw materials, and for a pace of growth that takes fuller account of various social costs has almost reversed these arguments. One can well imagine a federal government opting today for somewhat slower growth than multinational firms might prefer and might generate, given the above mix of objectives and a specific set of prices. Provincial governments have the same set of concerns, although in some cases the developmental and revenue pressures are greater on them.

Impact on the Economy

The domestic economic impact of the activities of multinational firms is a third area of conflict. Two points on this have been given much attention in recent Canadian discussions. One emphasizes the effects on the economy as a whole and on different sectors, as a result of major resource development and related transportation projects. This view emphasizes the negative effects that major capital imports and raw material exports would have, via a higher exchange rate, on the development of processing or manufacturing industries, which are also accorded a higher preference in such studies. The other and related point is the backward and forward linkages of such natural resource projects, as compared with alternative industrial projects. Natural resource projects, it is argued, may not lead to large domestic purchases (backward linkage) or the effects on the development of processed or manufactured goods via lower supply prices may be small (forward linkage). Given a relatively capital-intensive type of project, moreover, there is likely to be less direct training of labor, while a relatively high propensity to import would mean fewer direct efficiency gains from the effects on other domestic firms. Some studies suggest that backward linkages are not as large as forward linkages and that the combined output effect may be low compared to other industries. The evidence is not unequivocal, however, and depends also on the type of industry and the country being considered. In particular, it would be important to distinguish those firms that have a high degree of vertical integration within Canada, such as some of the major petroleum firms, from those that have a high degree of vertical integration with a parent abroad, such as some of the mining firms.

What needs to be asked here is whether the answers to these questions depend on the country of ownership of the firm in some convincing way. There are an increasing number of studies in Canada of specific aspects of performance, including particularly some that take account of the effects of foreign ownership when estimating the impact of proposed resource projects. However, systematic studies that would permit an answer to that question in the natural resource industries simply have not been made in Canada. It would be impossible to compare the performance of firms by country of ownership in the petroleum industry since all the major integrated firms are foreign-owned, but such a study in mining should be revealing. With relatively minor exceptions, the expressed policy preferences of Canadian governments for more processing of raw materials before export and more domestic sourcing of suplies appear to be directed toward all major existing firms regardless of ownership. There also appears to be a growing recognition that the major obstacles to trade in highly processed goods are tariff and nontariff barriers.

Form of Public Control

The fourth set of issues on which governments and firms may find themselves in conflict is the question of the form of control—that is, in the desire to have national interests, private or public, involved in the industry, partly in an attempt to resolve the issues noted above. This has led to small tax incentives to encourage foreign-owned subsidiaries to issue some shares, although, it must be added, many major foreign-owned firms in petroleum and mining have long had minority share-holdings available to the public. This set of issues has led also to a modest degree of tax discrimination in favor of smaller Canadian firms. The Foreign Investment Review Agency must consider the degree of Canadian participation in ownership of the subsidiary, among other things, when considering whether to approve foreign business investment in Canada. There is also a growing preference for joint ventures with private or public Canadian interests, a preference underlined by a federal policy statement, still to be defined in law in cooperation with the provinces, that all major new natural resource projects would require at least 50 percent Canadian ownership. Finally, there are several new public firms intended in part to compete with existing ones and some selective ventures into government ownership or participation in resource firms.

The pressure for public participation is likely to be particularly toward joint ventures, in an attempt by governments to get a larger share of control over basic production and investment decisions and a larger share of any net gains than they believe can be secured by regulation, by taxation, and by the outcome of market forces in these industries. Such involvement in exploration and in high-risk investments, such as tar sands, also exposes governments to the higher initial risks and the industry to a much higher degree of public involvement than before. Government corporations in the natural resource sector, such as the newly established federal petroleum company, permit similar possible gains or losses.

The issue of nationalization, which is less immediate than the forms of public participation just noted, serves a more complicated set of motives. Canada, like other countries, has a small but vociferous group that sees nationalization or at least patriation as the ultimate solution to the problems of multinational firms, especially in a "basic" industry such as petroleum. At a certain point a high degree of public regulation, participation, and attention, through both tax treatment and public expenditure, may well raise the question whether to internalize the inevitable administrative and other problems through nationalization of some firms —and perhaps also to avoid or at least to disguise the need to match external tax and market incentives in order to secure any given level of output or investment. Needless to say, the divided constitutional jurisdiction over resources would greatly complicate moves in this direction in many cases. It should be added that the provinces, even those with conservative governments, are not averse to threatening such moves in their tug-of-war with the federal government over resource taxation.

Whatever the preferred form of public participation, whether regulation or some type of participation in ownership, there is an overriding need for better information flows to and from government agencies and to the public. Information on such matters as reserves, demand, technological change, and substitutes are critical to any consideration of alternative policies for the future, as well as for resolving current issues. Unless the public has information of a high degree of reliablity, it is all too easy for the firms, the government agencies, or both to escape their responsibilities.

Conclusion

In sum, Canada, which someone once described as rich in resources and poor in policy, is busy rectifying the latter. The considerable contributions that multinational, particularly United States, firms have made to resource discovery and development in Canada in recent decades are now being looked at in a new light. With large and well-established firms, with the need and opportunity for major resource investments that will have enormous economic and political and social effects, with more public knowledge of the issues, and with a growing sense of a consequent need to consider the national interest closely and effectively, it is not at all surprising that the Canadian view and approaches to resource development today are very different from those in the resource boom of the early 1950s. It is inevitable that questions about foreign ownership of the natural resource industry are receiving renewed attention, not least because of the high visibility of the energy sector and the fact that the major integrated petroleum firms are all foreign-controlled, as are many of those in the mineral and forest-product industries. A number of issues frequently associated with foreign ownership, though not always due to it, are receiving attention. Ranking high among these issues are transfer pricing and the relation to the attempt to collect economic rent; the appropriate rate of investment, production, and export; a higher degree of processing for export and more sourcing in Canada; and more public participation in decision making and ownership, including better arrangements to disclose and evaluate information. Underlying all of this is a growing view that market forces are not the best means for deciding on the rate of exploitation of depletable resources, particularly when projects are very risky, heavily capital-intensive, and with long gestation periods.

So far as foreign ownership is concerned, there is a presumption in much of the literature and in policy that the net economic benefit from foreign investment in the natural resource industries is not as high as in manufacturing, that some aspects of such investment can be secured at less economic and political cost by alternatives to multinationals, and that the special problems and opportunities in this sector require a large and continuing government presence in any case. It is not at all clear, however, how many of the difficulties noted here are mainly due to foreign ownership of the industries concerned rather than to the economic setting of the industries or to governmental policies. The high degree of foreign ownership in these industries in Canada inevitably lumps all these concerns together in public discussion.

There are certainly more opportunities for the exercise of transfer pricing when a firm has affiliates abroad and is engaged in foreign trade, for example, but most major firms in the industries concerned, including those controlled in Canada, are in this position. It is not apparent why a Canadian-owned firm is more likely to take environmental concerns into account, or to have a rate of production for a depletable resource that takes adequate account of the *social* need to balance present and future use. Natural resource firms in Canada, regardless of ownership, face similar foreign-trade and transportation barriers to the efficient export of highly processed resources. It is true that substantial dividends accrue to foreign owners and that this would be a net social cost, compared to payments to domestic owners, if other things were equal. But it was partly because these other things (capital, knowledge, and markets) were not equally available by or through domestic sources that Canadians relied on foreign sources.

A key question regarding independence, as noted above, is whether governments find the costs of policy implementation higher in an economy with many multinational firms, and whether these costs are sufficiently high to offset any advantages. The usual response to this question in Canada is that a multinational that has its headquarters in Canada is more susceptible to the pressures of Canadian governments and less to that of foreign governments than a multinational with headquarters abroad. Present information and analyses do not enable one to know how much weight to give this point and in what respects. Certainly one can cite a number of examples of extraterritorial application of United States laws to subsidiaries in Canada, examples that have led to concern about the effects on Canadian sovereignty of a high degree of foreign ownership of industry. Nevertheless, it is difficult to know how far to apply the general question posed here to those primary resources that are clearly within the control and ownership of the states concerned and often lack the mobility and complexity of much of the manufacturing industry. There are plenty of recent examples to indicate the power that states have over their natural resources if they wish to exercise them, including some fairly formidable price, tax, production, investment, and marketing controls on the largely foreign-owned petroleum industry in Canada.

The fundamental issues are the problems of determining and implementing an optimal resource policy or set of policies for Canada and of determining and implementing the kinds of policies appropriate to the large, oligopolistic firms characteristic of primary resource industries. Specific difficulties or potentials posed by multinational firms will need consideration in some given policy contexts, but the fundamental issues posed here are likely to be far more important concerns than those associated with the country of ownership of the firm.

Two other important issues arise in considering these questions, namely, relations between governments. The first is the ways in which Canada-United States relations have been affected by the relatively strong position that Canada enjoys in some natural resources and by a determination to exploit that position more fully than in the past and to do so with more Canadian participation. While the Canadian position is not as strong as some would have it, given the many problems involved in bringing forward future supplies, it is significant so long as economic substitutes are not available. There is also likely to be a continuing high degree of Canadian dependency in some other aspects, such as the need for some forms of technical and capital access or for markets. There are clearly possibilities for joint maximization between the two countries, given these circumstances, as distinct from proceeding on the assumption that the actions by one country are unlikely to affect the other, or are unlikely to lead to reactions from the other. It is dangerous to assume in bilateral relations that the actions of the two parties do not affect the total returns available. The difficulty, of course, is the fear of many Canadians that Canada has fewer cards to play in any game with the United States, because of the disparate degrees of dependency. Hence the attempt to establish closer contact with the European Common Market; hence, also, the fact that the recent Canadian proposal to export more raw materials, if others also took more Canadian semiprocessed goods, was put in the context of multilateral trade negotiation.

The second intergovernmental issue that demands attention is the competition between federal and provincial governments over revenue and control of the natural-resource sector. In a decentralized federal state such competition is unavoidable and, in terms of the assumptions of federalism, the overlap of responsibilities is desirable. There are, however, some important consequences. In dealing with large firms in any primary resource sector, the bargaining power of governments is affected by a number of factors; for example, the ease of access to such resources elsewhere, the degree of competition or monopoly among firms, and the degree of cooperation among the national governments controlling the resource. The Canadian situation is complicated further by the competition among provinces to attract resource development by offering generous concessions, sometimes with disastrous consequences, as in some forest projects. The outcome is to reduce the net gain from such investments to the host country. Moreover, the lack of coordination in areas of shared constitutional jurisdiction can at times get out of hand, to the detriment of both public and private interests. The dispute over royalties and taxes in petroleum and mining is a case in point, as are the uncertainties in supply engendered by different approaches to pricing, production, exports, and investment. All of these questions must be put in the context of the fundamental need to make a major set of long-term investment decisions, especially on northern energy supplies and on southern alternatives to present supplies, and to determine the appropriate balance between public and private interests and initiatives in implementing these decisions.

The author is grateful to H. Edward English and Leonard Waverman for their helpful comments on this essay.

Foreign Investment in Manufacturing

H. EDWARD ENGLISH

Canada has attracted relatively more direct investment in both resource development and manufacturing than any other country, and the majority of it has come from the United States. Professor Safarian's essay in this volume deals with the rather different effects and policy issues posed by foreign ownership or control in the resource sector. In that sector, the rent (or sharing of revenues) and the conservation (or rate of depletion) questions are of major importance. How much of the rent from scarce natural resources can be captured by the people who claim those resources as a "birthright"? To what extent should rent be sacrificed as an inducement to invest in Canada (or any host country) in order to compete effectively with other host countries having similar resource endowments? Does the rate of resource exploration and exploitation adopted by the private company depart significantly from the rate that would result in the maximum net social benefit to Canada? In the manufacturing sector all rents are quasi rents (or monopoly or oligopoly profits) and therefore subject to erosion by the encouragement of competition. Furthermore, the location of a manufacturing plant is not primarily related to the presence of national natural resources, so it is not national but world resource allocation that becomes relevant, and the rate of use of international resources is a lower priority question for each national government (whether or not it should be).

In this essay the study of Canadian experience with foreign controlled enterprise and policy options, considered and sometimes adopted, will be reviewed in the context of other evidence relating to the organization and conduct of large manufacturing enterprises. The object is not merely to evaluate Canadian experience but to try to identify those issues arising out of foreign direct investment that are most substantive and deserve continued attention now that a decade of experience with these issues in North America and elsewhere has made it possible to gain some perspective on the relative importance of the various impacts of multinational enterprises.

Main Themes in Canadian Literature on Multinationals

In the considerable Canadian literature on the multinationals in Canadian manufacturing, the issues most often cited relate to perceived restraints on Canadian growth of several kinds:

(a) The multinational company appears to restrict Canadian manufacturing activity because it limits the possibility of exports from Canada in order to avoid competition between the subsidiary and the parent or other subsidiaries, or to meet labor and other political pressures in the home country of the parent firm, etc.

(b) The multinational appears to restrict the development of distinctive Canadian technology and the consequent export of distinctive Canadian products. This is perceived to be a consequence of the ease of application of foreign, especially United States, technology to Canadian needs, even when better Canadian adaptations might be possible. These Canadians options are sometimes seen as precluded because foreign technology is available at less than full cost.

(c) The assignment to Canada of producing units to supply only local markets and the limitations on development of Canadian technology appear to be at the source of the phenomenon called "truncation"—less than fully integrated Canadian manufacturing concerns. Truncation is also believed to frustrate the development of an adequate skilled management group in Canada.

In addition to these allocation effects, it is often suggested that the pricing policies of multinationals frustrate the capture of income by Canadian governments. This is because much trade in components and even in finished products takes place in non-arms-length transactions so that real prices and costs can be masked in an effort to avoid taxation by the host government.

Thus, multinationals in manufacturing are seen as having questionable effects on the allocation of resources and on the distribution of income between the home and host countries. In fact, most of the foregoing perceptions are highly questionable. Much of the more polemical literature on the multinationals implies that they are monolithic economic power centers able to operate not only beyond the influence of national governments, but also immune from the forces of competition within the industry. Neither of these simplistic implications is valid. While restraints and artificial allocations undoubtedly occur, they are not primarily the result of foreign ownership. The empirical evidence available on industries in which multinational enterprises are common suggests that the phenomena listed are to a large extent the consequences of the circumstances in which the firms operate.

The two major sources of unsatisfactory industry performance are the public policy environment created by the host government (sometimes abetted by the government of the parent firm's home country) and the wasteful aspects of the oligopolistic rivalry that occur in certain manufacturing industries and that also happen to be conducive to foreign direct investment activity. Both of these phenomena can be readily illustrated in the Canadian case.

Importance of the Policy Environment

Many of the criticized actions of private enterprises, foreign and domestic, can be explained by the policy environment provided by the host government and by other governments. For example, tariff and nontariff barriers bear much of the responsibility for uneconomic activities of multinationals. During the 1960s, Canadian economists pointed to considerable evidence that the lack of export activity by Canadian branches of multinational manufacturing enterprises was the consequence of the inability (and lack of incentive) of such branches to compete at international prices, an inability that resulted from the foreign trade barriers they had to overcome and from the prevalence of small scale and high cost plants that could operate profitably in Canada behind Canadian trade barriers.[1]

Similarly, United States-owned companies that invest or acquire patent rights on new products in Canada have found that they can more profitably start production of such products in their United States plants because access to their largest market is thereby assured. To be sure, market access is not the only advantage of technologically intensive enterprises located in the United States. Specialized research skills of all kinds are more likely to be developed in a larger industrially advanced country. Furthermore, the stress on training in applied science, and on business administration, gave American enterprise at least a temporary advantage in the postwar era. (Such writers as Servan-Schriber placed some emphasis, and should have placed more, on this aspect of "the American challenge.") But the European Economic Community and

---

[1] A. E. Safarian, *Foreign Ownership of Canadian Industry* (Toronto: McGraw-Hill, 1966); H. E. English, *Industrial Structure in Canada's International Competitive Position* (Montreal: Canadian Trade Committee, 1964); and two government reports, Task Force on the Structure of Canadian Industry, *Foreign Ownership and the Structure of Canadian Industry* (Ottawa, 1968) and *Foreign Direct Investment in Canada* (Ottawa, 1971). The last two are known as the Watkins report and the Gray report, respectively.

Japan, with their large domestic markets, have already largely overcome any United States lead in these areas. For Canada, apart from upgrading its scientific and managerial skills, a vital requirement in order to achieve competitiveness in complex manufacturing activity is assured equal access to markets of one or more of its larger trading partners. Given geographic proximity, the United States market is clearly the main target and at the same time the base on which capacity for competition overseas in technologically intensive goods might evolve.

Evidence on the Role of Oligopolistic Nonprice Competition

Market access, while vital, may not be everything. For some industries, at least, complete removal of trade barriers would leave some industrial markets under the influence of a group of large oligopolistic enterprises. One sector that already illustrates this condition is farm machinery.[2] Even though free trade has been almost universal in this sector since 1944, a group of five or six major firms is engaged in a kind of oligopolistic rivalry that raises serious doubts about the optimality of resource allocation. The main problem in this instance lies in the marketing or distribution system. It is symbolized by the strong incentives given to "independent" franchise holders to press the sale of new brand-name machines (mainly through interest-free inventories) and the discouragement of sales outlets that carry several brands.

Essential distribution and servicing costs in this market are undoubtedly higher relative to most other manufactured products. But many of the activities that are incorporated in distribution and servicing are the consequence of the efforts of each large oligopolist to preserve and, if possible, to extend its share of the market by pressuring the buyer to buy what he would not buy in the absence of that pressure. These efforts include offering new models or varieties of products when style and accessories are more significant than improvement of essential functions, subsidization of new product sales as an inducement to sales staff activity, various efforts to tie sales of one product to a commitment to purchase other products not necessarily related, advertising, and relative neglect of servicing. These are important elements in the multinational activities of farm machinery enterprises, and indeed they appear to be important in many of the other manufacturing industries where multinational enterprises are most active. The Canadian manufacturing sectors that have a high percentage of foreign control include petroleum, rubber, tobacco, transportation equipment, chemicals, and electrical products. All of these

[2] Royal Commission on Farm Machinery, *Report* (known as the Barber commission) (Ottawa: Information Canada, 1971). This report gives a detailed account of the characteristics of this industry, especially in chapters 7-11 and 27-30.

are marketing-intensive sectors where nonprice competition is relatively more important than for other manufacturing industries. Among the types of nonprice competition, marketing-oriented product modification and tied sales seem to be more important than substantive product improvements.

It is necessary, however, to examine more evidence on this matter, and it is easiest to focus on United States evidence since American scholarship has played a leading role in industrial structure analysis. Furthermore, the size of the United States market has provided ample scope for the exploration of economies of scale and of other forces that explain market structure.

From the earliest major empirical work of Joe S. Bain[3] in the 1950s to the more specialized work of recent years, the evidence has accumulated on the economies of scale of plant and firm. The relevant evidence may be summarized as follows:

(a) Economies of scale within the plant are significant, though their significance varies greatly among industry sectors, but the economies of mass production have frequently been exaggerated. For most sectors, minimum efficient scale can be achieved at levels of output that are relatively small in relation to the United States market—less than 5 percent and in most cases much less.

(b) The most concentrated industrial sectors are concentrated, not because of the economies of large plants, but because multiplant firms have been able to develop and compete effectively with those having fewer producing units. The main reasons for multiplant firms in the manufacturing industries relate to product differentiation—the creation of real and imagined modifications of products through research and development, style changes, packaging, and advertising—all to distinguish one producer's brands from those of rivals and to maintain that distinction.

Bain, Scherer, and others have demonstrated that product differentiation contributes to firm size through expanding the market, spreading quasi-fixed costs over a larger volume of business, and building brand or product loyalties. The spreading of fixed nonplant costs (for example, the costs of research and development) will in itself give a firm an advantage over smaller firms. The development of brand loyalties will

---

[3] Joe S. Bain, *Industrial Organization* (New York: John Wiley & Sons, 1959), especially chapters 7-8. A recent study by F. M. Scherer et al., *The Economics of Multi-Plant Operation* (Cambridge, Massachusetts: Harvard University Press, 1975) has provided much more evidence of the nature of economies of scale in multiplant firms. To quote one summary (by D. J. Daly), the book concludes that many companies are "much larger than the size necessary to obtain most of the benefits from the scale economies that can be quantified."

have the same effect but need not be cost-reducing, because it is intended primarily to reduce the elasticity of demand for the products of the firm engaged in selling activity of all kinds.

Application to Multinational Enterprises

In the international market this analysis has direct application. Firms will be tempted to go abroad if this will help them to spread the fixed cost of product innovations and exploit brand loyalties in new markets. But in foreign markets there are certain additional considerations, relating mainly to the choice between exporting and foreign investment. Either way costs can be spread and brand loyalties can be established and exploited. The choice between exporting and investment is also affected by the trade barriers imposed by national governments and by the differences in consumer tastes between national markets. The work done recently by Richard Caves, Tom Horst, and others[4] has contributed to the following evidence on product differentiation:

(a) Although many forms of product differentiation are present in the industrial sectors in which multinational enterprises predominate, the choice of foreign direct investment over simple export is more common for those sectors where brand loyalty and marketing activity are relatively more important than real product innovation.

(b) For these same sectors, it may be observed that the barriers to trade are higher than for sectors where research and real product innovation are relatively more important. This is not surprising, because it is in sectors supplying final consumer goods that the highest formal and informal trade barriers exist, as well as the most marketing activity.

To be more specific, United States export statistics show that the ten most important categories of manufactured exports are of construction and mining machinery, office and computing equipment, special industry machinery, aircraft, scientific and measuring equipment, general industry-machinery, chemical products not elsewhere specified, photographic equipment, other machinery except electrical, and electronic components. Note that these are research-intensive sectors producing mainly producer durables and other intermediate goods.

By contrast, the relative importance of foreign direct investment is

4 Richard E. Caves, *International Trade, International Investment and Imperfect Markets*, Special Papers in International Economics, No. 10 (Princeton University, November 1974); Thomas Horst, *At Home Abroad* (Cambridge, Massachusetts: Ballinger, 1974). The listings of leading industrial sectors in export, direct investment, and advertising appearing here are from data gathered for a forthcoming study, Fred C. Bergsten, Thomas Horst, and Theodore Moran, *American Multinationals and American Interests* (Washington, D. C.: Brookings Institution, forthcoming).

greatest for soap, drugs, soft drinks, office machinery, photographic equipment, petroleum refining, hardware and cutlery, optical goods, grain mill products (including breakfast foods), and rubber products. These are predominantly final consumer goods.

Five of these are among the ten manufacturing categories for which advertising expenditures are relatively most important, i.e., soap, drugs, grain mill products, soft drinks, and cutlery and hardware. Other sectors for which the advertising expenditure is relatively large are not important in either foreign trade or investment activities. This is strongly indicative of the importance of marketing activity as a stimulant to foreign direct investment in manufacturing.

There are, however, two important problems arising out of the limitation of advertising expenditures as a measure of marketing activity and out of the complex nature of some of the industrial sectors. Marketing-oriented product differentiation encompasses many activities besides advertising, e.g., style change, packaging, and sales force activity. Furthermore, for quite a few industry sectors these marketing activities are close substitutes for real product changes, and the boundary line between model or accessory changes and product improvement is not readily drawn.

Nevertheless, the pattern which appears to emerge is that the greater the importance of real product variety, the greater the significance of export activity, while the greater the importance of marketing-oriented product differentiation, the greater the significance of foreign direct investment. For those industries that involve both real product variety and intensive marketing activity, their export activity appears to concentrate on supplying components or specialized (lower volume) products by international trade and major lines of finished products by branch-plant activity.

These tentative conclusions should be further tested, especially for those mixed categories (i.e., most completely differentiated products) by a more detailed examination of the practices and strategies of the firms and sectors involved. The evidence indicates, however, that it is quite misleading to suggest, as some writers have, that multinational enterprises dominate all markets and that their oligopolistic behavior is virtually equivalent to monopoly and is the inevitable result of the advantages of large-scale operations. If the tendency to market dominance by multinationals in manufacturing is based primarily on rival marketing efforts intended to hinder entry of new competition and to fortify market shares to established competitors, efforts to modify or restrict nonprice competition could actively encourage more price competition and easier entry of new competitors and thus somewhat restrain concentration of economic power by multinational enterprises, without undermining their more useful contributions to the world economy.

It is obvious that established multinationals may not like to see their market shares eroded by policies that would constrain nonprice competition on which, along with trade barriers, their secure position in each national market may depend. But the choice they face over the next few years may be between modification of selling practices and encouragement of price and product quality competition, on one hand, and, on the other, more direct regulatory measures now being suggested by some economists and politicians.

This line of analysis also points to the great ambiguity of profits. Evidence from Comanor and Wilson,[5] among others, indicates that advertising activity in United States industries is broadly compatible with high levels of profit. But there is also evidence that multinational firms, especially during the process of becoming established in new markets such as Canada, have been prepared to accept low profits or even losses for extended periods in order to acquire a share of the Canadian market that is comparable to the share of the United States market they supply. This has happened in industries such as automobiles, chemicals, and home electrical and electronic appliances. The consequence of limiting the nonprice rivalry that occurs among large firms could well be to reduce the wasteful duplication of expenditures, and it is not clear that gross revenues would necessarily be reduced by more than costs. The only reason for believing that they might be is that barriers to entry would be somewhat reduced and demand elasticities increased, with the consequence of both lower prices and somewhat lower profits.

Implications for Policies of Host Country Governments

Successive Canadian governments have considered many policies for the guidance of multinational enterprises and have adopted a few. Most of these have little to do with the issues posed here. The most substantive measures have been those that limited foreign investment in sensitive sectors, such as banking and the media.

In manufacturing and other goods-producing sectors, major attention has, in recent years, been directed to the new Foreign Investment Review Agency (FIRA). Established in 1973, it has the power to review takeovers and investment by new or established foreign-controlled firms in new lines of business. It could be extended to cover all major investment by established enterprises, though this would require amendment of the act. Until recently, the agency has been exclusively concerned with takeovers. It has proceeded cautiously, and the fact that the cabinet must

---

[5] William S. Comanor and Thomas A. Wilson, "Advertising, Market Structure and Performance," *Review of Economics and Statistics* 49 (November 1967), 423-40.

finally accept or reject the agency's recommendations further demonstrates the government's desire to watch closely the administration of the legislation. In fact, during the first year of operation, FIRA and the cabinet accepted sixty-three of the ninety-two cases that were resolved. Of the remaining cases, only twelve were rejected, while seventeen were withdrawn. It is not, of course, known how many takeovers were precluded by the very existence of the agency. In fact, the average size of the firms that were "targets" of takeovers was about $6.5 million in assets, with 158 employees. Most of the cases concerned secondary manufacturing enterprises or "tertiary" industry enterprises being acquired to service such enterprises.

At first, the agency did not indicate the grounds on which its recommendations were based, but more recently it has given a summary of the more important benefits perceived in the sixty-three takeovers allowed.

Percentages of cases in which the particular benefit was expected:

Compatibility with industrial and economic policies	96.8
Improved productivity and industrial efficiency	73.0
Increased employment	68.3
New investment	57.1
Canadian participation as shareholders or in management	54.0
Improved product variety and innovation	47.6
Enhanced technological development	46.0
Increased resource processing or use of Canadian goods and services	41.3
Additional exports	34.9
Beneficial impact on competition	30.2

Among these, the least ambiguous are the second, sixth, and last. Many of the others beg questions about the efficiency of the resource allocations involved. But the basic shortcoming of the FIRA approach, apart from the costliness in the time and money of the regulatory process, is that it has almost no relevance to the problem of restrictive national trade barriers that promote oligopolistic industrial structures, or the problem of nonprice rivalry itself, cited earlier.

It is apparent that policies for stimulating competition by reducing trade barriers and limiting nonprice rivalry would be more effective if there is international action, or at least parallel action, by the major industrially advanced countries. However, Canada might introduce some measures unilaterally and urge parallel international action. The policy directions contained in the report of the government's task force, *Foreign Ownership and the Structure of Canadian Industry* (Ottawa, 1968), still seem valid—removing barriers to international trade, strengthening competition policies, and improving information flows between business and government.

Some steps have been taken in these directions, but on the whole Canadian policies affecting industrial structure still lack focus. Each policy area has a different administrative tradition, and new measures reflect the bureaucratic and political constraints associated with that tradition rather than a coordinated perception of the ways that the policies for restructuring industry could collectively serve agreed Canadian objectives such as sound economic growth and distinctive quality of life.

Canadian trade policy is forced to inch forward to satisfy the traditional GATT bargaining criteria that treat Canadian tariff reductions as "concessions" to be minimized rather than the necessary conditions for achieving efficiency in Canadian industries and a fully competitive position for Canadian manufacturers in world markets. Happily the recent report of the Economic Council of Canada on commercial policy (*Looking Outward*) points to bolder approaches compatible with the needs discussed here. This report points to the need for Canadian industry to be put on equal terms with competitors in the United States and the EEC. This is particularly important to Canadian producers attempting to launch distinctive products on the world market. But freer trade also encourages more price competition and real product variety, as one can observe from the impact of Japanese and European competition on the United States automobile market.

Canadian competition policy also continues to be limited by its traditional mechanisms, which have not proven to be well suited to the control of differentiated oligopoly. Interdepartmental suspicions in the federal government continue to make it difficult to dovetail those elements of policy that affect competition but lie outside the jurisdiction of the department primarily charged with the promotion of a competitive economy, e.g., commercial policy and the regulation of multinational enterprises and the traditional utilities. Even the effort of the Department of Consumer and Corporate Affairs to replace the traditional rigid criminal court approach to restrictive business practices by an administrative tribunal that might at least identify and recommend packages of remedies to resolve the structural deficiencies of an industrial sector has been handicapped by political pressures. Some of these have come from private industry groups that pay lip service to competition but seem unwilling to have competitive policies freed of their legal straitjackets. Such an attitude is a guarantee of the continuance of the current trend toward increasing government intervention of an ad hoc variety, the desperate last resort of conservative politicians trying to solve the unemployment-inflation trade-off and of liberal left politicians willingly accepting any evidence of the ineffectiveness of market disciplines.

Most surprising, at first glance, is the difficulty of attaining an efficient information flow between business and government. Disclosure arrangements have been periodically reviewed and some improvements made, but efforts are still handicapped by the suspicions of industry and by the cost burden placed on industry by the proliferation of reporting activities required by government departments and agencies (and at more than one level of government). The suspicion grows that effective disclosure arrangements can only emerge when government bureaus cease to regard the privacy of their own data sources as essential to their power or influence in interdepartmental (and even cabinet) bargaining.

The Foreign Investment Review Agency, which reports to the minister of industry, trade and commerce, provides a good example of the consequences of uncoordinated gathering of data on industrial markets. Had data about industrial structure and conduct from all government information sources been available to agencies responsible for competition policy, a whole new data gathering effort might not have been necessary to evaluate the merits of takeovers. Furthermore, had FIRA's activities been linked more clearly to Consumer and Corporate Affairs with its greater familiarity with the relevant social policy criteria affecting industrial performance, the review process would almost certainly have adopted fewer and more defensible criteria. It is difficult to imagine a competition policy tribunal or a tariff board accepting "gross employment contribution" as a justification for a takeover unless that employment can clearly be achieved without sacrifice of better alternative uses of the same resources or without indefinite continuance of protection against imports. In any case, the public interest is not served by the common practice of secreting information in order to optimize bureaucratic power positions. As the post-energy crisis inquiries by the United States Congress have demonstrated, both private and public agencies are probably guilty of this practice.

In addition to the improvement and better coordination of existing policies, some new policy measures may be necessary. The most obvious of these are some disincentive to unrestrained marketing activity and possibly a more positive incentive to real product improvement and price competition. It is noteworthy that the French government recently announced its intention to encourage product improvement and to limit a perceived deterioration in product quality. It is not known whether it is the French intention to attack this issue through disincentives to the full range of activity short of real product improvements (i.e., from advertising to annual model changes). The broadest approach would be a limit on model change, selling, and related expenses that could be charged against income for tax assessment purposes. The limit might be a general one or it could differentiate between purely marketing activity and product modification, leaving research and development expenses fully recoverable. In any case, an absolute floor should be incorporated in any such measure, which would make it possible for new firms to compete effectively but would impose constraint on established firms whose customary level of expenditure has risen well above that level in the familiar quest for secure market shares. Some such measures could have a salutary effect on the share controlled by the largest firms in the major industry sectors where multinational enterprises operate. It could, if combined with trade barrier elimination, considerably heighten the competitive capacity of smaller, or newer, nationally based enterprises.

If such a policy were adopted by Canada alone, it would face the challenge of spillover marketing through the media that reaches both the United States and Canadian markets. This is a difficult but perhaps not insoluble problem. At best, these policies might encourage the development of distinctive, perhaps more durable, and better Canadian products that would find a competitive advantage in the United States and other foreign markets.

The same objective could, in principle, be achieved by consumer product research activities accompanied by sufficiently wide distribution of the results so that the intrinsic merits of rival products would become well known to consumers, making it less easy for large companies to fortify positions of market strength or high-profile styling and high-pressure packaging and selling alone. Price competition could be in a measure restored and a new competitor with a superior product would have fewer problems in entering the market under these circumstances.

The foregoing policies are less restrictive or disruptive than some that are being proposed for the encouragement of competition among multinationals, e.g., the divestiture of major subsidiaries and promotion of competition between parent and subsidiaries. However, divestiture is a rather blunt instrument to deal with the specific need to reduce the competition-restricting effects of marketing, if on further study this proves to be the major source of market concentration by multinational enterprise and manufacturing.

In conclusion, the burden of the argument is that the Canadian interest in foreign direct investment in manufacturing consists primarily in identifying those ways that public and corporate policies make large enterprises less competitive than they could be and devising policies, with as much international cooperation as possible, to make the market discipline do what governments otherwise may find themselves politically compelled to do with less efficiency and sensitivity.

Deterrence, Détente, and Canada?

ROGER FRANK SWANSON

East-West détente appears to be one of the new realities of the international community. The present state of détente is both the cause and effect of fundamental alterations in the international community as a bipolar United States-USSR power structure has gradually disintegrated into a less rigid configuration. This alteration has been due to such centrifugal forces as Europe's resurgence and its attempts at unity, Japan's emergence as an economic power, China's reentry into global councils and its rift with the USSR, and more recently the Third World's new assertions, most notably through the oil cartel. Meanwhile, the two superpowers had reached a nuclear standoff and were themselves attempting to absorb domestic and international changes; for example, both the Nixon and Brezhnev doctrines reflected an attempt to redefine more manageable spheres of influence. The current era of détente can therefore be seen as an attempt on the part of all nations to adjust to and manipulate the sources of international change, and these attempts themselves have become part of the new realities that characterize the highly fluid international community of the mid-1970s.

Defined in the most general sense as the reciprocal attempt to improve relations between two nations or blocs, East-West détente has five dimensions—security, trade, science and technology, environment, and humanitarian cooperation. This essay concentrates on the security dimension, which has as its core the threat of nuclear weapons. While the other dimensions of détente are both important and interrelated with the security dimension, security matters retain an awesome priority, given the potentiality of a nuclear confrontation. If détente is one side of the coin, deterrence as the means of inflicting unacceptable damage on an aggressor is the other side.

On one hand there must be an attempt cooperatively to define areas of joint interest while reducing areas of tension; on the other hand, a sufficient level of armaments must be maintained to ensure stability and a sense of security between adversaries. The search for East-West détente is therefore a relative give and take, a juxtaposition of cooperation and national security assessments that must be continually balanced by both the United States and the USSR. While progress in détente depends primarily on the ability of the superpowers to define concentric interest areas, its impact on other nations and on the solidarity of alliances can be profound. Indeed, all United States allies, including Canada, are subject to the vagaries of the superpowers. However, unlike the other United States allies, Canada is at once more secure and more insecure.

Given the superpower confrontation, the fundamental and irrevocable reality facing Canada has been its geographical contiguity with the United States coupled with its location between the United States and the USSR. Thus, Canada has been more secure than the other United States allies because there was never any doubt about the United States strategic guarantee of protection. Geographically, Canada constituted an integral defense-in-depth component of the United States deterrence. But at the same time Canada has been more insecure than other United States allies because there was never any doubt that Canada would be targeted along with the United States in the event of hostilities, precisely because Canada was geographically a part of the United States deterrence. Moreover, because Canada, as a middle power with limited capabilities, is geographically isolated in North America with the United States, there have been varying degrees of Canadian concern about sovereignty. That is, given the extraordinary disparity in power between Canada and the United States, the greater Canada's defense involvement with the United States, the greater has been the Canadian fear of a loss of sovereignty to the United States. Canada has indeed had a "special relationship" with the United States, and the result has been an ambivalence in Canadian policy that sometimes bordered on the neurotic.

The geographical reality facing Canada necessitated two oftentimes contradictory Canadian policy responses. First, geography called for a Canadian cold war defense policy of intimate cooperation with the United States in an attempt to deter the Soviet threat. Secondly, precisely because its geographical location could automatically involve Canada in a superpower confrontation in which it had little or no say, Canada has had a special interest in détente whereby cooperation would replace confrontation. The common denominator in the Canadian approach to both deterrence and détente has been Canada's attempt to steer some semblance of a sovereign course by interjecting its voice, with varying degrees of timidity and gusto, into the superpower councils and especially those of the United States.

Speaking for all nations with capabilities similar to that of Canada, the Canadian foreign minister noted in 1969: "The capacity of the superpowers to affect the destiny of other nations is so great that middlepowers must clearly be vitally concerned about the policies of the USA and the USSR. Middlepowers have a right and a duty to seek to influence the actions of the superpowers."[1] The fact that the pursuit of this "right and duty" was easier said than done is not the point. The point is that Canada, highly vulnerable to the fluctuations of the international community, had no alterntive.

If other nations had a duty to influence the superpowers, it seems that Canada had a special right, given its participation in the development of atomic energy during World War II. After the German victories in Europe, the British moved their atomic energy program to Canada and located their laboratories at Chalk River. Moreover, Canada had supplies of uranium, and many have thought that the material for the first atomic bombs came from Canada's Eldorado mine on Great Bear Lake.[2] Canada was subsequently a wartime member of Washington's Combined Policy Committee, and its prime minister, W. L. M. King, participated in the November 1945 Washington meeting between Truman and Attlee, which resulted in the Joint Declaration on Atomic Energy.

Contrary to the intent of the declaration, cooperation did not replace rivalry as the international community unsuccessfully grappled with these new forces of destruction. Meanwhile, the nuclear club grew in membership with the first nuclear detonation test by the USSR in 1949, the United Kingdom in 1952, France in 1960, the People's Republic of China in 1964, and India in 1974. Although Canada could have become a member of the club, it chose not to do so. The Canadian government decided in 1946 to forego any weapons program with the work at the Chalk River laboratories proceeding in the peaceful application of atomic energy. Thus, although it was not a nuclear weapons state, the fact that Canada was a nuclear power seemed to ensure Canada's centrality in the post-World War II international community. However, any Canadian euphoria about a central role was quickly dispelled with the advent of the cold war.

The United States Deterrence

The worst fears of a Canadian author writing in 1938 seemed to have been fully realized by the late 1950s. Canada was "like a person on a bicycle who is being towed behind a motor car by a rope: the driver of

[1] Mitchell Sharp, *Statements And Speeches*, 69/16, October 20, 1969.
[2] Robert W. Reford, "Problems of Nuclear Proliferation," *Behind The Headlines* 35 (May 1975), 3–4.

the car might have every intention of telling the rider of the bicycle about every other car approaching, what turns he was going to make, etc., but as traffic got thicker and the pace faster, he would limit himself to shouting perfunctory directions over his shoulder and the fellow on the bicycle would have to take his chances although still on the end of the rope."[3] The United States was driving the car, Canada was riding the bicycle, and the tow rope was the United States-Canadian defense relationship. Two factors had locked the two countries in an escalating, expensive defense involvement, made necessary entirely new strategic concepts, and limited Canada's ability to make its own international decisions. These factors were the United States and Canadian perceptions of the increasing severity of a Soviet threat and the technological-military advances that made this threat more and more imminent as the decade of the 1950s progressed.

NATO was established in 1949, including of course the United States and Canada, but it became apparent that NATO had to be embellished with "continental" defense arrangements in North America. The critical decision to embark on a United States-Canadian defense program was made during the autumn of 1953 when the Eisenhower administration approved a series of recommendations growing out of a scientific study group in the summer of 1952. This decision culminated in the development of three early warning systems (Pine Tree Line, Mid-Canada Line, and the Distant Early Warning Line), new communications systems, improved means of interception, the 1958 establishment of the North American Air Defense Command (NORAD), which consisted of an integrated defense command for the United States and Canada, and an extensive joint program of defense production and development sharing. Apart from Canada's substantive defense contributions, which lessened the United States burden, Canada's geography gave the United States three advantages: first, additional warning time against Soviet bombers; second, defense-in-depth in that the northward extension of the air defense system meant that enemy bombers would be engaged before reaching their targets; and, third, increased range and speed of the United States striking force by locating United States strike and refuelling aircraft at northern bases.[4] Thus, by the late 1950s, Canadian complicity in the United States deterrence was complete, a fact that did not go unnoticed in the Soviet Union. For example, a 1958 Soviet broadcast beamed to North America took note, for the first time, of the flights of United States

[3] A. R. M. Lower, "Canada Can Defend Herself," *Canadian Forum* 17 (January 1938), 344.

[4] Samuel P. Huntington, *The Common Defense* (New York: Columbia University Press, 1961), pp. 328-29, 339.

nuclear-armed bombers over Canadian territory and ominously warned Canada that it was "seriously jeopardizing its own security" in running the risk of being "automatically drawn into an atomic war."[5]

Ironically, while the United States and Canada were furthering their defense relationship of unprecedented intimacy, many of the strategic rationales underpinning the relationship were being eroded. There are two reasons for this. First, the spiralling cost of weaponry had made it almost impossible for nations like Canada to participate meaningfully in collective defense. The Canadian role in its bilateral defense relationship with the United States reflected these changes. For example, the 1958 establishment of the United States-Canadian defense production-development sharing program was in part a response to the establishment of NORAD, an admission that military integration called for integrated defense production. However, it was also a Canadian concession to the overwhelming technological fact that Canada could no longer expend resources necessary for the independent development of major weapons systems. Second, Canadian geography was becoming strategically less important because of technological innovations in weaponry. For example, if Canada could contribute interceptors to a bomber defense system, it could offer little besides its territory to an antiballistic missile system, and even that was seen as not being necessary by the United States.

Complicating the ability of the United States-Canadian defense relationship to adapt to technological changes were changes in national and international forces. The feeling of mutuality between the United States and Canada on strategic matters that had underpinned their defense co-operation in the 1950s began cracking in the middle and late 1960s. Three factors account for this erosion: first, the Vietnam war, which suggested for the first time during the postwar period that the United States might be involved in a conflict in which Canada was not an ally. Second, perceptions of the Soviet threat itself were receding with the post-1962 relaxation in East-West tension, which tended to erode the solidarity of the Western alliance and raised questions about the necessity for astronomical defense expenditures. Third, there was an increasing Canadian concern about United States economic and cultural domination that resulted in a challenging of some of the basic assumptions of United States-Canadian interdependence. All of these factors seemed to be coming together in the late 1960s, with the year 1968 especially reflecting changing developments. In the United States, President Nixon was elected and, with the unleashing of Henry Kissinger, was to embark on a foreign policy with global reverberations. In Canada, Prime Minister Trudeau came into power with the promise of a com-

[5] *USSR Survey* (May 8, 1958), Foreign Broadcast Information Service.

plete defense and foreign policy review, sending out ripples of his own. By the mid-1970s, the United States had reassessed its deterrent posture, including Canada's potential contribution to it.

At present, the United States deterrence is geared toward three key military balances.[6] The first is the strategic nuclear balance, which for the United States consists of a mutually supporting triad of heavy bombers, ICBMs, and SLBMs (sea-launched ballistic missiles). The second is the balance of power in central Europe, with the United States deterrence including the NATO alliance, in addition to major contingency planning regarding the Middle East and Northeast Asia. Third, there is the maritime balance with a United States emphasis on sea control, including surveillance, and the projection of power ashore through attack carriers and amphibious forces. The fundamental reality facing the United States is the fact that the expenditures and defense capabilities of the USSR are increasing, while those of the United States and its allies are decreasing. For example, the United States defense share of the GNP has slipped from 9 percent to 5 percent in recent years, while the Canadian defense effort has declined some 20 percent.[7] The United States is therefore deeply concerned about a worldwide strategic imbalance, notwithstanding an era of détente, that could threaten the Western allies within a decade if present trends continue.

However, the fundamental Canadian defense goal is the surveillance and protection of Canadian sovereignty against foreign incursions. This is of course the basic defense goal of any nation, but, insofar as it affects the United States deterrence, the Canadian case is especially interesting for two reasons. First, if Canada's geographical North American isolation coupled with a United States strategic guarantee during a cold war era meant that Canada would be automatically targeted with the United States in a nuclear exchange, this same geographical isolation during an era of détente means that Canada is far removed from potential theaters of nonnuclear conflict while still enjoying a United States strategic guarantee. This suggests that Canada, if it so chooses, has the luxury of a strategic free ride whereby a minimal contribution is made toward the United States deterrence and the Western alliance, enabling Canada to concentrate on national surveillance. Second, given Canada's immense geographical size, the attendant difficulties and costs of domestic surveillance and protection are enormous, especially for a nation with a

[6] James R. Schlesinger, Secretary of Defense, *Report to The Congress on the FY 1976 and Transition Budgets, FY 1977 Authorization Request and FY 1976-1980 Defense Programs* (February 5, 1975).

[7] Joint Press Conference of Secretary of Defense James R. Schlesinger and Canadian Minister of Defense James Richardson, Ottawa, Canada, September 16, 1975. U.S. Department of Defense transcript.

small population and relatively limited economic resources. This means that Canada must get maximum mileage out of any given defense expenditure, concentrating on multiple-roles of defense equipment and forces. Too concerted an emphasis on national surveillance might therefore financially preclude any meaningful defense contribution to the Western alliance.

United States concern was succinctly stated by Secretary of Defense James Schlesinger during a September 1975 visit to Ottawa: "The basic premise, I believe, is that unless we are prepared to defend parts of the world other than the North American continent, we will soon have nothing more than the North American continent to defend and that would be a calamity from the standpoint of both our nations."[8] In short, United States officials were becoming increasingly concerned that Canada's preoccupation with national surveillance, which they welcomed to the extent that it would enhance North American defense, might be at the expense of Canada's other contributions to the Western alliance. These include Canada's NATO contributions to central Europe and Europe's northern flank, and its maritime role of shipping protection in the North Atlantic. Nor was this concern confined to United States officials. Other members of NATO, already distressed by the fact that Canada had reduced its NATO forces by 50 percent, were themselves increasingly critical about Canada's delay in reequipping its remaining forces. Indeed, NATO Secretary-General Joseph Luns had been quite outspoken in suggesting that Canada should both reequip its European forces and increase its level of defense spending.

These concerns were to a great extent neutralized in November 1975 when the Canadian government announced the conclusions of the first stage of its defense structure review.[9] This most recent Canadian defense review confirmed the priority defense roles of an earlier review. Canada's fourfold commitments were reiterated regarding, first, the defense of Canada; second, the defense of North America; third, collective security within NATO; and fourth, Canada's contribution to international peacekeeping. Although not disinterested in these Canadian reaffirmations, United States and NATO officials were rather more interested in the review's decision to undertake a Canadian reequipment program involving over $1 billion. Canada will replace its "Argus" aircraft with the purchase of a fleet of eighteen Lockheed P-3 long-range patrol aircraft, costing some $950 million. This aircraft will be relevant for both NATO and North American defense, while also providing long-range surveillance over the Arctic and Canadian territorial waters. In addition, Canada will update

[8] Ibid.

[9] Canada, *House of Commons Debates—Official Report*, "National Defence: Statement of Defence Structure Review", vol. 119, no. 213, 30th Parliament, 1st sess., November 27, 1975, pp. 9502–9503.

its main-battle tanks for NATO, at an as yet unspecified cost, either by modernizing or through the acquisition of new tanks. Also encouraging was the fact that the Canadian government announced an increase of 12 percent, in real terms, in capital expenditures each year for the next five years, until these expenditures reach at least 20 percent of the total defense budget. The final Canadian posture toward deterrence remains to be seen in that the Canadian defense review has now entered its second stage with the consideration of the replacement of fighter aircraft and ships. However, notwithstanding future uncertainties, the conclusions from the first stage of the review left officials both in the United States and in the Western alliance with a sense of relief.

East-West Détente

There are conflicting assessments of both how meaningful the present state of détente is and whether its momentum will increase or decrease. There are also conflicting assessments in the United States as to whether the United States approach toward détente has been entirely to its advantage. These assessments all reflect the relativity of a state of détente and the difficulties in balancing East-West cooperation and national security. To date, the most dramatic year in the dynamics of détente was 1972 when President Nixon made his visits to Peking and Moscow, the first president to visit either capital. From the former came a rapprochement of historical proportions; the latter marked the first time agreement had been reached between the superpowers limiting the arms race. Meanwhile, Canada had been pursuing détente on its own, at a somewhat faster pace than the United States.

In 1969 Ottawa decided to seek the exchange of diplomatic representatives with Peking, and it did so after extensive negotiations. In 1971 Prime Minister Trudeau visited Moscow, the first Canadian prime minister to have done so, and signed a "Protocol on Consultations." That autumn Premier Aleksei Kosygin was the highest ranking Soviet official ever to visit Canada. Moreover, Canada took the major unilateral step of reducing its NATO force contribution by 50 percent, much to the dismay of the United States which regretted the Canadian deemphasis on NATO, feeling that if troop reductions were to occur, they should do so within the context of multilateral balanced force reductions between NATO and the Warsaw Pact.

The United States and Canada were now proceeding at a markedly deterrence. Equally significant for the United States-Canadian defense re- with the United States, Canada was tending to emphasize détente over deterrence. Equally significant for the United States-Canadian defense relationship was the fact that Canada was now using détente as a counterweight to the United States in an attempt to secure greater independence in its foreign relations. While in Moscow, Prime Minister Trudeau best explained this linkage between détente and counterweight by noting that his visit to the USSR had been motivated by concern about the "overpowering presence" of the United States. He went on to observe that Canada sought to "diversify our points of contact with significant powers of the world" and that regular contacts with the Soviet Union "might permit us to arrive at as independent an opinion on world affairs as we can possibly formulate."[10] Indeed, it was in Moscow that Prime Minister Trudeau noted that the presence of the United States posed dangers to Canada's "national identity from a cultural, economic and perhaps even military point of view," an observation that was not well received in Washington.[11]

Still, there was nothing particularly new about Canadian attitudes toward East-West détente under the Trudeau government. The primary difference was that international conditions had been altered to the point that Canada could actively pursue these attitudes. Traditionally Canada has been rather indifferent to the ideological rigidities of the United States and the USSR and unconvinced of the inevitability of hostilities. For example, there was serious Canadian concern about the reliability of United States strategic bloc leadership triggered by "McCarthyism" and the Dulles concept of massive retaliation. Unlike the United States, Canada continued to trade with Castro's Cuba, and although it did not recognize China until later, ever since Mao Tse-tung's forces assumed power the Canadian position had been that contact should be established and that China should not be isolated from the international community. This Canadian position toward China had been reflected in diverse ways, such as wheat sales and an exchange of newspaper correspondents.

Currently, however, the main lines of United States and Canadian approaches toward the four principal forums of détente are, in a general sense, more similar than divergent. The first forum is SALT, which refers to the strategic arms limitation talks being conducted bilaterally between the United States and the USSR. Progress was made with the signing of SALT I at Moscow in May 1972 by Nixon and Brezhnev and the Vladivostok meeting in November 1974 with Ford and Brezhnev. The second round of SALT talks began in November 1972 in Geneva. Concentrating on the attempt to put a ceiling on the number of offensive strategic weapons, the final negotiations have yet to be reached. Given the bilateral nature of these discussions, Canada has not been relevant, although Ottawa has pointed out with satisfaction that the SALT talks were origi-

[10] Quoted in Roger Frank Swanson, "East-West Détente and the U.S.-Canadian Relationship," *SAIS Review* 16 (Spring 1972), 4.

[11] Ibid.

nally prepared in NATO and that the United States was keeping its NATO allies informed of their progress.

The second principal forum of détente, MBFR, refers to mutual balanced force reductions in Europe. NATO and Warsaw Pact countries have been meeting in Vienna since October 1973 in an attempt to maintain a balance of power in central Europe, but at a reduced strength and cost. The United States places major importance on these talks, especially because of the drive in Congress for unilateral cuts. Canada, as has been noted, already has taken unilateral steps in reducing its NATO forces. The third current forum of détente is the CSCE, which refers to the Conference on Security and Cooperation in Europe, which culminated in the August 1975 Helsinki "Final Act." It consists of declarations of good faith regarding such elements as inviolability of borders and economic, scientific, and environmental cooperation. Most of the nations of Europe, in addition to the United States and Canada, signed the declaration. United States and Canadian policies differed toward CSCE in that United States support came slowly and, according to some United States officials, only after major Soviet concessions on Berlin and MBFR. In contrast, Canada gave early and enthusiastic support to the conference.

The final major forum in East-West détente is the CCD, which refers to the Conference of the Committee on Disarmament which has been meeting in Geneva since 1962. It is the principal forum for negotiating multilateral arms control agreements. Discussions in this forum have led to most of the major multilateral arms control agreements to date, including the 1963 limited test ban treaty, the 1968 nonproliferation treaty, the 1971 seabed arms control treaty, and the 1972 biological-weapons convention. It is apparent that none of these multilateral agreements could have been reached without the concurrence of the United States or the USSR. As for the Canadian approach to the CCD, it has been stated by its former representative to Geneva: "The aims of Canada at Geneva have been pragmatic and have had to recognize the limitation imposed on Canadian initiative which results from being an ally of the U.S., both in Europe as well as for purposes of North American defence. . . . Thus in pursuit of our pragmatic but catalytic course, Canada has put first priority on ending the nuclear arms race, and first and foremost on ending nuclear testing, which is the outward and visible sign of the ongoing contest."[12]

And Canada?

One of the "inescapable realities" of Canadian policy, concluded the Trudeau foreign policy review, was that of "living distinct from but in har-

[12] George Ignatieff, "Canadian Aims and Perspectives In The Negotiation of International Agreements on Arms Control and Disarmament," *Canadian Perpspectives on*

mony with the world's most powerful and dynamic nation, the U.S."[13] This reality has been the primary external force affecting Canada's approach toward deterrence and détente. In conclusion, therefore, it is important to review the differences in the United States and Canadian approaches and to identify those factors that are currently preventing these differences from becoming destabilizing problems.

To summarize, Canada's approach toward deterrence seems to have an inward looking orientation that concerns United States strategic planners, who see the need for a greater European emphasis. Canada's approach toward détente is similar to that of the United States, although Canada traditionally has been a few steps ahead of the United States in intention if not in fact. An additional factor distinguishing Canada's approach from that of the United States is Canada's attempt to use détente as a counterweight to the United States influence. Despite these differences, there are at present no abrasive problems between Canada and the United States in the areas of either deterrence or détente. Five factors appear to be acting as a stabilizing force.

First, there has been an emphasis on consultations between the United States and Canada, especially since early 1975, whereby one party informs the other of its policy developments. For example, Canada kept the United States informed of its progress concerning its NATO force reduction and its diplomatic recognition of the People's Republic of China, while the United States kept Canada informed of developments regarding the SALT I talks. Such consultations do not necessarily mean that one party concurs in the policy of the other, but they do serve to neutralize exaggerated concerns based on misinformation or misperception. This ad hoc consultative arrangement has been assisted by a rapport between President Ford and Prime Minister Trudeau that was established during their December 1974 Washington meeting and furthered by their May 1975 discussion during the Brussels NATO summit meeting and their conversations during the August 1975 Helsinki summit gala.

A second factor concerns policy priorities. While Washington is concerned about deterrence and détente, it is the economic dimension, especially energy, that is currently found to be most troublesome regarding Canada. Thus, although certain officials in Washington might be distressed by a certain Canadian action or lack of action regarding deterrence or détente, Washington, as a matter of policy, is not willing to push Canada too hard at this point because of the other, more pressing issues of an economic nature.

International Law and Organization, ed. R. St. J. Macdonald et al. (Toronto: University of Toronto Press, 1974), p. 696.

[13] *Foreign Policy for Canadians* (Ottawa: Queen's Printer for Canada, 1970), pp. 20–21.

A third factor stabilizing the different United States and Canadian approaches toward deterrence and détente concerns the United States reading of Canadian domestic forces. There is the belief in Washington that Canadian internal preoccupations constitute a counterweight to Canadian policies that might be too disadvantageously divergent from those of the United States. Such internal concerns as federal-provincial relations and economic problems, especially as they become more acute, tend to dampen enthusiasm regarding highly innovative foreign policy directions. In short, Washington is willing to absorb a great deal of rhetoric about divergences because it sees the Canadian government as being able to go only so far in its disengagement with the United States in the areas of deterrence and détente before the constraints of internal difficulties and public opinion become operable.

A fourth factor concerns Canadian readings of the United States scene. Ottawa is not unaware of the fact that all the divergent initiatives that Canada has taken have, in varying degrees, been suggested or embraced by influential Americans. Senator Mansfield's call for United States troop reductions in Europe is an example. Making his own case for a reduction, Senator Mansfield at one point noted that "Canada, under Prime Minister Trudeau, one of the greatest statesman of this hemisphere, if not the world, is also in the process of reducing the Canadian contingent to NATO. . . ."[14] Such endorsements tend to mitigate against an excessively hard line toward Canada on the part of Washington officials precisely because the United States is far from being of one mind on these issues.

The fifth factor concerns the respective national interests of the two countries. One of the greatest stabilizing forces regarding United States and Canadian approaches toward deterrence and détente is the simple fact that there can be United States-Canadian agreement on a given policy, but for entirely different reasons. For example, Canada might not agree with United States security assessments regarding NATO, which after all are grounded in United States national interests as a superpower. However, if Canada sees Europe as a counterweight to the United States in its definition of its national interest, the Canadian attempt to establish some sort of consultative mechanism with the EEC countries becomes important. The price that Canada might have to pay for this link could be a European insistence that Canada more adequately "pay its dues" regarding NATO. Another example of reaching the same policy goal, but for different reasons, can be found in NORAD. In 1971 the Canadian defense minister described NORAD as protecting Canadian sovereignty "not just against a Soviet incursion, but also against potential American

14 Quoted in Swanson, p. 16.

incursion."[15] While this assessment of NORAD's usefulness received somewhat less than unanimous agreement in Washington, the fact remains that NORAD was renewed in May 1975 for an additional five years.

Canada's approach to deterrence and détente fundamentally involves its own assessment of its national interests. During the height of the cold war there was a United States-Canadian consensus that the interests of the two countries were basically the same. At present there is the feeling in Canada that the national interests of the two countries are significantly different. The cold war consensus and rhetoric of common interests went too far in obscuring the fact that there are two distinct actors in North America with differing perceptions and needs.

The question now is, Will the lack of consensus during an era of détente go too far the other way in precluding legitimate United States-Canadian areas of agreement that are grounded in their different national interests? That is, will it be remembered in United States and Canadian assessments of their national interests that major differences do not necessarily mean that the two countries will differ in actual policies. Or will Canada's attempt further to define its separate identity from that of the United States result in the policy temptation to differ for the sake of differing? In itself that could have a mischievous and destabilizing quality that both the United States and Canada would ultimately deplore.

At present, the policy positions of the United States and Canada toward deterrence and détente constitute differences in approach more than differences in concrete policy outcomes, and it remains to be seen where Canada goes from here. Serious in intent, if unsure in its method, Canada will continue to grapple with the duality of deterrence and détente, while worrying about and luxuriating in the United States hegemony. Of necessity Canada must attempt to neutralize its vulnerability in a world that still has two superpowers and counter its geographical isolation in a continent with one of them. In matters of deterrence or détente and in situations of confrontation or cooperation, Canada's fundamental foreign policy objective is the same now as it has always been. A Canadian author writing in 1938 perhaps best captured the objective with this thought: "Whatever our fate, it is to be hoped that our own government shall decide it."[16]

---

[15] Interview with Defense Minister Donald Macdonald, Toronto *Globe and Mail*, February 1, 1971.

[16] Lower, p. 344.

The Energy Challenge

PHILIP H. TREZISE

Any consideration of the "energy challenge" must begin with an answer to the question, What is it? This is not at all a facetious comment. The energy challenge—more commonly known as the "energy crisis"—has continued for two years or more, and it is by no means clear that either its substance or its dimensions have been sorted out adequately. It is necessary to come closer to the specifics before one can assess the impact of the energy situation on Canadian-American relations or on anything else.

One way to get more nearly to a definition of the energy challenge is to state what it is not. First, it does not inhere in a predictable early exhaustion of energy resources in the limits to growth sense. While deposits of oil, natural gas, and coal are finite and nonrenewable, known reserves are still very large. They are likely to be the principal energy sources for a long time to come. As time goes on, old reserves of these fuels will be exploited more efficiently, additional reserves will be found, and new technologies will make it possible to conserve on their use. But as price relationships change and oil or natural gas become (or remain) more costly relative to other fuels, they doubtless will increasingly be supplanted by less expensive sources of energy. It is idle to try to prophesy when the shifts will occur or what forms of energy will dominate in later centuries, but all human experience indicates that in time the requisite technological response will occur.

Second, for the near future, it is certainly not a matter of the high income countries' being unable to afford the higher costs of energy purchased from the Organization of Petroleum Exporting Countries. Even supposing that the real price of the principal energy source, petroleum, were to remain at present levels (a supposition that could be debated), the burden on the consuming countries would be easily within bearable limits. A crude but relevant measure can be found in the increased costs of oil imports as a share of the total national income or output.

The industrial country hardest hit by the oil price escalation of 1973-74 was Japan, where the immediate increase in out-payments for oil amounted to almost 3.0 percent of the gross national product. For Western Europe the figure was 2.4 percent, for the United States about 1.0 percent, and for Canada something above zero but not much above. Imports have since fallen, so these percentages will have been somewhat lower in 1975. The absolute sums involved are of course very large—all told, on the order of $62 billion in 1974—but they can hardly be said to be outside the rich countries' capacity to pay. One year's normal growth in their GNP would far more than make up for this unexpected draft on the total supply of goods and services.

Third, the energy challenge is not a question of a forthcoming catastrophe in financial markets or of OPEC raids on vulnerable currencies or of intolerably large Arab investments in vital Western industries. All of these fears were expressed by pundits and publicists, some of whom should have known better, throughout 1974 and into 1975. They have almost disappeared from the editorial pages and columns and journals, perhaps not so much because common sense has been restored as because it is difficult to continue presenting, as imminent disasters, happenings that seem steadily to recede from reality. International financial markets have operated quite smoothly in handling the new requirements placed on them, there has not been the slightest evidence that the OPEC countries ever gave thought to the quixotic idea of trying to disrupt currency relationships, and the Arab investment bugaboo seems to have gone quietly away.

There is a closer question as to the consequences for overall economic management of higher energy prices in the industrial countries. In retrospect, it is clear that the meaning of the very large boost in oil prices in early 1974 was misinterpreted by most officials in most or all countries. This is not so surprising, for the scene was a clouded one. On one hand, the new oil prices gave a strong new push to an inflation that was already extremely troublesome, politically and otherwise. On the other hand, the higher oil prices amounted to a kind of excise tax—a drain of consumer purchasing power from spenders to nonspenders—that operated in the first instance in a strongly deflationary manner on the rate of economic activity. The common policy reaction, understandably, was to focus on the inflationary push, the known and immediate evil. This meant, however, resorting to restrictive fiscal and monetary measures that only heightened the deflationary influence of the oil price rise. It cannot be doubted that the result was to hasten and greatly to worsen the downturn or recession from which the industrial countries have not yet fully emerged and the losses from which are of much greater magnitude than the tribute paid to OPEC thus far.

One may say that the lesson has been learned and that another sharp price rise would be met by more skillful and balanced policies. But the problems of demand management in this situation are inherently complex and difficult, and the outcomes of alternative policy choices are not always certain. Perhaps another external shock would be handled in a less costly manner than in 1974, but perhaps not.

That brings one to what may properly be termed the energy challenge. By accident of geography, a few countries have oil deposits within their boundaries so large in relation to world demand as to give them the capability of imposing important changes on the economic life of the consuming countries. It is conceivable that three or four oil producing nations, or fewer for that matter, could impose an outright embargo or such steep reductions in production and exports as to cause severe economic distortions in countries dependent on oil imports. In the extreme case of an extended embargo, normal economic activity in importing countries would be seriously disrupted. At least, as in 1974, additional inflationary pressures would be unleashed while new deflationary transfers of purchasing power were pushing economies toward recession.

Apart from the economic problems that could be posed, the political implications of the oil producers' potential leverage on the consumers are evident and sizable. The import-dependent areas, Western Europe and Japan, are for the time being substantially hostage to the oil suppliers, that is, if one assumes that exports from the major producers might be interrupted over a lengthy period. The United States is less immediately vulnerable, but a situation in which the economies and thus the political well being of its principal allies were put in jeopardy could only be seen as a major threat to American policy interests.

The most obvious answer to the putative power of the oil producers is to develop alternative and secure sources of energy. Under present price relationships there is every reason to suppose that this will happen, although the requisite investments will be costly and the lead times in many cases are likely to be long. If OPEC acts as an alert and efficient cartel, it will observe this process carefully, having in mind the possibility at strategic points of making temporary price reductions that are sufficiently deep to undermine higher cost alternative energy supplies elsewhere. The tactic is not without precedent in the history of the oil industry, and it seems bound to be considered by the OPEC monopoly as and if it feels itself endangered by the appearance of competitive suppliers.

It is not necessary to overstate the disruptive potential of the oil producers or the cartel. That potential is in fact liable to a good many limitations, not least of which is the differing underlying interests of some of the principal parties concerned. But oil is a commodity that occupies a quite crucial place in modern economic life and will continue to do so for some extended period to come. The OPEC states have noted the benefits of common action to raise prices, and the supposition must be that they will make the effort to continue their profitable collaboration. And the political and military situation in the Middle East, where most of the oil is located, is volatile enough to make almost any expectation credible except one of stability. Anyway, the risks appear to be sufficient to justify considering feasible actions to diminish or eliminate them.

I

Where does the energy challenge, put in these terms, fit into Canadian-American relations? By now, one would think, extravagant notions in the United States about the extent and relevance of Canadian resources to continental energy security have generally been brought down to earth. It should be evident that, for the present, Canada offers no solution to American dependence on OPEC oil. Proved reserves of petroleum in established fields are on the decline. New finds in the Arctic or from offshore sites are possible, but their contribution, if any, is for the future. Similarly, the extensive tar sand deposits in western Canada cannot be exploited on a significant scale with present technology, and large supplies of hydrocarbons from this source are probably for the late 1980s or later. Prospects for natural gas production from new fields are brighter, but transportation facilities must be built before these can be realized. For the next few years, the principal hope must be that Canadian exports of oil and natural gas to the United States will not be cut back so quickly or sharply as to cause acute problems for the regions that are uniquely reliant on transborder supplies. The magnitudes involved are not great, but the local adjustment difficulties will be sizable and unwelcome as supplies from Canada are reduced.

Recognition that the Canadian endowment of energy resources is modest should also have deflated the idea, which attracted some popular following in Canada at the outset of the oil crisis, that energy provided Ottawa with special leverage over Washington. At official levels in Canada there was no such illusion. In a report made public in 1973, the government took pains to point to the "minor role" of Canadian supplies in the United States energy economy and to the dependence of eastern Canada on American coal for power and for steel making.[1] The truth is that

[1] Department of Energy, Mines, and Resources, *An Energy Policy for Canada* (Ottawa: Information Canada, 1973).

the two energy economies are closely tied together—e.g., Canadian pipelines run through United States territory—so that a game of tit-for-tat would be possible, but also silly and unprofitable. And there is enough in the way of shared interests that their responses to the OPEC energy challenge ought to be for the most part parallel.

Canada was of course able to absorb the initial shock of OPEC's 1973 price hikes more equably than was the United States. The initial deflationary impulse from higher fuel prices was much less strong in a then self-sufficient Canada, and the Canadian recession, no doubt partly for that reason, was a good deal milder than the American one. Canada could not wholly escape inflationary pressures from rising fuel costs, however, and some fraction of the price level problems that preoccupy Ottawa is traceable to the continuing influence of the oil price explosion on the general price indexes.

At all events, Canada has now become a net importer of oil. Although this may not be a permanent circumstance, it undoubtedly will persist into the 1980s. And even if exports of other fuels—specifically, natural gas—give Canada a positive balance in energy trade, the national interest will still be in avoiding economically disruptive boosts in energy prices. As a prospectively high-cost producer of oil and natural gas, moreover, Canada will have a lively interest in seeking insurance against predatory price cutting by the oil cartel.

It need be remarked only in passing that Canada cannot possibly benefit from either recession or general inflation in the United States. With some 16 percent of the gross national output destined for markets in the United States, the level of business activity in Canada cannot be divorced from events south of the border. And inflationary influences from the United States cannot be contained at the boundary, except at unacceptable costs. Distressing as it understandably is to many Canadians, Canada's economic fortunes are tied to those of the United States.

Not so surprisingly, then, Canada and the United States are charter members of the International Energy Agency (IEA), the grouping of oil consumers established under the umbrella of the Organization for Economic Cooperation & Development in Paris. The IEA, which may well turn out to be among the most durable and important of Secretary of State Kissinger's accomplishments (it grew directly out of the energy conference called in Washington in early 1974), provides the mechanism for concerted consumer action in relation to the OPEC. It has already brought understandings on sharing of supplies in emergencies and on stockpiling against possible export embargoes or restrictions. It could give direction and order to energy research and impetus to national conservation measures. It is the forum for deciding on common defenses against cartel price policies that might be aimed at stifling the development of alternative energy supplies.

This multilateral answer to the energy challenge makes so much sense that even a cynical view about the ability of the governments of the affluent countries to cooperate to protect common interests still leaves ground for believing that the IEA may prove to be an institution within which Western Europe, Japan, and North America can work effectively together in coping with OPEC. By comparison, there are no bilateral options of promise. The principal proposition—to which France has given more attention than anyone else—is that favorable bilateral deals might be struck by individual consuming nations with the oil producers. No one, however, has explained why producers at this juncture should be expected to make serious concessions to customers. None have.

If most of the eggs thus belong in the multilateral basket, there are some peculiarly North American energy relationships which can be manipulated, for better or for worse, in meeting the overall energy challenge. Anything that can be done to stretch or increase energy supplies in the United States and Canada will mean an improvement in the consumer country position in general. For a topical example, more natural gas in North America will tend to reduce total claims on world oil output, to the benefit of importers in Japan and Western Europe. (This is why it does not much matter, so far as the energy challenge is concerned, whether North Sea oil is used in the United Kingdom, on the continent, or in the United States, and the same applies to Alaskan oil; the point is to reduce the size of OPEC's market, worldwide).

It would be stretching matters well beyond accuracy to say that either Ottawa or Washington has been making energy policy decisions that have been exclusively for the better, or in ways that have contributed much to transborder amity. Neither country has accepted the OPEC challenge so far as energy conservation is concerned. There have been avoidable irritations over energy issues. And constructive bilateral policies, where these seem possible, are only at their beginning. But the amount of harm done can be exaggerated, too, and the current outlook is not all bleak.

II

One issue, which seems in some respects to have been wildly misunderstood, has been the Canadian tax on crude oil exports, which earned a condemnatory resolution from the United States Senate. The import of the tax is not that it raised prices to American consumers. That would have happened anyway as Canadian export prices adjusted to world market prices. Rather, the point of the policy was to capture for Canada a sudden access of windfall profits, or economic rents, that otherwise would have gone to the oil companies operating in Alberta and Saskatchewan.

The export tax policy may have been unwise, on at least three grounds. First, it preempted profits that might have been ploughed back into exploration and development. Second, it stirred up federal-provincial differences that might better have been left to lie dormant. Third, because the proceeds of the tax have been used to subsidize petroleum product prices in eastern Canada, consumption has not been discouraged to the extent that would have been desirable. But few would really have expected Canadian politicians to allow the returns from high oil prices to go principally into the earnings of private firms, mostly foreign owned firms at that, or to pass over the opportunity at least temporarily to hold down gasoline and fuel oil prices nationwide. United States policy has not been different in its thrust; free markets and price mechanisms as instruments of energy policy have been distrusted and hindered south as well as north of the border.

More important than the export tax in direct impact has been the Canadian decision to begin supplying eastern Canada with crude oil from Alberta. Until the oil crisis, Ottawa had chosen not to permit a pipeline connection that could bring western Canadian crude to Montreal, on the sensible if somewhat mercenary ground that the oil could be sold above world prices in the United States while eastern Canada could be supplied with low priced imports from Venezuela and the Middle East. (It should be observed that Canadians west of the so-called Ottawa Valley line paid more for oil than eastern Canadians.) This policy was abandoned after the embargo scare and the price increases of 1973, and an extension from the terminal in Sarnia on Lake Huron to Montreal is under construction. The intention in Canada is that the crude sent to Montreal refineries be subtracted from the permissible volume of exports to the United States. The result will be to add to the adjustment problem that American refineries in the upper Midwest have in store as available Canadian oil reserves run down. It will not, of course, add to or subtract from the amount of non-OPEC oil in the world and thus has only a marginal relationship to the energy challenge.

Whether the Montreal pipeline will contribute, as originally advertised, to Canadian oil security is not beyond argument. Eastern Canada's needs for crude far exceed the 250,000 barrels a day that the pipeline is expected to deliver. Unless new oil fields are found in western Canada, supplies for the pipeline could fall off from this level (Ottawa's official estimates foresee that by 1982 there will not be enough crude for Canadian markets, including the 250,000 barrels for Montreal.) And if the import price of crude was to drop below the price of domestic oil, there would surely be pressure from Quebec to reverse the flow of the pipeline and send imported oil from Montreal into higher priced markets to the west. Instead of reducing Canada's dependence on OPEC, the opposite might be true. Anyway, it seems that the pipeline extension will bring at best very limited security returns for an expensive investment.

Natural gas has been the other large Canadian energy export to the United States, providing at peak about 4 percent of American consumption. As with crude oil, the Canadian reserve position in terms of transportable natural gas has been declining, and new export contracts have been prohibited by the National Energy Board since 1971. Finds of natural gas in the Northwest Territories open the possibility for a major venture in North American energy cooperation at a future date. Meanwhile, attention has focused on finding a "just" price for Canadian natural gas exports.

The typical export contract for natural gas has provided for deliveries over a long period, usually twenty-five years, at prices negotiated between the private parties, subject to the approval of both the National Energy Board in Canada and the Federal Power Commission in the United States. When the price of oil rose to high levels, all of the various prices that had been set for natural gas at American border points fell far short of the National Energy Board's guideline, which called for export prices not appreciably less than the prices of alternative fuels. But the price adjustment clauses in the private contracts made no provision for changes based on higher costs for oil or coal. If the natural gas exported to the United States was to sell at its "commodity value," special measures would be needed.

In the end, the Canadian decision was simply to declare a standard export price of $1 a thousand cubic feet, effective on all export contracts as of January 1975. Importers unwilling to accept the new pricing conditions were given the option of continuing under the old contractual terms for two years, after which their contracts would be terminated. By the end of 1975 the export price had been raised twice to $1.40 and then to $1.60.

This arbitrary, though apparently legal, adjustment of outstanding contracts has been accompanied by increases in prices for natural gas charged to the Canadian consumer. In fact, gas moving between provinces in Canada is considerably more costly to the end user than interstate gas is in the United States.

If the objective is to reduce dependence on OPEC, there is a good deal to be said for Canadian natural gas policy. The regulated low price for interstate shipments of natural gas in the United States surely promotes a casual use of this premium fuel where it is available, and it must work to discourage not only production but also exploration for and development of new supplies. Canadian pricing, even with a differential in favor of the domestic consumer, works on the whole in the opposite direction. While this may offer small comfort to Americans whose fuel costs in some cases may have quadrupled, there can be little doubt that all United States natural gas prices per BTU (British thermal unit) eventually will have to rise toward those of other fuels.

III

Now that scheduled reductions in Canadian exports of crude oil to the United States have become realities (the most recent projection is that the flow will end entirely in 1981) and the natural gas pricing decisions have been made, the next question is whether the two countries can turn successfully to the possibilities that may exist for strengthening the North American energy position.

Realistically, these possibilities are quite limited, at least for the present decade. Romantic notions about a massive investment program to take advantage of the large hydrocarbon potential of the Alberta tar sands have been dashed by a better understanding of the costs, including the environmental costs, of exploiting the deposits near the surface. At some later point, perhaps, an *in situ* process will be developed to get at the main, deeper lying reserves. In that case, a binational or multinational investment arrangement might be in order, since the costs seem likely to be of considerable magnitude. But this will depend on how fast the provincial and federal authorities will wish to proceed with the development of the tar sands at some still unforeseeable date in the future.

It is arguable that Canadian policies toward foreign investment will discourage risk taking in energy resources as well as in other fields. Although the screening procedure introduced by Ottawa has not been visibly overrigorous, the thrust of the policy is certainly not to make Canada a more attractive place to invest. On the other hand, the pace of exploration for oil and natural gas is mainly a function of expectations about royalties and taxes in Canada as against those in other jurisdictions. Canadian decisions on this score may not be what investors will wish, but no one should expect these matters to be influenced by official attitudes or actions in Washington or to be established through bilateral understandings.

The most important short-term energy project for Canadian-American combined action undoubtedly is the proposed natural gas pipeline from the Alaskan North Slope through Canada to the United States. The natural gas associated with petroleum in the Prudhoe Bay field on the North Slope is estimated at 26 trillion cubic feet, or more than 10 percent of proven United States reserves, and the likelihood is that larger amounts will be found in Alaska in due course. In the Mackenzie River Delta region in Canada, gas reserves of a much smaller order—4 trillion cubic feet—have been proved, and it is supposed that enough will be discovered to make a pipeline commercially feasible. A single pipeline from Prudhoe Bay, with a spur to the Mackenzie Delta, could tap both fields and serve consumers in both countries.

An all-Alaska line from Prudhoe Bay would require that facilities be built to liquify the gas for shipment by special liquified natural gas tankers to the lower United States. If the Alaskan route were to be chosen, then a Canadian pipeline will have to be provided to tap the Mackenzie Delta gas fields, and one has already been proposed. To build two costly pipelines plus ancillary facilities, where one and a fraction would suffice, would obviously be an excessively wasteful way to manage energy affairs. There will be environmentalist objections to any pipeline route, so the choice of an Alaska-Canada line will not expose the governments to wholly new political problems.

The Departments of State and External Affairs have sensibly undertaken to negotiate a general, reciprocal treaty on pipelines between Canada and the United States, to provide the legal and political basis for an understanding on the line through Canada from Alaska. The terms of such a treaty would cover the Maine to Montreal line through which most of eastern Canada's crude oil imports move, the interprovincial crude oil line that runs from Alberta through the upper Midwest to Ontario, a portion of the trans-Canada natural gas pipeline, and in some respects perhaps other oil and gas lines into the United States. If completed and ratified, it would provide the legal underpinning and requisite assurances to permit consideration of additional possible international pipelines—for example, from deep water ports in the Maritimes to carry crude oil into the midcontinent—when these seemed to be commercially feasible.

From one point of view, it seems extraordinary that Canada and the United States should consider it necessary or desirable to go through the formal treaty process to make possible a transportation line to carry American gas to American consumers and Canadian gas to Canadian consumers. Even if it were feared that some future Canadian government might consider imposing discriminatory and burdensome conditions on the operation of the line, the retaliatory capacities of the United States are so formidable in the energy area alone, to say nothing of those in transborder commercial and economic relations generally, that these fears ought to be largely discounted. But apprehension about each other's regulatory policies are not new in the Canadian-American energy relationship. In the 1950s, Ottawa subsidized an east-west natural gas pipeline so that it could be run north of Lake Superior rather than along an easier route that included United States territory. In 1966, when the original line reached capacity, the cabinet's first decision, subsequently reversed, was to reject a southern route for the needed new loop. And an Alaska-Canada line to bring the Prudhoe Bay oil to the American market was given only cursory consideration in Washington before the decision was taken to have an all-United States route.

In fact, a treaty and the ratification procedure that it entails may do the essential service of putting Canadian-American energy relations into perspective. Continentalism, in the sense of a full coordination of energy policies, is obviously politically dead in Canada, but a treaty debate would help to remove it and its abrasive connotations from the North American energy vocabulary. Awareness that neither country is self-sufficient in energy resources will be advanced, and so will understanding of the genuine links that geography and complementarity have imposed on the two energy economies. These links are represented in very considerable part by existing pipelines that cross United States territory, so a pipeline treaty could not fail to highlight them.

If a treaty debate did help clear the air, then one might expect that the quality of the general American-Canadian dialogue might be enhanced as well. That dialogue has not been distinguished in recent years, at official or other levels, by a maximum of concern for mutual interests or, sometimes, for facts. While it would be too much to imagine that other issues would automatically be made more malleable by ratification of a pipeline accord—some of them, after all, involve touchy intra-Canadian questions of provincial versus federal jurisdiction in a country where there are wide regional political differences—anything that put more realism into the discussions could hardly fail to be constructive.

The Evolving Trading System

HARALD B. MALMGREN

Both Canada and the United States in recent years have been reexamining their respective roles in the world trading system. The United States has tended to carry out its rethinking on a global scale, focusing on the broad outlines of the world economy and the general rules of the game that govern world trade and payments. The rhetoric of United States policy pronouncements has tended to emphasize issues of principle and the need for reform of the world trade and monetary systems. Canada's rethinking, on the other hand, has tended to be more narrowly oriented toward promotion of Canadian economic growth and Canadian independence. Consequently, Canadian thinking appears to concentrate on the pattern and nature of Canadian dependence on the United States and other national economies, and on the structure of Canadian industry and the pattern of regional impact of Canadian external relations.

Surprisingly, the two countries rarely give much thought to the conduct of their overall relationship with each other. The last major effort by the United States government to address Canada directly and in a comprehensive manner was in connection with the August 15, 1971, economic measures taken by the Nixon administration. From August to December of that year, led by then Secretary John Connally, the United States sought significant bilateral economic negotiations with the European Community (EEC), Japan, and Canada. The purpose was to find a package of actions in each case that could, in conjunction with exchange rate adjustments, ease the balance-of-payments difficulties of the United States, which in turn would ease the adjustment of all currencies in relation to each other during a period of monetary crisis. The EEC and Japan were somewhat reluctant, but nonetheless agreed to discuss trade and monetary matters in depth. The results were not earth-shaking, but these two economic entities did engage in a process of diplomatic exchange aimed at easing the economic and political stress at the time (in spite of the somewhat abrasive United States tactics and statements). Canada, on the other hand, objected vigorously to the unilateral actions and pressure tactics of the United States, and behind this posture of objection Canada refused to participate in meaningful talks.

Secretary Connally wanted unilateral trade concessions and agreement to a new set of rules to govern exchange rates. Behind this objective, however, was a more basic objective: the United States sought formal recognition that it had been under disadvantage and that actions would be taken by other nations to rectify this situation. The Canadian government felt that this objective bore no relationship to Canada and that pressure on Canada was especially unwarranted since Canada had floated its exchange rate much earlier. It was felt that the Canadian float had in effect paved the way for a new exchange rate system and that this should be viewed as Canada's contribution to the adjustment process.

Canada as a "Loner"

Much of the blame for the diplomatic tension generated in late 1971 might well be placed on Washington, given its public tactics. The result, nonetheless, was to make Canada, in the eyes of Congress and the United States Treasury, appear to be an obstinate loner that refused to play the game of "restoring world order." In Congress, the perception was that Japanese and EEC relations were improving while United States relations with Canada were worsening.

During the congressional consideration of the Trade Act of 1974, especially in the Senate in late 1974, various senators argued that Canada was acting as a "free rider." The persistent unwillingness of Canada to carry on a general trade dialogue bilaterally with the United States was brought up repeatedly as an argument in favor of the need for drafting tough provisions into the law relating to the conditions under which developed nations might benefit from the negotiations. A special provision penalizing "free riders"—nations that might decide to opt out of meaningful concessions in any new round of negotiations—was written into the law by the Senate Finance Committee. Although the language of the act refers to developed countries generally, the "no-free-riders" clause was specifically aimed at Canada (indeed, at one point, the committee seriously considered writing in a specific reference to Canada).

The Canadian–United States tensions, however, are not limited to this general area of doubts about Canada's "cooperativeness." Between the two nations there are periodic skirmishes over specific trade issues, reflecting very narrow political preoccupations. Some of the questions that come up in the natural resources area are in fact difficult ones involving provincial-federal relations in Canada, which inevitably condition the posture of the Canadian government toward the United States. Energy is such a problem area.

In other cases, the disputes cause political resentments on both sides of the border out of proportion to the importance of the issues. In agricultural products, for example, there are frequent outbreaks of trouble over trade in potatoes, eggs, chickens, turkeys, and meat products. Instead of quiet problem-solving, the two governments tend to dramatize the issues publicly, widening the range of political impact. In the eyes of Congress and the domestic-agency cabinet officers in Washington, many of these problems arise out of what appear to be unilateral actions on the part of the Canadian authorities. While the United States is by no means innocent of unilateralism, it sees Canada as acting unilaterally on small and big issues alike, whenever its domestic politics suggest the slightest need for it. The United States, on the other hand, has usually resisted special interests that sought unilateral action.

Occasionally, there were privately expressed suggestions from the Canadian side that some regularized framework of consultations and guidelines for actions on trade issues between the two countries was needed, but neither side ever followed up on these suggestions. In spite of the tensions and the fact that the mutual interests of the two nations far exceed their differences, very little thought has been given in either capital to the overall United States-Canadian relationship. The policy planning process and day-to-day diplomacy of the two nations are engaged in other matters. Even the diplomats personally are in an awkward position, because in economic disputes the relevant cabinet officers and civil servants talk directly to each other over the telephone, or see each other periodically without fully utilizing their respective embassies. Often the diplomatic system, bypassed by direct communications and uninformed about their nuances, is unable to smooth out the political and diplomatic elements of the problems.

World economic issues fascinate Washington. When the United States government thinks about the world, however, it thinks in terms of "big power" maneuvers. This results in concentration of diplomacy on the larger nations of the EEC, on the USSR, and on Japan. France, West Germany, the United Kingdom, and to a somewhat lesser extent, Japan, get primary attention. Canada is often mentioned, but much as an afterthought introduced into interagency discussions by the State Department. In the interrelated foreign policy system of officials and former officials who will likely return with a change in administration in the United States, foreign policy discussions focus on what has become popularly known as trilateralism. While some people intend to include Canada by referring to the North American leg of the triangle, most have in mind the big three: the United States, the EEC, and Japan. This leaves Canadians often wondering if they have somehow been cut loose from the main activities of world economic affairs. Canada officially objects, not surprisingly, when it is forgotten.

This neglect of Canadian considerations has not been limited to the United States. The French and Germans very definitely did not wish to have Canada included in the presidential economic summit at Rambouillet, France, in the autumn of 1975. It was felt in Europe that Canada would act as a loner, tending to define points of difference, when the purpose of the meeting was to find points of agreement on both policy and philosophy. Moreover, in less polite and private discussions preceding the summit, it was said that Canada had nothing to contribute.

This assessment was unfair in many respects. Certainly the role of John Turner, when he was minister of finance, played an important role in international monetary deliberations, acting as intermediary in the North-South confrontations as well as among the developed nations. And in the early years of the General Agreement on Tariffs and Trade (GATT), it was Canada more than any other nation that supplied men of high caliber to act as honest brokers and innovative problem-solvers in the maneuvers between other nations.

But this important special role of Canada has been declining. John Turner's role as chairman of key international committees was viewed by other nations as an exception. Whether one can list examples that suggest greater Canadian imagination and global diplomacy does not matter much. What matters is the perception elsewhere that Canada is increasingly a loner, going its own way, on the basis of its national preoccupations.

Canadian diplomacy in recent years has in fact reflected a rather narrow conception of Canada's problems and interests. In multilateral meetings, Canada has been less and less likely to propose general solutions or to act as middleman. Instead, when multilateral proposals were made by one of the "big three" or by international secretariats, Canada would seek to differentiate itself and to seek exceptional treatment or the inclusion of a Canadian reservation. The 1974 OECD Trade Standstill Agreement is a recent example. Most countries agreed on the basic elements of an understanding that would limit the freedom of national governments to take unilateral actions in the trade field during the period of economic recession and adjustment to the abrupt change in world oil prices. Among the agreed points was a widely supported desire to include some restraint on possible national actions to impose export controls. Even the United States, which had had resort to export controls in 1972 in connection with domestic anti-inflationary policy, was willing to agree internationally to restrain itself. On the other hand, Canada wanted to keep its options open on the export side. Canada's only ally on this point was Australia, which admitted that it was preoccupied with negotiations with Japan on raw materials supplied to that nation.

Given the loner role that Canada has increasingly tried to play, it is not surprising that some of the other nations got together selectively without giving adequate thought to Canada. Should Canada be surprised when it is left out? Although, in economic terms, Canada is a great power, it has not played its diplomatic hand as one. In comparison, a nation like France plays its diplomatic hand far more aggressively in every international forum and therefore is itself brought into all of the inner circles of Western economic affairs. This happened in spite of the fact that most of the French maneuvers were based on narrow, domestic motivations.

This perception of Canada's role is not a necessary reflection of Canadian desires to have a "differentiated" foreign policy with a national character of its own. Every nation should have its own way of dealing with external affairs, and the orientation will necessarily depend on national interests. If Canadian policy were a mirror image of United States policy, Canada would not be credible, either to the United States or to other nations. Differentiation is essential. It is the method of differentiating its approach that gives rise to these appearances of Canada acting as loner.

Pursuit of a special relationship with the EEC, for example, seems in Canada to be a way of diffusing Canada's economic dependence on the world economy (that is, a way of reducing dependence on the United States). In the EEC there is puzzlement and resistance to the thin edge of a North American wedge, while in the United States there is irritation over what is perceived as anti-United States initiatives. The United States perception has to be put in a context in which the United States has been vigorously attacking the special trading arrangements of the EEC with the nonmember countries like Sweden and Switzerland and the associated countries in the Mediterranean, Africa, and elsewhere. Differentiation through a special arrangement with the Community of the Nine has been thus waved off as a domestic Canadian gambit worthy of little European attention and some American irritation. A special relationship with the USSR is less irritating in the case of the United States, since it is not perceived as having any real content. If such an arrangement were to become substantive and involve close economic and political ties between Canada and the USSR, the reaction in the United States would of course be entirely different.

The real question, then, is why Canada chooses to differentiate its external affairs in this way, instead of playing a role as an independent force in the multilateral economic system. At present, the United States and the European nations are often at loggerheads over key economic and institutional issues. The Japanese government has been reluctant in these circumstances to intervene, or even to play a middleman role. Other nations feel they are too small in economic terms to have much influence. Canada could, if it chose, play an important role in suggesting new initiatives that might resolve or help get around the United States-European impasses and that would not only be of value to the workings of the international economic system but also of great value to Canada's own national interests and objectives.

Canada's Preoccupation with Vulnerability and Dependence

The preoccupation in Canada with political issues of vulnerability to United States economic developments and excessive dependence on United States investors, technology, management systems, marketing style, and government policies, is understandable, particularly in political terms. Yet Canada is dependent on the international economy as a whole, to a much greater extent than the United States. In the ten years between 1963 and 1973, exports from Canada as a share of gross domestic product rose from 17.2 to 24.1 percent, and imports rose from 16.0 to 22.0 percent. Exports and imports now stand at over half of the output of the goods-producing industries of Canada (agriculture, fishing, forestry, trapping, mining, manufacturing, construction, and utilities). To the extent that Canada wants to diffuse its relationships and reduce economic dependence on the United States, it is the world market that must pick up the balance. The Canadian economy is far too intertwined with trade to trim back the United States relationship without stepping up the relationship elsewhere. But this cannot easily be accomplished by bilateral deals. Instead, Canada has to look to general trade expansion and evolution of the rules and workings of the trading system as a whole in a direction that meets Canada's needs. What this means is that Canada, even more than the United States, should be concerned about multilateral initiatives and negotiation, in its own national interest.

The external elements of the Canadian economy are critical to domestic growth and anti-inflationary policy. Canada's internal problems with inflation and weak recovery in the mid-1970s cannot be dealt with through reliance on internal Canadian economic measures, because of the large-scale interaction of Canada with the rest of the world. The inflation and recession were more or less synchronized phenomena in most of the industrialized nations. World demand consequently pulls on the internal markets of each nation at about the same time; and when there is a falling off of economic activity, in any one part of the system, it has of late come at the same time as decline in other industrialized economies, reinforcing the downturn.

It has not been possible in the 1970s to insulate individual national economies from world forces while instituting domestic economic measures. The United States tried to implement price controls within the domestic economy and soon found itself stuck with an apparent need to introduce export controls, to prevent bleeding of products in short supply to higher-priced foreign markets. Even import restrictions were reviewed to determine if temporary liberalization could bring domestic relief. The problems resulting from international pressures were only partly moderated by these devices. It is much more difficult for Canada to attempt to insulate itself. So, if Canada looks inward with a view to altering its domestic economic circumstances through domestic actions alone, it will usually fail to achieve its objectives. For internal reasons, even if for no other reason, Canada should consequently be looking outward and should be among the most active nations internationally in multilateral economic activity, seeking improvements in the methods of coordinating economic policies among the larger trading nations in the OECD and seeking to restrain the unilateral actions of other nations in the trading and monetary systems that might distort the external forces working on Canada to its disadvantage.

From another perspective, it is traditional, in Canadian self-examination, to put heavy weight on problems of economies of scale and the relatively small size of the Canadian market to provide a basis for argument concerning Canada's competitive position and vulnerability to United States trade and investment. Canada is not alone, of course, in pursuing this type of argument. Similar arguments have been made in other nations in connection with their respective neighbors, particularly in connection with the debate on formation and enlargement of the EEC. This was especially true in the British debate on entry into the community. Such a line of reasoning can be a little misleading if it relies solely on questions of market size and economies of scale. If one looks at the position of West Germany, or even more tellingly, at Japan, the performance of these economies demonstrates that exports can make up for economic limitations of market size at home. They also demonstrate that exports can cross tariff and nontariff barriers and still compete exceptionally well. Indeed, the performance of West Germany in the face of continuous appreciation of the DM is nothing short of remarkable. Again, the lesson is that Canada's worries about size of market in connection with its United States relationship is the wrong focus; it is the world market opportunity that is relevant to Canada's internal development potential.

Internally, it is also notable that Canadian industry is relatively highly protected, compared to United States and European markets. Behind this protection, industries function in what economists call an oligopoly situation—a few firms dominate key sectors and act in a manner that least disturbs each other in a desire to preserve a profitable but quiet life. To promote efficiency and a global outlook, in line with domestic growth and anti-inflationary policies, the government of Canada needs to promote liberalization of trade at home and abroad. Canada, for domestic reasons, probably needs this more than most of the other industrialized nations.

But these global thoughts are not the focus of Canadian thinking. Instead, United States-Canadian relations are viewed as a bilateral matter, in one compartment of external affairs; Canadian-European relationships constitute another bilateral matter, in another compartment; Canadian-Latin American or Caribbean relationships are elsewhere; and the link with Japan is something of a special adversary relationship, because of import competition. The United States-Canadian dialogue concentrates on border problems, as noted earlier. Even where there might be much to be gained diffusing the management of these border issues by drawing them into a multilateral context, this has been rarely done.

A good example of bad management, admittedly on both sides of the border, has been the Canadian-American automotive agreement. A clever solution to a potentially explosive problem, the agreement has been under attack in the United States Congress almost continuously since its inception. In the period of the late 1971 monetary upheaval and United States pressures for trade and monetary talks, this agreement became a central issue, with Washington pressing for some adjustments in its operation. The specific details are not so important as the fact that both sides then chose, and have continued to choose, to take polarized positions in public. The pressures consequently continue and periodically break out in congressional debate. It is a matter of time only until something unfortunate develops because of lack of management of the pressures.

Surprisingly, the underlying views of the industry itself are not the source of the controversy. And even more surprising is the fact that in the mid-1970s the unions are not upset either. The United Auto Workers in the United States favor the agreement. In a little-noticed statement adopted unanimously by the UAW International Executive Board on September 24, 1975, in Michigan, the UAW indicated some embarrassment over the fact that the United States Treasury was investigating possible dumping of Canadian-manufactured automobiles as part of a broader investigation of imports from Europe and Japan. The statement called for review of the Canadian-American automotive agreement, but it certainly did not suggest abandonment or wholesale restructuring of the present arrangements.

Assessing the agreement's effects is not easy, since even the basic statistics of the two governments are in a state of unusual disarray. Yet, because of the stonewalling of the two governments and the unfavorable picture developed by some analysts on the United States side, nothing positive has been done, and the irritation grows. Senator Hartke, through the powerful Senate Finance Committee, asked for a major review and analysis of the agreement by the International Trade Commission. The commission issued its report early in 1976, and its conclusions were extremely negative about the value of the agreement to the United States economy. This development could have been avoided. Long ago the two governments should have appointed a joint commission to analyze the problems and recommend adjustments from time to time, as well as to explain the workings of the agreement to the public.

This unwillingness to bend slightly and give the appearance of close cooperation appears to be difficult for Canadian politicians in the context of a preoccupation with the image of overdependence on the United States. The problems of United States-Canadian relations would be much easier to deal with if Canadian officials could shift the focus of attention away from vulnerability and dependence in connection with the United States and toward the opportunities for Canada in global economic activity. As far as the United States-Canadian official discussions are concerned, when they do take place from time to time, the two sides tend to remain polarized. Only occasionally do the officials on both sides meet to discuss their mutual interests in connection with their respective dealings with the rest of the world. Yet the sheer magnitude of their mutual economic relationship and the importance of both in the world trading system makes the absence of a more broadly based dialogue difficult to understand.

Opportunities of Multilateralism

The thrust of the 1975 report of the Economic Council of Canada, entitled "Looking Outward: A New Trade Strategy for Canada," puts heavy emphasis on the need for Canada to look to world developments and to take an outward-looking and liberal orientation in its trade policies. The general thrust of this report makes much sense for Canada, but it cannot become meaningful without a complementary change in Canadian diplomatic activities in most international economic meetings.

There would also be a need for a closer exchange of views between Washington and Ottawa, in order to exploit the leverage of the two nations. In this connection, Canada will at times have conflicting interests and at other times mutual interests. There will also be cases where the interests do not overlap and are neither conflicting nor common but where one can help the other out of multilateral difficulties. Where there are mutual interests, particularly where domestic Canadian political interests can be benefitted, the two parties should be moving in mutually supporting ways.

The field of trade policy and trade negotiations provides some examples. The major issues of multilateral trade policy and trade liberalization are commonly thought to be those covered in the GATT negotiations, or in the current Multilateral Trade Negotiations (MTN), which include many nations not members of the GATT but which utilize the GATT secretariat to provide supporting services for the negotiations. These issues of impediments and distortions to trade are important. They are usually conceived of in terms of tariff and nontariff barriers to trade. But these problems can no longer be viewed in isolation from government policies relating to regional or industrial development, nor can they be looked at separately from broad policies toward developing nations, including commodity policy, development assistance policy, and food policy. Increasing economic interdependence has combined with increasing political activism on the part of developing nations and with periodic materials scarcities and synchronized business cycles among the Western industrialized nations. Internally, aids to industry that have a direct or indirect effect on exports or imports are coming under international scrutiny, so that domestic policies are increasingly being considered fair game for discussion and negotiation among nations.[1]

In connection with the negotiations (MTN) taking place in Geneva in the mid-1970s, United States and Canadian negotiators do meet periodically to exchange observations about respective tariff-cutting proposals and the specific objectives of each in nontariff barrier negotiations. But the need goes far beyond this commendable informal dialogue. The broader issues of North-South confrontation or of maneuvers with the USSR under the heading of "détente" or of United States policies toward OPEC are not brought into consideration. (It is probably fair to say that the negotiators in Geneva for these two governments are kept relatively uninformed by their capitals about what is taking place in other diplomatic or negotiating contexts.)

Resource, raw material, and commodity policies in the mid-1970s are being discussed in a different kind of context than previously. The influence of the oil-producing nations of the OPEC group, together with ups and downs in various commodity markets combined with political efforts to manage commodity flows and prices by some of the developing nations, has created a new kind of political climate in North-South dealings. The so-called producer-consumer dialogue (renamed the Conference on International Economic Cooperation, or CIEC, in late 1975) in Paris quickly spilled over from oil price issues to all North-South economic relationships. The OPEC nations and some of the European nations insisted on bringing into the dialogue a number of non-oil-producing nations, to get at the fundamentals of the problems. Side by side with this development was an important debate in the UN General Assembly, in Special Session, in the mid-1970s, which gave rise to a variety of proposals by the industrialized nations, the most notable of which was the statement made by the United States on September 1, 1975, on behalf of Secretary Kissinger. This and other international activity have created an entirely new negotiating environment.

In this context, neither the United States nor Canada has been particu-

---

[1] For an explanation of the interactions of domestic and international aspects of these trade questions, see Matthew J. Marks and Harald B. Malmgren, "Negotiating Nontariff Distortions to Trade," *Law and Policy in International Business* 7 (Spring 1975), 327-411.

larly imaginative in developing new concepts for dealing with resource and raw material problems. It is difficult to understand why this is so. Canada has its own internal needs and political pressures for new policies of developing its domestic resources. There has been in Canada public discussion of the need to promote development of key sectors of the economy and in turn the need for sector negotiations in international trade negotiations to focus on the problems of specific sectors of interest to Canada. The purpose, of course, is to find means of developing processing industries that can be built on the Canadian raw material base. When it comes to international discussion, however, what exactly is on Canada's mind is not clear to other nations. The United States, for reason of internal domestic political pressure, also wished to develop negotiations within the framework of key sectors, but over several years in the early and mid-1970s was unable to ascertain what Canada really wanted to do. In other words, the two countries, for perhaps different reasons, had the same tactical objectives but were unable to find a common approach, or even explain to each other the line of thinking in their respective capitals.

In agriculture, one would think that the broad objectives of the two nations would be similar, if not identical, since both are major producers and exporters of grains. In the mid-1970s, the United States ideas on what should be done in the international grain trading system are very unclear. Most negotiating efforts seem to come to a stalemate on procedural issues because neither the EEC nor the United States seems able to disengage long enough to suggest new concepts or initiatives. The United States position can be described as a more or less ideological one, in opposition to measures that would alter free market forces and especially in opposition to measures which would establish and manage world food prices. The EEC, on the other hand, favors negotiation on the basis of commodity agreements that would stabilize the conditions of trade. Canada would probably come out somewhere between these two positions, in light of its own national interests, and therefore is in a unique position to act as an independent initiative-taker and middleman. Canada could, if it chose, put forward ideas that met its own needs and that would probably be welcomed by the United States and Europe as a way out of deadlock. Certainly, at a minimum, Canadian ideas would be brought home for debate and counterargument in the other capitals, which would in turn start capitals thinking about what they really want.

This is a complex subject, and philosophic statements shed no light on what is in fact negotiable. Almost any proposal put forward in precise detail would be taken seriously and given careful examination. From Canada's own political point of view, it would seem an ideal context for ministers, particularly given the importance of grains to the western provinces and the Canadian economy as a whole. In other words, one might excuse confusion and indecision in Washington, but the absence of a well-planned strategy and an activist role on the Canadian side is much more difficult to understand.

The structure of tariffs, from raw materials through processing stages to finished products, ought to be a subject of common interest in North America. The methods of coping with commodity instability in developing nations, and the ways in which potential solutions might affect the economies of the industrialized nations, should be of great common concern to the two nations. The use, or potential use, of export controls by any supplying nation (whether a developing nation or Canada, Australia, or the United States) is a complex and challenging area for the policy process in both nations. The interests are similar, and the search for international rules in this area ought to be a common pursuit, but it is not.

The prospects for the Multilateral Trade Negotiations in this context are consequently unclear. To the extent that Canada continues to play a "loner" role, the pressures from developing nations will tend to dominate in shaping tariff structures, as well as commodity buffer stocks and commodity schemes, because of the absence of either intellectual leadership or coherent and coordinated thinking among the Western nations.

In energy, almost no thought is given to North American problems, while Canada and the United States go their separate ways. This is a most sorry spectacle in the light of the common interests throughout North America in relation to the world as a whole. This criticism is not limited to oil and gas. The international uranium enrichment and nuclear power picture, for example, is thoroughly confused by spreading autarchy—which in turn has highly unfavorable consequences for global problems of proliferation of nuclear weapons materials.

In questions of international regional policies the two nations are on divergent paths. The United States argues philosophically about the need for great powers to avoid bilateralism, although it persists in flirtations with bilateralism in its dealings with the oil-producing nations, other Middle Eastern nations, and the Eastern European nations, especially the USSR. The United States plays its "big power" games without thinking much about Canada. Canada, on the other hand, pursues its narrow interests in grain sales in the short term by negotiating special arrangements, such as those with China and the USSR. Canada also toys wistfully with the idea of a special arrangement with the EEC (an idea that is likely to go nowhere). Yet the Pacific, where Canada's long-term growth is likely to be greater than in the Atlantic, receives scant attention. The natural policy alliance of Australia, Canada, and the United States in agriculture and other raw materials is never given a second thought. Occasionally, some economic or political analyst will write about a Pacific area free trade arrangement or a Pacific area coordination group, but in the broad sweep of policy these ideas are left out of sight.

The winding down of the unfortunate Vietnam war could have been a fine diplomatic opportunity for Canada and Japan jointly to call for new economic cooperation in the Asian Pacific, with corollary proposals for exploring common interests and conflicting interests in trade policy toward each other and toward the rest of the world. But this type of imaginative perspective is not found in official circles.

In the meantime, the wide variety of international negotiations now under way, in the International Monetary Fund, in the World Bank system, in the Multilateral Trade Negotiations, in the Paris producer-consumer dialogues, in the OECD and UN discussions of multinational enterprise and international investment, in the UN bodies such as the General Assembly, Special Session, and UNCTAD, and in the regional negotiations (including the evolution of the Lome Convention linking the EEC to over fifty developing nations), and the bilateral dealings of governments, all portend change. Governments in such a high state of diplomatic and negotiating activity will no doubt find it necessary to reach at least some agreements, to show for their efforts. The interests of both Canada and the United States are likely to be affected in substantial ways by the outcome of all this activity, yet the two think very little about the commonality of their predicament.

In the United States in the mid-1970s the sentiments for increased protectionism are by no means dead. The passage of the Trade Act of 1974 suppressed some of the pressures and created formal channels for many of the special interest groups, slowing down their attacks on liberal policies. But the passage of that Trade Act also seems to have put many people into an unguarded frame of mind. It will take very clever management of trade policy internally and internationally by United States trade officials to keep under control the forces of unilateralism, protectionism, and isolationism. It is doubtful whether these forces can be kept fully under control. A multiplicity of actions drawing on various protective provisions of the new Trade Act are not part of a master design of United States trade policy, but rather are symptoms of the continuing pressures facing the administration and therefore facing other nations that trade with the United States, including Canada.

The short-sighted, narrowly constricted vision characterizing both Ottawa and Washington in connection with these global questions is regrettable. Yet of the two nations, Canada loses more by it.

The report of the Economic Council of Canada mentioned earlier states at one point, "There is also the growing tendency of major nations to speak of a 'tripartite' organization of international affairs. . . . Such an arrangement seems to throw Canada arbitrarily into the U.S. orbit—a prospect that disturbs many Canadians." That development, which is increasingly true, is as much the result of Canada's way of dealing with global questions and with the United States, as it is of Washington's habit of ignoring Ottawa.

Conflict over Industrial Incentive Policies

SPERRY LEA
JOHN VOLPE

In recent years, considerable controversy between Canada and the United States has stemmed from certain governmental policies in both countries to assist domestic industry. Described here as industrial incentive policies, they are more typically viewed, in terms of their real and alleged trade effects, as "nontariff distortions." The potential for continued and heightened bilateral conflict over industrial incentive policies is apparent from the realities of the Canadian-American economic relationship, a recent discussion of which made the following observation: "Conceivably, the greatest source of bilateral friction arising from new Canadian policy would not come from foreign policy initiatives but from the external impact of ones aimed basically at domestic problems. For instance, given the high percentage of Canadian production exported to the United States, Canadian policies to head off unemployment through subsidizing production might often appear in American eyes to be export subsidies, and be answered as such."[1]

This essay approaches the subject by first seeking a better way to understand industrial incentive policies, both generally and as they appear in the Canadian-American context. It then reviews their actual economic impact on both countries through a summary of recent findings.[2]

[1] *The New Environment for Canadian-American Relations,* A Statement by the Canadian-American Committee (Washington, D.C., and Montreal: National Planning Association and the Private Planning Association of Canada, 1972), p. 34.

[2] John Volpe, *Industrial Incentive Policies and Programs in the Canadian-American Context,* The Canadian-American Committee (Washington, D.C., and Montreal: National Planning Association and the C. D. Howe Research Institute, January 1976).

Among developed countries in general, industrial incentive policies are widespread and spring from similar perceptions and trends. The most basic national objectives, domestic well-being and world security, are seen to require certain economic achievements, of which a partial list includes an acceptable level of economic growth with control over inflation, reasonably full employment, technological advancement, and a rough balance on international payments. To attain these ends, there has arisen an increased reliance on governmental management of economic affairs which, given industry's central role in creating wealth, providing employment, earning foreign exchange, and building and maintaining an arsenal for defense, has meant growing government involvement in the process of industrialization. Though specific policies differ widely in scope among the developed countries, they have always included a variety of steps, applied either across the board or quite selectively, to encourage or protect domestic industry—in short, to influence how resources would be used and how the income from their use would be distributed.

Impediments to imports, traditionally the most common form of assistance to domestic industry, have been reduced significantly over the postwar period by international negotiations, leading both to an ever-greater access by the products of one developed country to the markets of others and to the development by governments of ways other than tariffs and quotas to support domestic industry—the so-called nontariff distortions. Viewing this trend, Robert Baldwin noted recently "a significant increase in the number and magnitude of government programs designed to subsidize production in various industries and regions [most of which] seem prompted by a greater sense of public responsibility toward improving economic conditions for those employed in depressed industries or regions and raising the rate of growth both generally and in selected industries."[3]

While Canada and the United States have shared in this process, special circumstances have created a unique North American condition:

1. In Canada, growing concerns over economic sovereignty, national unity, and new employment opportunities to accommodate the fastest growing labor force in the developed world have bred determined governmental policies to encourage further processing of that country's raw material endowment, to promote exports of its manufactured goods, and to place new industries in its disadvantaged regions. The last objective is served by the Department of Regional Economic Expansion (DREE), established in 1969 to create employment where people already live and where jobs are needed.

2. In the United States, other forces have been at work. The dramatic

---

[3] Robert E. Baldwin, *Nontariff Distortions of International Trade* (Washington, D. C.: The Brookings Institution, 1970), p. 110.

events between mid-August and the end of that year—the import surcharge, the devaluation of the dollar and the end of its convertibility into gold, and the Smithsonian agreements—signaled acute American anxiety over its international economic performance. Thereafter, the United States was more keenly sensitive to what it considered unfair competitive practices by other countries—now suddenly including Canada, which it no longer considered a special case deserving preferential treatment and with which it passed a winter of discontent in often abrasive confrontations over a wide variety of "trade irritants."

3. Quite apart from these events, an unusual market situation was being shaped between the two countries by the coincidence of several factors unique to them. These include the propinquity of major population and production centers; a common language; well-coordinated communications and transportation systems; and widespread American ownership of Canadian industry, which has led to production in the two countries of many items of similar designs, specifications, and brand names. Thus latent opportunities were generated for a homogeneous North American market and increasingly realized as traditional worldwide trade barriers were being reduced over the postwar period. One evidence has been the substantial rise in fully manufactured goods as a share of Canada's exports to the United States, from approximately 12 percent in 1959 to about 40 percent in 1975.[4] The largest portion of the increase is in automotive exports, but nonautomotive manufactures have almost doubled their share over the same period.

Given the current concerns in Canada and the United States and the homogeneous North American market for manufactured goods—in some respects more truly "common" than that achieved by the Common Market—it is only natural that the industrial incentive policies of the two countries will occasionally work at cross purposes. Two recent policies are notable for leading not merely to considerable bilateral friction but eventually to the adoption of countermeasures.

One was the United States DISC legislation of late 1971, which permits firms in that country, including those foreign owned, to establish affiliated "Domestic International Sales Corporations" and thus gain a significant tax deferral for substantial export volume. The announced purpose was to shift some production for foreign markets from subsidiaries abroad that enjoyed certain tax benefits to DISC-affiliated plants at home. Canadian authorities began objecting to this plan a year before its adoption, perceiving three potentially adverse effects: greater competitiveness of existing United States exports in both Canada's domestic and foreign markets, a new incentive to American firms to service the Canadian mar-

---

[4] Sources: Statistics Canada, *Summary of External Trade,* cat. no. 65-001; and *Summary and Analytical Tables, Trade of Canada,* vol. 1, cat. no. 65-201.

ket from domestic production rather than from their Canadian subsidiaries, and a lure to Canadian-owned firms to locate or expand manufacturing south of the border instead of increasing domestic investment. Partly to offset these anticipated effects of DISC, the Canadian government offered what one might call "countervailing tax incentives" to its own manufacturing and processing industries in the spring of 1972. It also closely monitored imports from DISCs until 1973, after which concern over adverse effects lessened.

The second, more notable example was the Michelin case, a package of benefits extended by three levels of government in Canada to this French tire company in 1969 and 1971 to locate two plants in Nova Scotia, considered an economically depressed region. Specifically, the federal government offered a $16 million grant and an accelerated depreciation allowance; the province of Nova Scotia extended a $50 million loan and a $7.6 million grant for capital and training; and the local government donated the plant site and reduced the property tax rate. Washington, responding to pressure from the country's tire industry and recognizing that three-quarters of the output of beneficiary plants probably would be exported to the United States, found Michelin to be violating United States law regarding "bounties or grants on exports," whereupon it applied a countervailing duty in January 1973.

A New Approach to Scoring

In traditional classification schemes, industrial incentive policies are placed among a wider range of "nontariff distortions" under single headings. Baldwin suggests twelve categories. While useful as an inventory device, this method does not do justice to the complex individuality of each measure. Table 1 attempts a new approach to correct this problem by permitting an incentive policy to be scored one or more times on five separate checklists, which are separated into three that denote basic characteristics and two that show actual effects at home and abroad. The first group is further separated into the "whys" of a policy (column A) and its "whats" (columns B and C). Perhaps the most important insight revealed by scoring a policy in this manner is the ambiguities regarding the national goals being served.

Disagreements arise between the original designers and ultimate administrators of such policies and between the more political considerations present at their conception and the generally more economically oriented arguments then made publicly on their behalf. Dunn and Lea recently concluded: "Listening to ex-officials who were involved in the decision whether or not to launch DISC, one finds that the higher one goes in the Washington hierarchy the less DISC looks like a move calculated to bring some net economic benefits to the United States, and the more it appears

TABLE 1

Industrial Incentive Measures
Checklists of Major Attributes

Basic Characteristics			Actual Effects	
A National Policy Goals	*B* Conditions of Application	*C* Techniques	*D* Domestic Effects	*E* Foreign Effects
1. increasing domestic employment	1. without restriction	1. direct subsidies	1. increasing domestic employment	1. decreasing domestic employment
2. improving the trade balance . . . through . . .	2. only when it is . . .	2. rebates for performance	2. improving the trade balance through . . .	2. impairing the trade balance through . . .
(a) encouraging increasing exports	(a) in specified localities	(a) related to production	(a) encouraging exports	(a) restricting exports
(b) reducing imports	(b) producing certain products	(b) related to exports	(b) reducing imports	(b) increasing imports
(c) encouraging import substitution	(c) with a certain size range	3. advantageous treatment on . . .	(c) encouraging import substitution	3. reducing incoming direct investment
3. reducing direct investment abroad by home-based firms	(d) experiencing certain labor conditions	(a) governmental procurement	3. reducing direct investment abroad by home-based firms	4. preempting technological growth
4. neutralizing regional disparities	(e) domestically owned	(b) taxation	4. neutralizing regional disparities	
5. furthering technology	(f) exporting a specified share of its production	(c) interest rates	5. furthering technology	
6. fostering national unity	etc.	(d) power costs	6. fostering national unity (mainly a Canadian concern)	
7. enhancing national security		(e) transportation costs	7. enhancing national security	
		(f) plant construction	8. costing the national treasury	
		(g) labor training		
		etc.		

Notes: Scoring of characteristics in Group A should distinguish between primary and secondary objectives. It should also recognize that policy goals underlying a particular measure can shift over time. Scoring in Group D should recognize the possibility of Perverse Effects (i.e., decreasing employment); effects recorded here that were not mentioned in Group A—even as secondary goals—are Inadvertent Effects. Effects listed in Group E typically represent frustrations of national policy in trade linked countries; whether such effects occur, and if so, to what extent, is often at the heart of contention.

to have been justified as serving one or another political game plan."[5] Among political explanations for DISC were the hopes of persuading a key congressional leader to accept the administration trade policy proposals, appeals to the American business community, and attempts to provoke certain trading partners (other than Canada) into negotiating the removal of their own export tax incentives. Further opportunities for disagreement arise between the country initiating incentives to production of internationally traded goods and its major trading partners. Usually the arguments center on the degree to which presumably beneficial effects for the implementing country (column D) translate into allegedly disadvantageous effects for another (column E). Canadian-American disagreement over DISC is a case in point.[6]

Of greater interest is a generally less prevalent form of dispute, but one perhaps more typical of the Canadian-American context, over just where among the five lists a judgment should be based. A clear example can be found in the different ways Canada and the United States score the aids offered to Michelin in Nova Scotia. For Canada, these incentives involve strictly domestic programs and therefore should be immune from countervailing actions. Thus Canada interprets the policy package basically as follows: desirous of fostering national unity (A-6) by neutralizing regional disparities (A-4), the federal, provincial, and local governments have offered to Michelin, provided it established production within a designated locality (B-2a), a series of different supportive measures (C-1 and several within C-3). The United States, however, views the policy package as an export subsidy justifying countervailing action by focusing on effects (columns D and E) rather than on announced characteristics. While recognizing that assistance was not contingent on export performance (B-2f or C-2b), the American view can be stated as follows: the actual effects in Canada of assistance to Michelin included increasing Canadian exports (D-2a), since about 75 percent of the output of the beneficiary plants was to be exported to the United States. Thus the counterpart effect on the United States was to impair its trade balance through increased imports (E-2b), in the process decreasing domestic employment (E-1).

These conflicting views of the crux of the Michelin dispute surfaced recently in two articles appearing a year apart in the same journal. In their criticism of the Washington decision to countervail, Robert V. Guido and Michael F. Morrone wrote: "The central problem posed in Michelin is whether the Canadian assistance was actually designed to encourage exportation to the United States by facilitating the location in Canada of

---

[5] Robert M. Dunn, Jr., and Sperry Lea, "U.S.-Canadian Relations: Some Problems and Paradoxes," paper presented to the Association for North American Studies, San Francisco, December 28, 1974.

[6] Ibid.

the Michelin Tire Corporation or was intended to bolster the sagging economy of the province of Nova Scotia."[7] In reply, two former United States officials, Matthew J. Marks and Harald B. Malmgren, denied the relevance of any such choice over basic intentions: "Although Canadian assistance to the Michelin Tire Corporation concededly was designed to bolster the economy of Nova Scotia, it does not follow, as [Guido and Morrone] assumed, that such assistance did not constitute the payment of a bounty or grant. The countervailing duty issue depends not upon the existence of a valid domestic purpose but rather upon the international trade effects caused by what may be admittedly a legitimate internal economic assistance measure. Analysis of this issue requires a pragmatic examination of the complex interaction between domestic and international policies."[8]

The tendency for industrial incentive policies to be judged in the initiating country on the basis of *raison d'être*—most benignly stated—but by its trading partners on the basis of actual or potential effects—stated in the worst possible light—emphasizes the importance of a better understanding of the economic consequences of such policies.

Evaluating the Net Effects of Industrial Incentive Policies

Industrial incentive policies have domestic and foreign effects that are difficult to evaluate. They are not particularly amenable to quantification, leading to assessments of their domestic and foreign impact based largely on subjective judgments. These, in turn, frequently are difficult to make because each industrial incentive policy operates in an environment containing many other incentive policies, initiated at home and in other countries. Taking these and other difficulties into account, this section will review the balance-of-payments impact and, to a lesser extent, certain microeconomic effects of the industrial incentive policies of Canada and the United States on each other.

Balance-of-Payment Effects. When employed by either country, incentive policies are perceived by the other to affect adversely its bilateral and multilateral balance-of-payments positions. Indeed, when considered individually, each policy has these effects to a greater or lesser extent. For instance, by favoring domestic over foreign producers, government procurement policies and practices restrict imports, while exports are promoted through tax rebates on export profits, favorable terms for finance

[7] Robert V. Guido and Michael F. Morrone, "The Michelin Decision: A Possible New Direction for U.S. Countervailing Duty Law," *Law and Policy in International Business* 6 (Winter 1974), 238.

[8] Matthew J. Marks and Harald B. Malmgren, "Negotiating Nontariff Distortions to Trade," *Law and Policy in International Business* (Spring 1975) 356, n. 116.

and insurance, and locational aids and other incentive devices. In addition, modifications of the domestic tax structure and other devices to assist domestic industry, though usually motivated by national needs and considerations, are often found to affect international transactions.

Yet an important and frequently ignored point about industrial incentive policies is that their balance-of-payments effects are at least partially offset in several ways. First, while the absolute level of any incentive policy may have important consequences for either country's domestic economy, its impact on the balance-of-payments depends only on its level relative to the incentive policy existing in the other country.[9] Since Canada and the United States employ incentive policies that are quite similar in kind, though in most cases not in magnitude, the payments balance effects of any policy are to some extent reduced.

Thus the impact of one country's procurement policies and practices is largely counterbalanced by the fact that the other country grants analogous preferences to domestic producers, and the same can be said for other import-restricting efforts. Similarly, export-promoting efforts by one country may increase the volume and change the structure and direction of its trade, but parallel policies utilized by the other country significantly offset any balance-of-payments effects. Finally, changes in the domestic tax structure by one country to aid domestic industry by enhancing its international cost competitiveness are largely neutralized by similar changes occurring in the tax systems of the other country.

A second offsetting factor exists because of the substantial degree of Canadian-American economic interdependence. The movement since World War II toward greater interdependence has been most notably evident in merchandise trade flows, patterns of direct investment, monetary and financial relationships, tourism, and trade union bonds.[10] The interdependence expressed by these and other direct links is largely asymmetrical in nature—that is, Canada is much more dependent on the United States than the reverse—and is reinforced by indirect linkages in the form of "spillover" effects on the Canadian economy that result from changes in demand pressures in the United States. Together, these direct and indirect links are responsible for transmitting business fluctuations from the United States to Canada.

Thus the Canadian economy is highly sensitive to economic develop-

[9] This section highlights the thorough analysis of this point by Richard N. Cooper, "National Economic Policy in an Interdependent World Economy," in *Changing Patterns in Foreign Trade and Payments*, ed. Bela Belassa (New York: W. W. Norton and Company, Inc., 1970), pp. 98-115.

[10] For a detailed discussion of the nature, problems, and prospects of Canadian-American economic integration, see Theodore Geiger, John Volpe, and Ernest H. Preeg, *North American Integration and Economic Blocs*, Thames Essay No. 7 (London: Trade Policy Research Centre, May 1975), pp. 1-39.

ments in the United States, while that country's economy in turn is affected in important ways by changes in Canadian economic activity. Given both the significant role of exports in the Canadian economy—particullarly in the manufacturing sector, which must specialize and have access to large-scale markets in order to increase competitiveness—and the primary importance of the American market to Canadian exporters, United States incentive policies that directly or indirectly have external repercussions can easily depress the Canadian economy producing, in turn, substantial negative or offsetting "feedback" effects on United States interests. For example, any decline in Canadian economic activity that results from United States import-restricting policies will reduce United States exports to that country and tend to impair its balance-of-payments objectives.

As a third offsetting factor, in the recent history of Canadian-American relations, the adoption of a trade-distorting policy by one country has provoked in the other not only significant criticism but also a specific response in the form of an offsetting countermeasure. Here, a careful distinction is made between *autonomous* and *induced* distortions; that is, between government incentive policies that initiate trade distortions and those government countermeasures that attempt to *offset* trade distortions introduced by the other country. As mentioned above, there are two important countermeasures: the United States countervailing duty imposed on imports of Michelin tires from Canada in response to Canadian government incentives granted to that company and the Canadian corporate tax reductions for manufacturing and processing industries that were, to some extent, a reply to the United States DISC program. These countermeasures are major links in the chain of economic effects of Michelin and DISC, in the sense that they weaken the intended trade balance impact of both programs.

While the United States countervailing duty was applied to offset the trade impact of the Michelin subsidies, the extent of the offset depends on the accuracy of the Treasury's determination of the subsidy element. Unfortunately, the Treasury policy in each case is not to disclose information on why it decides to countervail nor on how it goes about determining the degree of subsidy element present. All that can be said is that the application of the countervailing duty in this instance offsets, to some extent, the trade impact of subsidies received by that company, though the greater (less) the subsidy, the lower (larger) the trade offset of the countervailing duty.

With regard to the second specific countermeasure, one way of approaching a determination of the extent to which Canada's corporate tax reductions offset the balance-of-payments impact of the DISC program is to calculate the expected percentage decline in prices—export prices for the United States and manufacturing and processing prices for Canada.

Recent studies have shown, with some qualifications, that if the benefits of both programs are fully passed on to buyers, Canada's corporate tax reductions at least approximately offset the expected trade balance benefits to United States exporters under DISC.[11]

The discussion thus far has implicitly assumed fixed exchange rates or variants of floating exchange rates, for, generally speaking, a *freely* floating exchange rate will tend to offset significantly any balance-of-payments effects of government programs instituted by both countries. However, automatic exchange rate adjustments and their effects admittedly are not easily predictable. When governments elect—as they often do—to intervene through the use of monetary and fiscal policies partially or totally to offset exchange rate movements whose sectoral effects they often find unmanageable, the consequences of their actions not only affect the actual value of the exchange rate but also may reinforce the objective of a given national policy. It should be noted also that a *freely* floating exchange rate system may work more in the direction of offsetting changes in the Canadian exchange rate than for the United States. This is because the Canadian economy is current account oriented whereas the United States economy is capital account oriented.

For Canada, any program that decreases the price of that country's exports will increase the demand for its currency, thus mitigating government actions. For the United States, however, changes in the value of its currency are likely to be more responsive to developments in capital markets, such as the capital market consequences of changes in the demand for oil and the Eurocurrency market, since the United States dollar is used also as the international means of payment. Thus a situation may exist, even under *freely* floating rates, where those factors are combining to lower the value of the dollar *vis-à-vis* other currencies that would then reinforce the *initial* currency depreciating effect of many payments-distorting incentives policies of the United States government.

Some Microeconomic Implications of Incentive Policy Programs. In addition to their macroeconomic impact, industrial incentive policies also generate significant microeconomic effects. Canada is concerned with the structure of its trade, particularly with more balance between its manufacturing and resource sectors. Historically, many Canadian resource industries have received very favorable tax treatment while manufacturers, though protected by tariffs, had fewer tax advantages and faced higher United States and foreign trade barriers. In general, such industries now require access to the United States market more to achieve the economies

[11] John Helliwell and John Lester, "Reviewing the Latest DISC: Simulations of Its Aggregate Impacts on Canada," *Canadian Tax Journal* 20 (July-August 1972), 291-98 and R. M. Hyndman, "The Efficacy of Recent Corporate Income Tax Reductions for Manufacturing," *Canadian Tax Journal* 22 (January-February 1974), 84-95.

of scale and specialization and are more susceptible to incentives and countervailing actions in the United States. Thus, Canadian objections to the United States DISC program were due not only to its expected balance-of-payments impact, but also to its perceived effects on the structure of the Canadian economy and on the structure of Canada's trade with the rest of the world. Similarly, the United States is concerned with foreign industrial incentive policies that impede trade expansion in sectors of the economy where it believes it has a comparative advantage, and it applied a countervailing duty in the Michelin case ostensibly because of an anticipated increase in tire imports and the consequent loss of output and employment within that industry.[12]

Generally, industrial incentive policies are not neutral in terms of their impact on sectors of an economy or on factors of production. Even when the objective of a given policy is national in scope, programs invariably operate through sectors and reallocate resources among competing sectors. Not only for Canada and the United States, but also for all industrialized countries, industrial incentive policies that promote exports change the export structure and distort the input composition of total exports—both for the country introducing them and for the countries affected. In some cases, fiscal devices to encourage exports shift mainly capital but also other factors of production into production for export and away from that for domestic consumption, leading to excessive export promotion and a capital-intensive mix for exports beyond what the factor endowments of many countries would otherwise suggest. Government procurement and other import-restricting policies can stimulate the growth of a particular industry or sector of the economy, reallocating resources in the process, particularly if the government purchases a significant percentage of the output of that industry or sector.

In addition to their effects on trade structures and on resource allocation among competing sectors of a given economy, industrial incentive policies tend to alter the tax structures of countries introducing them, and many countries have found it necessary to alter their tax structures to meet the artificial, competitive challenges introduced by other countries. Canada, for example, changed its domestic corporate tax policy in part to meet the challenge of the United States DISC program. Recent changes in the domestic tax structures of many industrialized countries have tended to reduce the overall taxation of capital and may have left countries with undesirable tax systems they would not otherwise have chosen.

---

[12] Not reported in the literature on this case is the interesting fact that the complaints of the United States tire industry (which controls most Canadian plants) appear to have stemmed more from the adverse effects of the new Michelin operation in Nova Scotia on production in their Ontario plants than on that in the United States.

In conclusion, while the industrial incentive policies of either Canada or the United States tend to have only a minor impact on the balance-of-payments positions of both countries, the microeconomic effects for both countries can be significant. Although the offsetting factors previously described mitigate balance-of-payments effects, they do not resolve the microeconomic issues raised above, and it is for this reason that the government in both countries should adopt a pragmatic, cooperative approach that could not only minimize the conflicts generated by these incentive policies, but also reduce their microeconomic effects. Given the prospect that both governments will continue to be involved, to a significant extent, in setting policies that will in some way affect the bilateral relationship, such an approach is clearly needed.

Canada-United States Environmental Relations

DAVID LEMARQUAND
ANTHONY D. SCOTT

Canada and the United States have the longest shared border in the world. The border is "artificial," for it is drawn across rather than along natural physical boundaries and does not recognize physical and ecological interconnections between the countries. As a consequence, Canada and the United States must share the same waters, airsheds, forests, game, and fisheries. When one country uses these resources, the harmful or beneficial side effects are transmitted across the border. Naturally, uncompensated damages to a shared resource can antagonize the neighboring country. A project that seems on balance a good idea to people on one side of the border who can weigh the environmental damages against the benefits from the project, will be seen far differently by people on the other side who will experience only environmental damages. There are a number of locations along the frontier where such environmental questions are actual or potential international irritants. Fortunately, many of the oustanding issues are being dealt with before they erupt into major controversies that can damage Canada-United States relations.

The first section of this essay presents a brief summary of most of the transfrontier environmental issues that currently concern the two countries (excluding fisheries questions, which would require an essay of their own). Brevity has made it necessary to ignore the history and many complexities of these issues and to present only snapshots that illustrate the present state of environmental relations. The final section offers brief comments intended to summarize the common characteristics of these issues. Here the concentration is on the Canadian initiatives or response. Factors that facilitate agreement are also discussed, especially the role played by the International Joint Commission (IJC), and some comments on future prospects are made.

Transfrontier Environmental Issues

Eastport. The Pittston Company in 1972 revealed plans for an oil refinery complex at Eastport, Maine. Eastport is one of the few undeveloped deepwater harbors on the United States east coast. Pittston plans to transport offshore oil in tankers of up to 250,000 dwt to the proposed refinery. The passage to Eastport is through a narrow and deep channel that is entirely in Canadian waters. Canadians objected to the refinery project, fearing the traffic of oil tankers through what they consider treacherous coastal waters would threaten fishery resources and recreation areas of high value.

Despite official Canadian objections, the Pittston Company has sought approval from domestic United States authorities for its proposal. The Maine Board of Environmental Protection held hearings and approved the project subject to a number of conditions, including the use of smaller tankers (150,000 dwt) with double hulls. Of more international significance, it made its approval subject to the approval of Canadian authorities for passage through Canadian waters or agreement from them that such approval is not required. Canada has objected to the project, and federal views were made clear to the Maine board, both in the State Department and in support of New Brunswick's appearance at the board's hearings. Otherwise, it has taken no action to stop the project. Ottawa has been reluctant to ban the tankers from Head Harbour Passage, in the hope that United States domestic processes would make such action unnecessary. However, the Maine board's action will force Canada to consider the Pittston project, provided Pittston considers that it can meet the conditions imposed by the board. Given Canada's initial and continuing objections, Pittston is unlikely to secure Canadian approval.

Although many groups in the United States also oppose the Pittston plan, those in support portray Canadian objections less as a reflection of Canadian environmental goals than as a strategy to get the refinery complex located in the Maritime Provinces where a number of developed deepwater ports might welcome the Pittston refinery. They also point to Lorneville, farther up in Passamaquoddy Bay in New Brunswick, as a deepwater port that Canadians have been able to accept while objecting to the United States project. Canadians respond that the two ports are not at all similar in the navigational and environmental risks they present. Lorneville is in open deep water whereas ships approaching Eastport must pass through an area of shoals, small islands, and a narrow channel only 400 yards wide near a major lobster pound at Deer Island. Also, the passage is subject to more extreme tides and stronger currents.

The Saint John River Committee. In September 1972 the Canada-United States Committee of Water Quality in the Saint John River was established by the two governments. The committee, which is made up of representatives from the two national governments, Maine, New

Brunswick, Quebec, and local planning agencies, was to study the water quality problems along the international sector of the river which forms part of the boundary between Maine and New Brunswick. Industrial activity on both sides of the border, principally the pulp and paper industry, has created significant deterioration of the river's quality upstream before it becomes downstream an entirely Canadian river. The IJC has been asked to review the committee's work and submit recommendations to the two federal governments. The committee has now submitted a report calling for a "mini Great Lakes Water Quality Agreement." This would establish water quality objectives for the international sector of the river, give to the IJC monitoring and surveillance functions, and outline a program of abatement to improve the river's water quality.

The Dickey-Lincoln Dams. The United States Corps of Engineers has proposed construction of a pair of dams on the Saint John River to provide hydropower and flood control benefits both in Maine and downstream in New Brunswick. The status of the dams in Congress is in doubt, but if the engineers wish to proceed, they must apply for permission from the IJC to raise the water level of rivers flowing out of Quebec. If Ottawa objects to the project, the IJC would probably not grant the approval; otherwise, an agreement would still have to be worked out between the two national governments, Quebec, and New Brunswick on the conditions for flooding and river regulation.

Lake Memphremagog. On Lake Memphremagog between Quebec and Vermont there has been a deterioration of water quality, caused largely by nutrient enrichment from the major city on the lake, Newport, Vermont. The Canada-United States Ad Hoc Group on Lake Memphremagog, which was established to study the problem, recommended a program of pollution control abatement in both countries, including nutrient removal at Newport. Quebec and Vermont are expected to exchange letters of commitment to carry out the program. The Department of External Affairs and the State Department will formalize the commitment through an exchange of diplomatic notes.

Lake Champlain-Richelieu River. Along the Richelieu River in Quebec and New York, annual flooding causes about a million dollars damage each year. Canada has a 1937 IJC Order of Approval authorizing works in Canada which would lower the level of Lake Champlain and thus permit better flow regulation of the river. United States conservation groups have objected that lowering the lake will cause major damage to the surrounding wetlands in New York and adversely affect migratory birds and spawning fish. In late 1973, the two governments made a reference to the IJC asking for recommendations on lake level regulation. The United States and the IJC do not want Canada to take any action until the United States completes environmental studies of the regulation. The United States has failed to fund the studies, however, and Canada objects to waiting another two years until the studies are completed. Nevertheless, Canada has expressed willingness to forego the 1937 order in favor of an environmentally less damaging regulation plan, even though it would cost $6 million more than need be spent under the 1937 order. Canada feels that further delay would cause more damage and thus will likely ask the IJC for approval to construct works to regulate the river. The problem is aggravated somewhat by the lack of agreement on the possible damages. Canada recognizes that the 1937 order will create environmental damages but feels that the New York conservation groups' objections to the newest regulation plan are unfounded.

Great Lakes Water Quality Agreement. In April 1972 the Great Lakes Water Quality Agreement was signed. The chief provision of this major agreement calls for scheduled construction of municipal and industrial treatment plants for all municipalities and industries within the Great Lakes system, with phosphorous removal for Lake Erie and Lake Ontario. In Ontario the construction of sewage treatment plants is well advanced, but the development of complex regulations made necessary through the passage in October 1972, over presidential veto, of extensive amendments to the Federal Water Pollution Control Act led to a two-year delay in construction. A further complication was the impoundment by President Nixon of all funds for sewage treatment plant construction under the act. These funds, impounded in the midst of Vietnam federal belt tightening have since been released and the regulations are now in operation. However, the setback in the deadline for completion caused concern in Ontario and Ottawa. At present, Ontario, Ottawa, and the basin states are worried about further slippage on the United States side. If present efforts by southern senators in Congress to reallocate funds under the act succeed, funds would be directed from the Great Lakes to other regions, thus creating further delay in meeting objectives under the agreement.

There have been other problems in implementation. The new permanent joint monitoring and surveillance institution established under the agreement has found that recent optimistic estimates of progress in reducing United States phosphate discharges have been based on erroneous assessments. Also, the water quality data, especially on the United States side, have been seriously inadequate, making it impossible for the commission to draw firm conclusions about the effects of programs under the agreement. In addition, measures taken to reduce the amount of toxic PCBs entering the Great Lakes have apparently been ineffective. The two federal governments and the IJC are studying these problems.

Great Lake Water Levels. In times of high water levels in the Great Lakes, considerable shore erosion takes place on both sides of Lakes Ontario and Erie and, to a lesser extent, Lake Huron. As a result, the United States has put pressure on Canada to agree to a plan whereby water could be stored in Lake Superior. Canada is cautious about deliberately moving disbenefits and benefits around the Great Lakes Basin in view of the problems of legal liability and compensation which could result. It is likely that the cost of establishing compensation would in Canada outweigh the benefits that the new system of regulation might offer. The IJC's own regulation plan, to store some water to reduce high-water levels downstream, does not go as far as the United States would wish. Ottawa is reluctant to proceed unless the United States underwrites the whole cost of compensation. As yet no agreement has been reached.

This is only the most recent of many issues concerning Great Lakes levels. The best known is the dispute about the diversion of water out of Lake Michigan at Chicago. There has also been pressure from New York interests to release more water out of Lake Ontario, even though this would increase flooding along the St. Lawrence, notably at Montreal. For a number of years the IJC has been studying the possibility of further regulation of the lakes by installing control works at the egress of Lake Huron and Erie, similar to those now at Lakes Superior and Ontario. It is generally recognized that this would be uneconomical. A future problem of some magnitude may emerge if efforts to use ice breakers to extend the navigation season continue.

Detroit-Windsor Air Pollution. Air with high sulphur dioxide levels and particulate matter often drifts across the St. Clair River from Detroit to Windsor and from Sarnia to Port Huron. The principal polluters are Detroit's coal-fired thermal power plants and other industrial coal-fired boilers. In December 1973 the IJC recommended an extensive abatement program with some expanded responsibilities for itself in surveillance, monitoring, and reporting of air quality. Ontario, Michigan, and Washington rejected such a major program. Washington and Michigan felt their own programs (under United States law) would eventually meet the IJC objectives.

Nevertheless, Ontario and Michigan have recently concluded a memorandum of understanding in which each side committed itself not only to a joint contingency plan for air pollution episodes, but also to a long-term abatement program. In a joint reference to the IJC, Ottawa and Washington agreed to the principles of the memorandum and pledged their support. The reference also asked the IJC to report on the progress of programs outlined in the memorandum of understanding and to monitor the air quality in the area. In itself this reference represents a breakthrough, for in effect it commits the United States to the contingency program and, more important, to switching to low sulphur fuel, a key element in meeting the sulphur dioxide objectives. Applications from the affected plants for low sulphur fuel are before the federal energy agency.

The Garrison Diversion. The Bureau of Reclamation has a project to divert about 2 percent of the upper Missouri River flow into central and eastern North Dakota for a multipurpose irrigation, flood control, water supply, recreation, and wildlife habitat improvement scheme. The project has been called the "salvation of North Dakota" and could cost up to a billion dollars. The first stage is expected to cost $400 million. The international problems arise from the fact that 84 percent of the irrigated lands will drain away from the Missouri basin northward into the Souris and Red River and into Manitoba.

Canada objects that the return water will have a high saline content, particularly damaging to the low-flow Souris River and the municipalities and industries dependent on it for water supply. Fear is also expressed that eventual added nutrient loadings to Lake Winnipeg will accelerate its eutrophication. There is also concern about the effect on Lake Winnipeg's whitefish industry and the introduction of coarse fish species from the Missouri system. Ottawa has made its concerns known to Washington in a number of official notes since 1969. In 1973 Canada formally informed the United States that it had concluded that the project as planned would violate article IV of the 1909 Boundary Waters Treaty, which states that "water flowing across the boundary shall not be polluted on either side to the injury of health or property of the other." The United States replied that no construction potentially affecting Canada would be undertaken unless it was clear that United States obligations under the treaty were met.

Although the project has strong local support in North Dakota, there is also significant criticism of the project by Americans questioning the expense and economics of irrigating land most suitable for dry-land farming and single-crop harvests. They also criticize the expected salt accumulation from leaching of the soil and possible environmental damages to the extensive wildfowl refuges in the area and the interbasin transfer of water from the Missouri to the Saskatchewan river system. Thus Canada has a number of private supporters in the United States of its objections, as well as the Council on Environmental Quality, the Environmental Protection Agency, the Office of Management and Budget, the General Accounting Office, and some congressmen. The State Department is also on record as saying that if the IJC finds that the project will cause damages in Canada in violation of article IV, it will actively oppose the bureau's project.

The IJC has no automatic jurisdiction over this issue, but the two governments have agreed to submit the necessary reference to the commission to study the problem and to make recommendations. There are expectations that under these circumstances the IJC could propose expensive modifications that would reduce or eliminate the project's adverse effects in Canada. Acceptance of such modifications would allow the project to proceed, much to the dismay of United States domestic critics. However, if the United States does spend considerable sums to meet the antipollution provisions of the treaty, it will be an important precedent.

East Poplar River. The Saskatchewan Power Corporation is constructing a coal-fired thermal generating plant on the East Poplar River, a small
tributary of the Missouri. The river will be dammed to create a cooling
pond. The United States is concerned because the plant could cause both
local air and water pollution in Montana, and the dam could reduce the
flow to an unacceptably low level. Saskatchewan and Ottawa have agreed
to meet the level of particulate removal that the United States seeks, even
though it is higher than Canadian domestic law requires. The two national
governments have also asked the IJC and its Air Pollution Advisory Board
for further advice.

Since the 1930s the IJC has had responsibility for recommending ap-
portionment of the river's flow. Now that there is a demand for the water,
the two national governments have asked that the IJC undertake an ap-
portionment study on an urgent basis. Avoidance of water pollution to the
satisfaction of the United States is more difficult because the possible
effects from operation of the plant are not known and there is also a lack
of data for the river, especially for the ambient water quality in Montana.
However, under a license issued by the federal minister of the environment in accordance with the International Rivers Improvement Act, the
Saskatchewan Power Corporation is obligated to meet the antipollution
provisions of the Boundary Waters Treaty.

Flathead River. Rio Algom Ltd. and Pan Ocean Oil Ltd. have been con-
ducting feasibility studies for development of two open-pit coal mines on
Cabin Creek, a tributary of the Flathead River in Canada, eight miles upstream from the British Columbia–Montana border. Montana would like
the Flathead River, which forms the western boundary of the United
States Glacier National Park, to be declared a "wild river" by Congress.
Environmental groups in Montana and to some extent in British Columbia
are worried about the effects of the $200 million mining operation on the
highly regarded wilderness area, especially the possible deterioration of
water quality from coal sediments. In February 1975 the Flathead Coalition was organized; it now has 68,000 members, mostly in Montana but
also from British Columbia. The coalition hopes, if possible, to stop the
project, or more realistically, to ensure that the river is protected.

British Columbia has assured those concerned about the project that it
will have the highest environmental standards both to satisfy provincial
environmental objectives and to meet Canadian obligations under article
IV of the 1909 Boundary Waters Treaty. Ottawa, for its part, is willing
to defend the company's interests if it does its absolute best to minimize
environmental effects. Ottawa is also somewhat annoyed that the United
States should contemplate unilaterally declaring the Flathead a wild river,
thus putting pressure on Canada to meet the highest United States water
quality standards for the river's headwaters.

Skagit River. In 1942 the IJC gave the city of Seattle an order of approval to raise its hydropower dam, the High Ross Dam, 126 feet subject to the condition that a compensation agreement be worked out with British Columbia for flooding the 5,200 acres of land as the reservoir backs up into provincial crown land. In 1967 a compensation agreement was finally signed: British Columbia was to receive $35,000 a year. When the details of the compensation agreement became known about 1970, provincial conservation groups protested against the project because of the environmental damage it would cause and the low compensation price. The ROSS Committee (Run Out Skagit Spoilers) was formed to fight the project. Environmental groups in the United States supported by the Washington State government, some members of the city council, and some United States federal departments are also opposed to the dam because of the environmental damages it would create on the Washington State side of the border.

In 1971, Ottawa and Washington referred the issue to the IJC. The IJC concluded that there would indeed be significant environmental damage in Canada, but it was restricted by its terms of reference from reconsidering either the merits or the other effects of the High Ross project. In the United States, hearings have been held by the city of Seattle, the Washington State Ecology Commission, and most significantly the Federal Power Commission (FPC). The FPC is now weighing the evidence presented before its hearings and is considering whether to approve the application. It is expected to approve it but with conditions that may make the project economically unfeasible. On the Canadian side a joint federal-provincial position on how to resolve the issue was frustrated at first because the provincial government that signed the 1967 agreement refused to reconsider its decision. Since 1972 a new provincial government has been opposed to the flooding, but it disagreed with Ottawa over tactics. Ottawa is awaiting the FPC decision before considering further moves. British Columbia has had secret discussions with the city of Seattle, without Ottawa's participation, which reportedly are directed at British Columbia's offering the city compensation to drop its project.

Juan de Fuca and Georgia Straits. In the early 1970s Canadians became concerned about the transportation of oil from Alaska down British Columbia's West Coast through the Juan de Fuca Straits and the difficult-to-navigate San Juan and Gulf islands. Oil refineries have been built south of the British Columbia-Washington border, and a large facility at Cherry Point is particularly close to Canada. Canada has strongly objected to large oil tankers in the coastal waters. These objections have received some support in the United States, where Governor Evans of Washington advocates that the major unloading facilities be located at Port Angeles on Juan de Fuca Strait or even further west, at points that have fairly open approaches for ships. The political viability of these proposals, which are supported by Canada, is uncertain.

Canada's credibility, or at least Ottawa's, has been reduced by Canada's decisions to transport its own oil out through the same waters. Already, in order to supply Montreal's refineries when they were faced with shortages, Alberta oil has been shipped in flag-of-convenience tankers through the Panama Canal. Furthermore, British Columbia may have to receive its future oil through the same waters if Alberta can no longer supply the British Columbia market. This realization that crude oil transportation is a common problem has led Ottawa to concentrate on making the Straits of Georgia and Juan de Fuca tanker route as safe as possible.

In 1973, an oil spill contingency plan was signed to facilitate the cleanup of oil in case of an accident. There are also advanced plans for a vessel-management scheme that would directly control all traffic in shipping lanes in the Juan de Fuca-Puget Sound-Georgia Strait area. However, the United States has higher priority areas, namely, the major east and gulf ports, for establishing this type of navigation system. In another joint project the two governments' agencies are now seeking funding to conduct joint marine and environmental scientific studies in the area. Under the trans-Alaska pipeline legislation, funds are available to meet compensation claims for cleanup costs arising from oil spills. Canadian claimants are specifically included in the legislation as possible recipients of the liability funds. Canada would like to work out some type of mechanism to facilitate the settlement of claims between the two countries, especially for private environmental damages not covered by "cleanup" terminology.

Perspectives

The issues just described span a continent and affect the air and water in heavily populated, rural, and wilderness areas. Such disparate issues and settings would appear to have little in common. Nevertheless, a few elements justify their being grouped together and distinguish them from otherwise similar situations in other parts of the world.

In the first place, Canada is more often the victim than the villain. Canadians suffer or fear that they will suffer from United States actions in connection with many of the issues discussed. The environmental intrusions or changes from the United States are not surprising, for it is much more heavily populated and industrialized than Canada. Many regions are under environmental stress, and the boundary areas are no exception. In the future, more damages may originate from Canada as it exploits its resources along the border and as the already established population concentrations in southern Canada become larger. The threats to the East Poplar and Flathead rivers in the United States from Canadian energy projects are an illustration of this possibility. However, at present, Canada still suffers more, and the disproportionate flow northward of damaging environmental intrusions will likely continue.

The frontier is open to environmental damages originating from projects in either country, but it often excludes the beneficial goods or services to which the projects give rise. Bringing no compensating employment or other benefits to local citizens, such damages become issues that are easy to exploit by local political leaders. In Canada, nationalist sentiment sometimes adds another dimsension. Many issues are essentially local, but they can easily flare up to hold national attention for brief periods. No domestic trade-offs need be made with other sectoral or regional interests, for no one benefits anywhere in Canada. Consequently, local politicians and interest groups worried about damages from across the border find a sympathetic ear at the national level. An appeal to national unity over the issue is not unusual.

The Skagit issue is an illustration. On the instigation of an opposition Member of Parliament from British Columbia, Parliament passed a unanimous resolution condemning Seattle's proposed project to flood into Canada. The Department of External Affairs abhors such spontaneous tactics, but it could find no supporters within the ruling Liberal party to challenge the environmentalist and nationalist resolution or to press for a more moderate approach. This case is typical; there are few conflicting political interests within Canada to moderate transfrontier issues at the national level. Not until the administration is faced with the problem of formulating a consistent policy does the Canadian position become subdued.

In any case, for many inland water controversies, Ottawa is constrained by the provinces in the responses it can make. For example, the 1972 Great Lakes Water Quality Agreement represents as much the culmination of diplomatic exchange and agreement between the two sovereign authorities of Ontario and Canada as between Canada and the United States. Again, in its attempts to resolve the Skagit issue, Ottawa has been restricted by the narrow range and, to Ottawa, unrealistic and unreasonable alternatives that British Columbia has offered. Of course, the United States is also a federal system, but the states do not have the provinces' powers over industrial, transportation, property, civil rights, water, and other natural-resource issues.

In some other issues, Ottawa has no national policy on which to work out compromise solutions with Washington. For example, the United States has felt the natural-resource and energy squeeze more intensely than Canada. As a result, the federal government has faced up to an agreed national policy, such as the development of Alaskan oil, at an early stage, whereas Canada has yet to formulate many aspects of taxation, export, or transportation policy for development of its oil and gas reserves in the Arctic.

By 1973 the United States was committed to developing its Alaskan oil reserves. At that time it may have been willing to meet Canadian objections to the transportaion of Alaskan oil through the Juan de Fuca Straits and San Juan Islands if Canada could have offered an acceptable alternative. An offer to the United States to participate in the development and use of a MacKenzie Valley Oil pipeline or to supply United States West Coast oil refineries with Canadian oil might have been acceptable. But these alternatives for solving the specific problem of West Coast oil tanker traffic close to Canadian coastal waters entail wide-ranging policy decisions. Such a policy might have to entail decisions about accommodating or ignoring native aspirations in the North, the timing of the exploitation of oil reserves and the construction of a pipeline, the possible export of oil to the United States in face of domestic fears of a "continental" energy policy, and the degree of energy independence to maintain. In short, for this and some other issues Ottawa is unwilling to let a local controversy force premature creation of important national policy with wide-ranging consequences.

In such circumstances, lacking for constitutional reasons a firm power base and lacking a formulated national policy, Ottawa has tended to bark rather than bite. Carping and complaining provide some emotional outlet when it is unprepared or unable to offer the United States constructive or forthright solutions. Of course, temporizing is not unique to Canada or its environmental foreign policy. However, it does little to improve relations between countries or to satisfy domestic political demands.

National foreign policy priorities also subdue Ottawa's diplomatic response to Canadian domestic protest against United States spillovers. Transfrontier incidents are regional in impact and, like all national governments, Ottawa must balance the regional issue against the broader perspective of bilateral relations between countries. It does not want unrestrained protest to poison the atmosphere. On some issues, therefore, Ottawa may simply ignore regional protests or downplay them. For example, in British Columbia the provincial government and many citizens feel that in the 1961 Columbia River Treaty the province and Ottawa made an egregiously bad bargain, and so they want to reopen the bargaining. But Ottawa feels it has no leverage with which to get any concessions from the United States. It does not even have domestic support to make concessions to the Americans to interest them in reopening the treaty. Further, such a move could only damage Canada's credibility when it signs other international agreements. Hence, it has simply ignored such regional demands.

The traditional channels and forms of communication between capitals have also dampened the audibility of Canadian dissatisfaction. The response of the Canadian government may be perfectly clear to the State Department, itself versed in the subtleties of diplomatic exchange, but when it reaches the politicians engaged in the hurly-burly of specific issues in Washington the Canadian response may emerge as irresolute and be misunderstood. For example, Canada evidently considers the Garrison case to be a black and white issue. In its own manner it has protested strongly and consistently against the proposal. However, by the time the Canadian messages filtered down to the congressional subcommittees responsible for funding the project the protest was termed "weak"; opponents to Garrison in the United States were reported as "bitterly disappointed" by the lack of a firm Canadian response.

Although External Affairs and other departments tend to stick to traditional channels of communication and exchange, there are many opportunities for them and Canadian interest groups to engage in transnational coalition building and other forms of intervention to pursue more forcefully Canadian interests in the United States. Groups in the United States that for their own reasons oppose projects like the High Ross Dam, the Garrison project, and the Eastport refinery look to Ottawa for support in their struggle. But, for the reasons that constrain Canadian protest mentioned above, Ottawa would prefer the issues to be settled within the United States. It would rather have its battles fought for it by the United States groups rather than make a strong stand itself and possibly irritate Washington.

In general, there are opportunities to use the whole network of transnational (nonofficial) relations, both for and against environmental changes. Trade unions and multinational corporations work on both sides of the border and have not hesitated to use personnel, funds, research, and propaganda media to obtain favorable domestic Canadian or IJC decisions. American energy policy is implicity represented at Ottawa by the goals of United States oil companies in Canada. Many of these circuits can be reversed.

In recent years, Canadian interest groups have taken advantage of opportunities for standing before United States domestic tribunals to present the Canadian views of United States projects. The ROSS Committee is an official intervenor before the FPC in its deliberations over permitting construction of the High Ross Dam. Canadian groups have participated in the court review of the trans-Alaska pipeline environmental impact assessment. However, such groups feel uncomfortable and find the experience of having to defend Canadian interests before United States tribunals distasteful. Furthermore, it already concedes to the United States jurisdiction which in some cases might still be in dispute. Also, with increasing nationalist feeling among Canadian groups, they are not inclined to seek out allies in the United States. The trend may be for interest groups to rely again more on Ottawa to convey their feelings to Washington.

Not all issues along the frontier are simple one-way spillovers. Where the resources are shared, as in the Great Lakes or on the Saint John River, environmental damages are reciprocal. Water quality problems can be particularly difficult to remedy because the problems emerge from the methods of production and patterns of settlement in a country. Policy in each country must be tempered by the need to make domestic trade-offs between groups resisting increased costs for pollution abatement and those who favor improved water and overall environmental quality. The costs of pollution abatement are easily determined, but the values that can be attributed to environmental quality are largely intangible and differ with the attitudes and perceptions of each country.

Fortunately, Canada and the United States have similar perceptions of environmental quality. The 1972 Great Lakes Water Quality Agreement indicates that where perceptions of the problems and of the desired objectives are similar fruitful cooperation can result. Significant problems can still arise in the implementation, for the priorities or methods of implementation that either side establishes for the cleanup of a shared resource may vary, but the nature of the problem is much less difficult than where there is no agreement in principle.

The shared perceptions between the two countries permits ready agreement on the need for resolution of specific issues. But between agreement on goals and final implementation, a number of domestic and international snags may frustrate solutions to the problems. It is in this context that the IJC performs such an important role in Canada-United States environmental relations. The IJC heads off some potential problems through its approval procedures for projects that alter the water levels at the border. Its orders of approval are granted only when there are no major objections to a water project from the other country. If there are no major objections, the orders usually take into account issues raised by either side.

The approval procedure is designed more for changes in water levels and flows than for pollution or other environmental issues. For these, there is typically a reference by both countries to consider a potential or existing environmental problem. Agreement on goals is already implied, and both countries can be reasonably assured through the past performance of the IJC that the solution it recommends will be within the range of alternatives they considered acceptable when making the reference. Thus the IJC provides a mechanism to produce impartial solutions that can be accepted by both sides. When the issue is very contentious and local passions are aroused, the IJC's greatest contribution is to provide a means of obtaining agreed and trusted technical and social data. Rarely, by the time it reports, are there any facts in dispute. In the absence of the IJC's technical board procedures, neither side would have the same confidence in each other's proposal, and the resolution of problems might be needlessly hindered by endless debate about technical issues.

The recognized impartiality of the IJC reports can also be used by the Departments of State and External Affairs to elicit political support or calm domestic opposition to proposals that both departments seek. The role of the IJC is important and its work is apparent in many of the issues discussed. The point should be emphasized, however, that it operates most successfully when there is a consensus between the countries on the possibility of solutions to specific problems and only quantitative issues must be resolved. Without this much agreement there will be no reference to the IJC. In general, the most difficult outstanding environmental problems between the two countries may still be worked out on a bilateral basis.

Overall, reaction to specific issues can be shrill and increase the heat between the two countries for brief periods, but the number is small and the impact of these issues on Canada-United States relations is not great. The shared demand for environmental quality, although not everywhere uniform and often distorted by the disproportionate distribution of damages, is perhaps the main reason why the environmental controversies do not play a more prominent role in Canada-United States relations. Another reason is the practice, in large part facilitated by the work of the IJC, to discuss problems before they blow up.

Environmental relations in the future may be strained by other aspects of Canada-United States relations that have an environmental dimension but have little to do with the transfrontier spillovers. United States participation in the development or purchase of Canadian energy is an example. The environmental damage in British Columbia from the Columbia Treaty Dams aggravates Canadian feeling toward the low economic return that critics of the treaty feel British Columbia has received. Dissatisfaction may arise in other projects where Canadians may sell their power to the United States, such as from the major hydrodams in northern Manitoba, Quebec, and Labrador. Possible United States participation in an Arctic oil pipeline scheme might also create similar antagonisms. The problems arise not from United States action but through Canadian failure to anticipate fully costs and changing values in working out agreements. The problems would in effect be Canada's own fault, but pressures from the United States to reach agreement and Canadian unwillingness to live with onerous terms of a commitment could work to antagonize all relations. Perhaps for these reasons there is considerable pressure at the national level to avoid continental energy commitments, although the provinces' sales ambitions for their resources are not easily restrained by Ottawa.

The future prospects for environmental relations otherwise remain much the same: periodic outbursts of indignation against specific proposals, but on the whole characterized by slow resolution of problems case by case, in part attributable to the need for the Canadian government to work out an agreement, not only with the United States, but also with provinces over the use of their natural resources. Some small changes might be expected. Canada could be the villain in more issues as its population expands and it develops its resources along the border. The slow incremental pace of resolving particular issues may not satisfy domestic critics whose toleration of compromise solution may be slight. If, for example, oil spills occur along the West Coast to confirm Canadian environmental fears, the incident may for a period flash into intense resentment. Issues involving reciprocal damages should be more amenable to agreement as each side shares similar evaluations of the benefits from eliminating transfrontier damages.

Transfrontier environmental conflict can be explosive because of the disproportionate distribution of benefits and costs and, at least in Canada, the ease with which nationalist feeling can be aroused and the independent position from the federal government the provinces can take. Thus considerable sensitivity is required in the management of environmental bilateral relations. But, if each side retains its understanding of the problems faced by the other, environmental issues need not escalate the level of tension between Canada and the United States.

The authors wish to express their thanks to Ray Robinson of Environment Canada for his invaluable information and comments in the preparation of this report.

The Optimum Use of
Canadian Resources

CARL E. BEIGIE

To Canadians, the title of this essay is likely to be provoca-
tive, at least when placed in the context of major issues in the Canada-
United States relationship. An ability to determine the rate at which a
nation's resources will be developed, and then the share of production that
will be made available for export markets, has come to be regarded by
many Canadians as the litmus test of sovereignty. This essay will therefore eschew any notion of a joint bilateral or North American determination of what is optimal in Canadian resource use. Furthermore, it will
reflect the author's view that a volume on Canadian-American relations
is not an appropriate place to enter into a normative evaluation of policy
decisions made in Canada regarding the use of Canadian resources.

What, then, is left to discuss? First, Canada has taken, or is contemplat-
ing taking, new directions in the field of resource policy that could affect
the bilateral relationship in fundamental ways. This essay will describe
briefly some of these new directions, explore the basic forces to which
Canadian resource policy initiatives are responding, and outline the most
important bilateral implications that are likely to arise from these initiatives. Second, if one accepts the principle of sovereignty in resource decisions, basic changes in those decisions that occur rapidly may have high
transitional costs on external parties. Examples of such transitional costs
will be provided here to illustrate the genesis of frictions in the bilateral
relationship. Third, Canada and the United States share certain resources
(air, water, migratory fish, and fowl), and in these cases it is appropriate
to consider optimum resource use in a bilateral context.

Resources cover such a wide range of topics, many of which could be
the subject of separate essays, that the approach here must be selective and
illustrative. Moreover, attention will be focused, at least at the outset, on

conceptualization of the optimum use question, with an attempt to integrate economic and political factors.

The term "optimum" must be distinguished carefully from the term "maximum." It would be possible to base economic policy on the goals of maximizing growth, employment, or price stability, for example, but it has proven impossible thus far to devise a set of policies to maximize all three goals simultaneously. When trade-offs are required, with somewhat faster growth achieved only at the expense of somewhat less price stability, say, an optimum balance among results must be sought. Thus the concept of optimization applies to situations in which at least two distinct policy objectives exist, neither of which is likely to be maximized in the optimal solution.

It is possible to determine whether a maximum has been achieved by reasonably objective criteria. For example, an engineering assessment can be made of the physical capacity of a production facility, and actual output can then be compared with this capacity estimate to see if the maximum level has been achieved. Optimality, in contrast, is often a highly subjective concept. One individual, or one nation collectively, may regard a particular solution to a set of policy targets as being more or less desirable than another individual or nation. Economists focus on such questions as: Have scarce resources been utilized with maximum possible efficiency? Or, in cases of multiple objectives: Would it be possible to move further toward the fulfillment of one goal without sacrificing the progress that has been achieved in fulfilling other goals? Economics, however, does not provide a foundation on which to judge whether one goal is inherently better or worse than another; the process whereby goals are ranked lies largely in the domain of political science.

Economists fall back on market forces to resolve optimality issues. Prices, it is argued, convey results that are determined by, and which in turn help determine, individual decisions regarding conflicting objectives. A basic theme in this essay is that Canadian policy directions generally, and in the area of resources particularly, appear to reflect a much more skeptical attitude toward a resolution of trade-offs in the marketplace than do United States policy directions. The foundation for this skepticism has not yet been fully explained or carefully analyzed. What can be discerned are the notions that markets are somehow being manipulated against Canadian national or regional interests and that markets, even when not so manipulated, fail to capture adequately all those factors that are perceived as being important in policy formation. In any event, it would be worth exploring some of the possible implications for bilateral relations that might emerge from fundamentally different attitudes and approaches regarding the role of the market place in the two countries.

The term "resources" is used in both a broad and a narrow sense in economics. In the broad sense, resources encompass a nation's labor supply, including various skill dimensions, its capital stock (e.g., buildings and equipment), its technological base, and its raw materials. It is only in such a broad context that a full discussion of the optimum use question can be provided. Still, current usage generally confines the term "resources" to commodities that are, directly or indirectly, the product of land. The reasons for focusing on this class of resources undoubtedly reflect the notions of a national "birthright" and territory, the essence of political sovereignty.

A distinction is traditionally made between "renewable" and "nonrenewable resources." This distinction has considerable emotional appeal as a basis for policy formation at a time when there is widespread concern over the possibility that the world is "running out" of essential resources. It is also a distinction that is nearly devoid of meaning in questions concerning the optimum use of resources.

At a global level, the output of, or from, virtually any resource—renewable or nonrenewable—can be expanded greatly through the application of a sufficient amount of labor, capital, and technology. The critical issue is the incremental cost of achieving this expansion of supply. It is conceivable, and even likely, that increased output from renewable resources (e.g., food from arable land) will be more costly than increased output from nonrenewable resources (e.g., energy from coal). Even if a resource is physically used up in the consumption process, resource-policy decisions that are optimal must reflect prospects for new discoveries, substitution of other means for meeting basic needs, and technological innovations. Moreover, some nonrenewable resources can be recycled in the consumption process.

The mistake is quite often made in the United States of thinking that Canada has an identifiable, unified approach to resource policy. This perception is inaccurate for at least two reasons.

First, the individual provinces have the power under the British North America Act to determine the terms under which resources within their territories will be developed. Differences exist among these provinces in basic areas such as taxation, ownership, and production for external markets. Moreover, the distribution of resources within Canada is quite uneven, leading to all the traditional problems in reconciling producer and consumer interests. A prime example is provided by the continuing debate over the appropriate domestic price for oil.

Second, even at a national level, where decisions regarding terms for supplying export markets are vested, essential ingredients of an overall resource policy are lacking. There has not been a determination, for example, regarding self-sufficiency targets. Nor has there been any clear enunciation of the government's objectives regarding the role of resources in the future evolution of the Canadian economy.

An appropriate description of Canadian resource policies would be that they reflect Canada's position as a resource-surplus, industrialized nation that continues to experience periodic balance-of-payments difficulties. This position involves complicated trade-offs between desires and realities and between national objectives and international constraints. The nature of these trade-offs in the context of the Canada-United States relationship is outlined below.

Canada As a Resource-Surplus Nation

A quick assessment of Canada's importance as a source of resources is provided in table 1, showing production and consumption of selected re-

TABLE 1

Canada's Share of Selected Resources
and Commodities (Based on 1972 and 1973 Data)
(percentage of free-world production and consumption)

	Production	Consumption
Asbestos	63.7	3.2
Nickel	50.0	2.4
Pulp	38.5	3.8
Newsprint	38.4	3.5
Zinc	27.8	7.2
Silver	26.5	5.4
Uranium	19.8	1.7
Hydropower	16.6	16.6
Lead	14.4	2.3
Copper	13.6	3.9
Iron ore	11.6	3.1
Grains	6.4	3.1
Gold	4.9	1.9
Wheat	4.5	1.3
Crude oil	3.5	3.1

Source: Greenshields Incorporated, *Canada: Resources and Potential* (Summer 1974), pp. 26–27.

sources and commodities. Crude materials are much more important in Canadian exports than in Canadian imports. If one excludes automotive products, which are affected by the special provisions of the Canada-United States agreement, crude materials represent 40 percent of Canadian exports, more than twice the share in imports.

The pressures on resource policy formation in Canada are similar to those in any other resource-surplus country at the present time. These pressures will be examined under the headings of rent collection, further processing, and market stabilization.

Rent collection. "Economic rents" arise when price exceeds the full cost of production (including a normal return on financial capital employed) of a commodity or good. These rents may be the result of a particularly favorable production location (saving transportations costs), an unusually rich ore deposit (saving on refining costs), an especially shallow and concentrated oil pool (saving on development costs), etc. In short, differential cost conditions are likely to exist for the variety of sources needed to meet demand, giving rise to differential rents. If these rents are not taxed away, through charges such as leasing and royalties, firms operating these various supply sources will have a range of rates of profitability reflecting these differential rents. However, companies are likely to be utilizing a number of sources with different cost conditions, in which case the range of profitability rates will be reduced.

It is natural to expect nations, or regions, within which resources are located to seek to capture the greatest possible share of economic rents. The problem is the extreme difficulty of determining how high these rents actually are and then collecting them in an efficient manner. Provincial governments in Canada are experimenting with new forms of resource taxation, but there is considerable evidence that several of them may have gone too far, reducing the incentives necessary to sustain production and additional investment.

In most instances, Canada is not the source of high-rent resources. Potential supplies of many resources are abundant, but they can be exploited only at relatively high cost. This fact has tended to be overlooked, however, as a result of recent sharp commodity price increases that accompanied worldwide shortages. Profits of many resource companies surged as price had to serve the function of rationing available supplies. These high but temporary profits attracted public attention and created pressures for governments, which were desperate for revenue to pay for rapid expenditure growth, to tax those profits away. In doing so, tax measures have been adopted that have the effect of raising costs permanently, or at least until market reactions force governments to reduce them.

As the adjustments to temporary shortages take place, sources of supply with high costs (inclusive of new taxes) are likely to have difficulty finding markets at prices high enough to cover these costs. Investment activity may shift to other regions. Governments, mistaking this process for a "show of force" by the producer companies, whose bigness makes them particularly vulnerable to government action, are likely to come to the conclusion that they must expropriate these companies, or get into the production business themselves with new companies, if rents are to be fully captured. This line of reasoning is one of the basic explanations for Saskatchewan's recent announcement that it intends to take over its potash industry, much of which is now operated by American interests, and for the decision by the federal government to establish Petrocan, a new national oil production and marketing company.

Canada is no different from most other resource-export countries in its objectives for collecting resource rents. The combination of high rates of inflation, which have complicated the task of determining true rents, and the difficulties of constructing an efficient rent-collection system has produced serious disruptions in private investment decisions. Risks have increased in the form of a greater likelihood of government expropriation and in reduced rewards for exploration and new production activities because of the likelihood that successful ventures will be heavily taxed, leaving inadequate incentives for taking chances on exploration. The probable result of this situation will either be a growing gap between resource needs and supplies as the world economy recovers from its recent recession or a greater involvement of public funds in high-risk resource ventures undertaken by government enterprises. It is doubtful that the Canadian public is going to regard the latter as an optimum use of general tax revenues when, as is inevitable in this kind of economic activity, government enterprises are announced.

A resolution of these issues probably requires three types of responses. First, inflation must be brought under greater control if large distortions in the true rent picture are to be reduced. Second, new and more flexible systems for rent collection must be devised. Third, private companies must take the initiative in responding to the public's "need to know" the true profitability prospects of its operations. This "need to know" and the perception that private companies hide basic information from the public represent key factors in Canadian decisions to take the route of greater participation by government enterprises in resource activities.[1]

Further processing.[2] Canada, in common with most other resource-exporting countries, is seeking to upgrade domestic value added in the processing of its resources prior to export. In pursuit of this objective, it has included further processing as one of the criteria for evaluating proposals for foreign direct investments falling within the terms of reference of the Foreign Investment Review Agency. In addition, in May 1974, Parliament passed amendments to the Export and Import Permits Act which empower the federal government to impose export controls to "ensure that any action taken to promote further processing in Canada of a resource that is produced in Canada is not rendered ineffective by reason of the unrestricted exportation of that natural resource."

It is generally known that tariffs in most countries (including Canada) tend to increase with higher stages of processing. This tariff "escalation" distorts optimum economic activity in both exporting and importing

---

[1] In the case of oil sands development, government participation has been sought by private companies because of the exceptional risks involved. See Judith Maxwell, *HRI Observations,* no. 10, *Developing New Energy Sources: The Syncrude Case* (Montreal: C.D. Howe Research Institute, 1975).

[2] This section relies heavily on Louis Silver's *HRI Observations,* no. 6, *The Pursuit of Further Processing of Canada's Natural Resources* (Montreal: C.D. Howe Research Institute, 1975).

countries and limits job opportunities that are perceived as attractive in the resource-exporting nations. There is also a view, shared by many in Canada, that there are high profits to be made in processing activities, although the theoretical foundation for this view is weak. To return to the concept of rents, nations with the resources have the power to capture these rents at the source; additional excess profits from further processing would have to be the result of market power in the processing and fabricating stages, independent of the resource rent. Of course, there is also an interest in the employment potential of processing activities, but here again the relative employment advantage of processing, as compared with other uses for labor, are not self-evident, especially since high income societies employ most of their labor forces in service industries, many of which are even more labor intensive.

It remains unclear how far Canada might go with its processing objectives. The concept of "sectoral approaches" to trade liberalization is being emphasized by Canada at the current GATT negotiations, but this concept has not been clearly defined in terms of priorities or negotiating mechanics, and Canada's position appears to be more selective that that of the nonindustrialized nations in UNCTAD.

The more serious bilateral issues arising in the area of further processing concern United States fears that Canada will add new distortions in access to supplies rather than simply trying to remove existing distortions in access to markets. Will Canada employ the use of export controls and two-price systems to create an artificial incentive to locate production facilities in Canada even when competitive cost conditions, if observed, favor location elsewhere? Will Canada restrict resource supplies out of a concern that these exports are being used to maintain operations in other countries that would, if built today, be located in Canada on cost grounds? It would be premature to try to answer these questions now, but it is understandable that the United States would have these fears in the face of an absence of firm trading rules and sanctions in the resource area.

Market stabilization. The traditional plight of resource-exporting nations is that of sharp fluctuations in international commodity prices. Canada has diversified its export earnings considerably in recent years, so commodity-price stabilization does not have as high a priority as in less-developed countries. Still, market stabilization figures in issues that have emerged in the bilateral relationship for two reasons.

First, government revenues in several of the provinces depend very much on resource developments. In the potash industry, for example, prices and quantities demanded have fluctuated markedly in recent years, and so has the revenue from taxation of the industry in Saskatchewan. The provincial government has supported attempts to stabilize the market, but the conditions in this industry are not conducive to stabilization in the absence of a degree of international coordination that is unlikely to be achieved. One of the reasons for the announcement by the province that it will take over the industry is a belief that government ownership will assist the stabilization process. In effect, the government is betting that it can run the industry with greater stability as a state monopoly than private firms could, even though one of the rationales used to explain the expropriation is that the perceived market power of these firms to control the market has worked to the disadvantage of provincial interests.

Second, income stabilization policies have appeared with increasing frequency in Canadian agriculture. These programs, involving marketing boards, insurance schemes, and price supports, need not create serious issues if they serve the sole purpose of income stabilization through, say, well-administered buffer stocks. But in a number of instances (e.g., eggs), stabilization is accompanied by restrictions on production or indirect subsidization of high-cost producers. These programs create a situation in which imports must be restricted in order to protect the domestic market. Alternatively, surplus production must be disposed of in external markets at prices below domestic support levels.

Canada as an Industrialized Nation

Canada is the most industrialized nation among the major resource-surplus nations. As a result, while it faces pressures similar to those in other industrialized nations concerning disruptions in world commodity markets, it has a somewhat broader range of options for dealing with these disruptions, at least in areas where a resource surplus currently exists. Its choice regarding the appropriate option to exercise is bound to affect the bilateral relationship, particularly when it is difficult to separate motives pertaining to Canada as an industrialized nation from those pertaining to Canada as a resource-exporting nation.

The area of energy resources provides sufficient latitude to examine the major points at issue. The actions of the Organization of Petroleum Exporting Countries (OPEC) cartel have forced all industrialized nations to reassess their domestic energy policies. For some of these nations (e.g., Japan), there is really no alternative to making the best possible arrangement to ensure a continuing access to external sources of supply. For others, including both Canada and the United States, domestic energy potentials provide greater flexibility. The fundamental issue concerns the optimum trade-off between the objective of least-cost sources of supply, on the one hand, and the most secure sources of supply, on the other hand. The resolution of this trade-off, which simply cannot be made on strict economic criteria alone, is summarized in decisions concerning the optimum degree of domestic self-sufficiency. Neither Canada nor the United States has made this decision, but to increase self-sufficiency in the short run Canada has taken actions that have affected the bilateral relationship.

Prior to the OPEC-induced disruptions in world energy markets, Canada met roughly half of its oil needs from imports from OPEC countries (principally Venezuela) and exported an approximately equivalent amount to the United States. (An interesting parallel exists in coal. Canadian production in the West is used for exports to third countries; eastern needs are supplied by imports from the United States.) In order to meet a greater share of its oil needs from domestic sources, a pipeline from the West is now being extended from Sarnia, Ontario, to Montreal, Quebec. In order to fill this pipeline, exports to the United States had to be diverted, since traditional producing regions have apparently passed their peak operating rate and cannot be counted on for increased output. This phasing out of exports was begun prior to the completion of the pipeline extension, with production being "shut in" on a temporary basis.

A related issue arising from the security of supply considerations concerns the pace at which new resources will be developed. Proved reserves may be regarded as an inventory of potential supplies—an inventory that increases a nation's future consumption options. Economists, as well as resource companies, are likely to stress the principle that resources should be developed when market price exceeds production costs. But suppose the nation, or province, that has these reserves decides that market prices do not adequately reflect the future scarcity value of resources. This may result from either greater skepticism about the future pace of advance in the development of technology or of substitutes for resources that are classed as nonrenewable, concerns about the well-being of future generations, or simply a desire to minimize future risks of external supply disruptions. There may be high costs associated with these views, but the choice of measures to respond to them may be made in full recognition of these costs.

There is one other important factor that arises from Canada's being both an energy-surplus and an industrialized economy. Major resource development projects may have a destabilizing impact on Canadian prospects in manufacturing sectors. The exchange rate may be boosted by the capital inflows to fund the project and the export earnings from the output of the project, wage rates may be bid up as labor is sought to construct the project, and inflation may be accelerated by the additional demands placed on the economy by the project. To the extent that there is discretion over the undertaking of the project, the above considerations may lead to delays and a stretching-out process. This may be widely interpreted as an unfriendly act by people in the United States who do not understand Canadian objectives for more balanced economic growth and the problems created in meeting these objectives by major resource projects.

There is a fairly widespread view in Canada that resources have been used to "bail out" the country from balance-of-payments deficits resulting from "spending beyond its means." In the early 1970s, Canada's trade account improved markedly, creating the impression that it had greater flexibility in its approach to foreign investment issues generally and resource issues in particular. Since that time, however, Canada's trade position has deteriorated badly, despite a so-called floating exchange rate, with a current account deficit of about $5.5 to $6 billion in 1975.

Canada has chosen to finance this deficit by attracting foreign capital inflows with interest rates significantly above those in the United States. It is probable that the deficit will narrow somewhat as the United States economy recovers its momentum, which will stimulate Canadian exports, especially in resource sectors and automotive products. But Canada faces serious problems in its external accounts: its unit labor costs have increased sharply in relation to those in the United States; a depreciation in the external value of the Canadian dollar would help exports, but it would also add significantly to domestic inflation problems; and there are major constraints and risks associated with a need to rely on high interest rates to attract foreign debt capital to offset a large deficit on current account transactions.

What this probably means is that Canada's resource decisions in the near term will have to reflect a need to develop supplies for export markets and to permit, indeed to attract, foreign investments to make sure that this development takes place. In short, the degree of independence in Canadian resource policies can be no greater than is allowed by Canadian decisions and behavior affecting the broader economy. This fact will be resisted by resource nationalists, but it will be reflected in the actions of policy pragmatists.

The United States has not been unsympathetic to Canada's announced intention to pursue new directions in its resource policies. This attitude is appropriate in that long-term resource decisions should be regarded as the prerogative of sovereign nations. Still, there are two types of friction generated by short-term dislocations emerging either from changes in resource policy directions, or from decisions required in the face of temporary supply disruptions.

The first type of friction is illustrated by the Canadian decision to phase out oil exports to the United States. The decision itself has been much less of an issue than the way it has been implemented. Instead of maintaining production and exports at existing rates (taking into account declines in physical capacity) until the Sarnia-Montreal pipeline extension was completed later in 1976, Canada shut in production temporarily. As a result, it will be able to extend its ability to supply the market east of the Ottawa Valley, at consumption rates projected for 1982, by a little over one year.

This modest extension has been achieved at a cost to Canada of the potential return from earnings that would have been made from earlier sales of this shut-in production. Perhaps this is a cost Canadians would be willing to pay, but the amounts have not been calculated for the Canadian public. What has not been figured in the cost-benefit calculation, however, is the impact of supply cutbacks to refiners in the "Northern Tier" states that established these facilities in anticipation of a continued interest on the part of Canada to maintain its exports. (Decisions to restrict natural gas exports to United States customers would be even more disruptive, since alternative sources and transportation facilities would be harder to obtain than in the case of oil.)

A second type of friction concerns the sharing of temporary supply disruptions, and the energy area provides another example here. In 1974, production problems in the British Columbia natural gas fields created shortages in western markets. These shortages were imposed on export customers in the state of Washington without proration and despite the fact that there were long-term contracts involved (in contrast to oil, which is exported under short-term permits). This was a decision of the British Columbia government and caused some embarrassment to the federal government. The point, however, is that in the absence of some bilateral understanding on sharing short-term shortages, frictions are inevitable.

It is interesting to compare experience with other resources. Because Canada and the United States occupy the same continent, certain natural resources are shared. These resources include rivers flowing across the boundary, lakes straddling the boundary, and air passing over the boundary. There have been many occasions when bilateral issues have arisen over shared resources; two recent ones were the Garrison River Diversion Project and the proposed raising of the water level at the Ross Dam.

These issues are rarely allowed to become points of serious friction. Both countries recognize common responsibilities, adhere to agreed procedures for resolving disputes, and accept the principle of compensation for injured parties. In fact, the main reason for mentioning this class of resources is to point up the difference with respect to resources that are not shared.

Conclusion

This discussion of the optimum use of Canadian resources has been confined to issues with a legitimate bilateral focus. Canada has, in this author's view, made some curious decisions relating to resource policy. For example, it is hard to comprehend why it continues to use general tax revenues to maintain the level of domestic oil prices below the price of imports now that Canada has become a net importer of oil. This policy discourages both conservation and supply expansion.

But what is the legitimate bilateral issue here? It can hardly be that Canada is in some sense wasting world resources, since it is not clear what the proper price for oil really is in the face of the monopoly power of OPEC and, in any event, Canada is paying the world price for its imports. Canada might be regarded as wasting its own resources in violation of some assumed set of international principles, but this is not a bilateral issue.

The serious bilateral issues in this case come down to two considerations: Does the low domestic oil price act as an artificial inducement for production activities to be located in Canada that would otherwise be placed in the United States? Does Canada's oil policy involve inappropriate short-term costs to the United States? The author's view is that the answer to the first question is probably no, so long as firms are aware of the medium-term oil supply outlook in Canada, which is not favorable. The second question deserves a qualified yes, the qualification being an assumption that both countries wish to maintain cordial, rather than strictly arm's-length, relations.

Two clear conclusions do emerge from an observation of the Canadian scene: "Waste" is a far different concept to an economist than to the politician, and much more readily accepted by the latter. There are substantial sacrifices involved in optimizing in a Canadian context alone.

The author's expectation would be that Canada will find that decisions concerning optimum resource use cannot be made in isolation from opportunities provided in the United States market. (An example is likely to be seen in the eventual decision to bring Arctic energy resources to markets using joint transportation facilities.) Some of the thornier issues arising in the resource field—such as export controls, sharing of temporary shortages, and two-price systems—are most likely to be resolved in a multilateral rather than a strictly bilateral context.

Index

Agriculture, 9, 126, 134, 171
Air pollution, 153
Aird commission, 64-65
Alaska pipeline, 121, 122
Alberta, 44, 45, 49, 50, 51, 78-79, 118, 121, 157
Anglo-Canadians, 10-11
Anti-American sentiment, 38
Atomic energy, 102
Automotive Trade Agreement (automobile pact), 7, 15, 17, 22, 131

Bain, Joe S., 92
Balance of payments, 124, 143
Banking systems, 5
Bilingualism. See Quebec, language issue in
Book publishing, 72-73
Bourassa, Robert, 31, 33-36
Broadcasting, 64-67
British Columbia, 157-62 passim
British North America Act, 51, 53-62, 166
Business community, 2-9

Canada Council, 73
Canadian: perceptions of the United States, 14-26; policy toward the United States, 16-17; studies, 1
Canadian Broadcasting Corporation (CBC), 65-67
Canadian Radio and Television Commission (CRTC), 66
Canadian Transport Commission, 47, 48
Canadian-U.S. Parliamentary Committee, 3
Central Canada, 41, 44
China, 100, 108, 110
Coal,
Cold war, 19, 22, 112

Columbia River Treaty, 3
Columbia Treaty Dams, 162
Committee for an Independent Canada, 74
Common Market: See European Economic Community
Confederation, 28, 33, 34, 54
Conference of the Committee on Disarmament (CCD), 109
Conference on International Economic Cooperation (CIEC), 133
Conference on Security and Cooperation in Europe (CSCE), 109
Conally, John, 124-25
Congress, U.S., 7, 17, 125, 126
Constitution Canadian, 78. See also British North America Act
Consumer and Corporate Affairs, Department of, 97, 98
Cuba, 108
Culture, Canadian, 20, 24, 26; homogenization of, 19-21
"Countervailing tax incentives," 140, 142

de Gaulle, Charles, 30
Détente, East-West, 100-102, 107-12
Deterrence, United States, 102-6, 110-12
Dickey-Lincoln Dams, 151
Diefenbaker government, 68
Domestic International Sales Corporations (DISC), 139-40, 142, 145-47
Duplessis, Maurice, 29

East Poplar River, 155
Eastern Canada, 116, 119, 122
Eastport, Maine, 150

Economic Council of Canada, 17, 21, 26, 97, 132, 136
Economic integration, 18, 21
Energy, 7, 113-23, 126, 135, 171, 174-75; policy, 49. See also Oil
European Economic Community (EEC), 86, 90, 111, 124-36 passim, 139
Export and Import Permits Act, amendments to, 169
External Affairs, Department of, 32, 122, 158, 161

Faulkner, Hugh, 69-70
Federal Power Commission, U.S., 120, 156
Federal-Provincial Tax Equalization Grant, 51
Film Development Corporation, 67
Films, 67
Finance Committee, Senate, 131
Flathead River, 155
Ford, Gerald R., 110
Foreign Investment Review Act (1973), 7-8, 38
Foreign Investment Review Agency (FIRA), 18, 26, 38, 83, 95-96, 98, 169
Foreign Ownership and the Structure of Canadian Industry, 96
Foreign Policy for Canadians, 24-25, 75
France, 30, 31, 98, 126
French Canada, 10, 27-39, 41, 63, 66-67. See also Quebec

General Agreement on Tariffs and Trade (GATT), 17, 97, 127, 132, 170
Garrison River Diversion Project, 153-54, 160, 174
Georgia, Straits of, 156-57
Government of Canada, 53, 58-59. See also Ottawa
Great Lakes water levels, 152-53
Great Lakes Water Quality Agreement, 152, 158, 161

Hartke, Vance, 131
High Ross Dam, 156, 160, 174

Industrial incentive policies, 137-48
Industry, Canadian, 26, 45. See also Investments, foreign
Inflation, 129, 169, 172
International Energy Agency (IEA), 117, 118
International Joint Commission (IJC), 16, 18, 22, 149-62 passim
International Monetary Fund, 136

Investments, foreign, 5-8; in manufacturing, 88-99; in primary industries, 75-87

Jamieson, Donald, 26
Japan, 91, 100, 114, 115, 118, 126, 131, 136
Juan de Fuca, 156-57
Judicial Committee of the British Privy Council, 55-61

King, W.L.M., 102
Kissinger, Henry A., 23, 104, 117, 133
Kosygin, Aleksei, 107

Labor unions, 2-3, 57, 160
Lake Champlain, 151-52
Lake Memphremagog, 151
Laporte, Pierre, 30
Legislatures, provincial, 53, 61
Lesage government, 29, 31
Lévesque, René, 31, 34
Luns, Joseph, 106

Macdonald, Sir John A., 54, 55
Machinery, farm, 91
Mackenzie River Delta, 121-22
Maine Board of Environmental Protection, 150
Malmgren, Harald B., 143
Mansfield, Mike, 111
Manufacturing, Canadian, 6-8
Marks, Matthew J., 143
Media, American, 20, 26
Mercier, Honoré, 55
Michelin Tire Corporation, 140, 142-43, 145, 147
Middle East, 116, 119
Montreal, 5, 35, 37, 119, 157
Mowat, Oliver, 55
Multilateral Trade Negotiations (MTN), 132, 133, 135, 136
Multinational corporations, 6, 77, 79-86, 93-95, 160; Canadian literature on, 89-90
Murray, Richard, 8
Mutual balanced force reductions in Europe (MBFR), 109

National Energy Board, 120
National Film Board (NFB), 67
National Transportation Act (1967), 48
Nationalism, Canadian, 9, 13, 19, 20, 23, 26, 73
Natural resources, 7, 75-87, 88
New Brunswick, 150-51
Newfoundland, 61
Nixon administration, 124

Nixon, Richard M., 24, 104, 107, 152
North American Air Defense Command (NORAD), 103-4, 111-12
North Atlantic Treaty Organization (NATO), 103, 105-11 passim
Northwest Territories, 120
Nova Scotia, 140, 143
Nuclear weapons, 100-112 passim
Nye, Joseph 16, 21-22

Official Language Act (1974), 34-35, 38
Oil, 7, 15, 49, 50-52, 81, 113-23, 172-75; Alaskan, 158-59; environmental issues of, 150, 157; price of, 79-81, 87, 115, 133
Ontario, 26, 45, 79, 152
Organization of Economic Cooperation and Development (OECD), 130, 136; Trade Standstill Agreement, 127
Organization of Petroleum Exporting Countries (OPEC), 113-20 passim, 133, 171-72, 175
Ottawa, 5, 22, 33, 45, 107, 122; and environmental issues, 153-60 passim; and the language issue, 34; and Washington, 81, 116, 118, 132, 136, 153, 154, 156; and western Canada, 43-44, 49

Parliament of Canada, 53, 54, 55, 58-60, 62, 66, 158
Parti Québécois, 31, 34-36, 39
Pearson government, 32, 68
Periodicals, 67-70
Pittston Company, The, 150
Potash industry, 170-71
Price controls, 80, 129
Professors, American, 70-72
Progressive Conservative party, 22
Provincial-federal relations, 11

Quebec, 26, 41, 119; and biculturalism, 27-39; and foreign affairs, 30; "Francization" of, 38; language issue in, 28, 32-39; modernization of, 29, 39; "quiet revolution" in, 29-31; secular revolution in, 10; separatist movement in, 30-34, 37, 39
Quebec Resolutions, 53

Reader's Digest, 68-70, 73
Regional Economic Expansion, Department of (DREE), 138
Regionalism, Canadian, 40-43

Richelieu River, 151-52
Rohmer, Richard, 15
ROSS Committee, 156, 160
Royal Commission on the Arts, Letters and Sciences, 73
Royal Commission on Bilingualism and Biculturalism, 27, 32
Royal Commission on Publications (O'Leary commission), 68
Royal Commission on Taxation, 78

Saint John River Committee, 150-51
Sarnia-Montreal pipeline, 173
Saskatchewan, 118, 170
Saskatchewan Power Corporation, 155
Schlesinger, James, 106
Securities and Exchange Commission, 5
Select Committee of the Canadian Senate on Mass Media (Davey committee), 68
Skagit River, 155-56
Soviet Union. See USSR
"Special relationship," 23-24, 101
State Department, U.S., 4, 68, 122, 126, 161
Strategic arms limitation talks (SALT), 108, 110
Supreme Court of Canada, 60-62

Tariffs, 6, 17, 82, 90, 97, 132, 133, 135, 137-38, 140, 146, 169
Television, cable, 26
Third option, 8, 16-17, 25
Time, 68-70, 73
Toronto, 5, 37
Trade, 8, 17-18, 26, 62, 93, 97, 124-36
Trade Act (1974), 136
Treasury Department, U.S., 15, 18, 21, 131
Trudeau government, 17, 32
Trudeau, Pierre Elliott, 3, 23, 25, 27, 33, 104, 107-11 passim
Turner, John, 127

Union Nationale party, 31
United Auto Workers, 131
United Kingdom, 126
United Nations, 136
USSR, 100-112 passim, 126, 128, 133, 135
United States: culture in Canada, 63-74; investments in Canadian manufacturing, 88-99 passim; investments in Canadian primary industries, 75-87; perceptions of Canada, 1-13. See also Washington, D.C.

Venezuela, 119
Vietnam war, 104

Warsaw Pact countries, 109
Washington, D.C., 81, 110-11, 126, 140. *See also* Ottawa

West Germany, 126
Western Canada, 40-52; and energy, 116, 119; and freight rates, 48, 49; and transportation, 46, 49
Western Economic Opportunities Conference, 44
Western Europe, 114, 115, 118